Lost in the Backwoods

Dedicated to the memory of
Alan Harry Daiches (1939–2006)
and Elizabeth Daiches Kettle (1946–2008),
born in the United States of Scottish parents,
lived and worked in England and Scotland.

'Man is born to endure': this could have been the motto of the many thousands of Scots who emigrated to North America, most of whom were not heroic in their aspirations, although many showed courage in their actions. In North America there was much to endure and often little or no support. Scots were early identified as robust material for settlement in the New World, and a spirit of resignation was an ingredient of their pragmatism. Both the ruggedness and the resignation often seem organic to the rigorous nature of their homeland; both were encouraged by their religious faith, particularly Presbyterianism.

In the accounts he wrote of his fur-trading and settler experiences, Alexander Ross is often critical of circumstances and people, and is sometimes querulous, but he is accepting. For most Scottish emigrants in the eighteenth and nineteenth centuries there was little option but to persevere, to play the cards they had been dealt. They were, by and large, wild cards. Some migrants, whether settlers or sojourners, would perish in extreme circumstances, destroyed by the cold, by flood or fire, by starvation or by hostile natives. Many more would be casualties of less dramatic situations: incessant toil, exhaustion, loneliness, disease, childbirth, accident.

The aim of this book is to examine the experience of the North American wilderness. I have chosen to focus on the Scottish experience not because it is necessarily more impressive or more illuminating than that of other nationalities, but because North America is so important an arena of Scotland's past. Scottish experience also provides a broad spectrum of individual and collective encounters with wild country and extreme conditions. There were many admirable achievers, like Alexander Ross, and a few spectacular figures – George Simpson, Donald Smith and John Muir are just three examples – who left a profound imprint on the developing nations of Canada and the United States. But most Scots transplanted a demanding existence in the old country to an often more difficult life in the new country's wilderness. Sufficient numbers persevered and survived to make an impact on both the physical and cultural environment of their new territory, although in most cases their individual stories are not chronicled. Names in today's telephone directories and reconstructions by the writers of fiction remind us that they existed.

There is no strict time span for this study, but a useful starting point for the story of Scots and the North American wilderness is 1773, a significant date on both sides of the Atlantic. In Scotland, Samuel Johnson and James Boswell set off in August 1773 to make the journey to the Highlands and Islands that became for many of the readers of their accounts an introduction to unknown territory. Boswell and Johnson did not get as far north as Loch Broom on the west coast, where in June the brig *Hector* had embarked for Pictou, Nova Scotia, with around 300 emigrants on board, but on Skye

Introduction

Even when we knew which tree he had gone behind there was the fear that what would come out when you called would be someone else.

Margaret Atwood, *Surfacing*

In the spring of 1812, Alexander Ross, from Moray, was alone with his dog Weasel in a cabin at the confluence of the Columbia and Okanogan rivers in what is now Washington State. He was part of a fur-trading expedition which had set out from the Pacific Fur Company's base at Astoria near the Pacific coast. The rest of the expedition, led by David Stuart from Perthshire, had pressed on through the mountains to the north. Ross was, he wrote:

> Alone in this unhallowed wilderness, without friend or white man within hundreds of miles of me, and surrounded by savages who had never seen a white man before. Every day seemed a week, every night a month. I pined, I languished, my head turned gray, and in a brief space ten years were added to my age. Yet man is born to endure, and my only consolation was in my Bible.[1]

Seven years earlier Ross had arrived in Lower Canada, now Quebec, where he had struggled to make his way as a schoolteacher. In 1811, he had joined John Jacob Astor's newly set up fur-trading enterprise as a clerk, a job for which teaching school in however raw a territory scarcely prepared him. It was a disillusioning experience in what Ross described, in a letter to his sister at home in Turriff, Aberdeenshire, as 'this dissolute, extravagant and butterfly country'.[2]

Ross 'languished' in the wilderness of the northwest, yet resignation and the Bible carried him through. He had little option but to continue in the fur trade, which he did with some success. By 1818, he had joined the North West Company, which ousted Astor's company from Astoria, and was in charge of Fort Walla Walla, near the Columbia's junction with the Snake River. He married an Okanogan woman with whom he had several children, and later settled at Red River, now Winnipeg, where he became a highly respected citizen and sheriff of Assiniboia. He never returned to Scotland.

All America lies at the end of the wilderness road.

T. K. Whipple, *Study Out the Land*

The ordinary man will not survive.

Anon. (quoted in Margaret MacDonell, *The Emigrant Experience*)

There is a pleasure in the pathless woods.

Lord Byron, *Childe Harold*

I found this place contrary to nature, every talent that was in my head has departed.

John Maclean (quoted in John Lorne Campbell,
Songs Remembered in Exile)

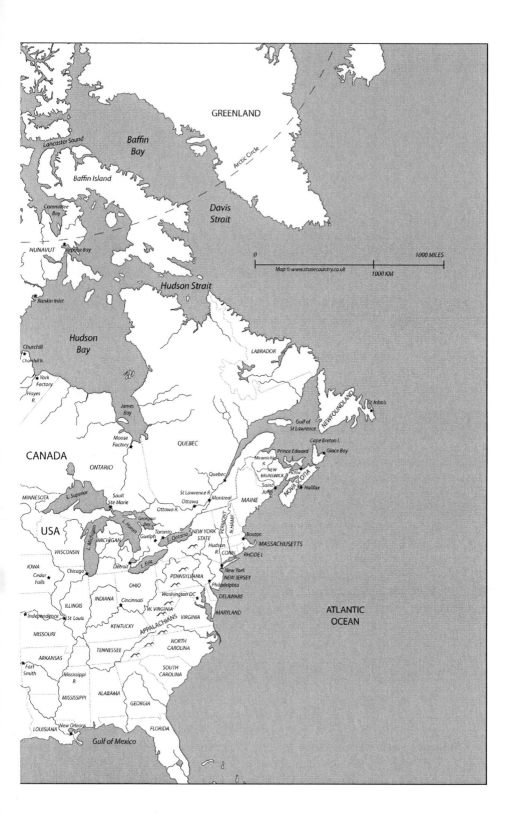

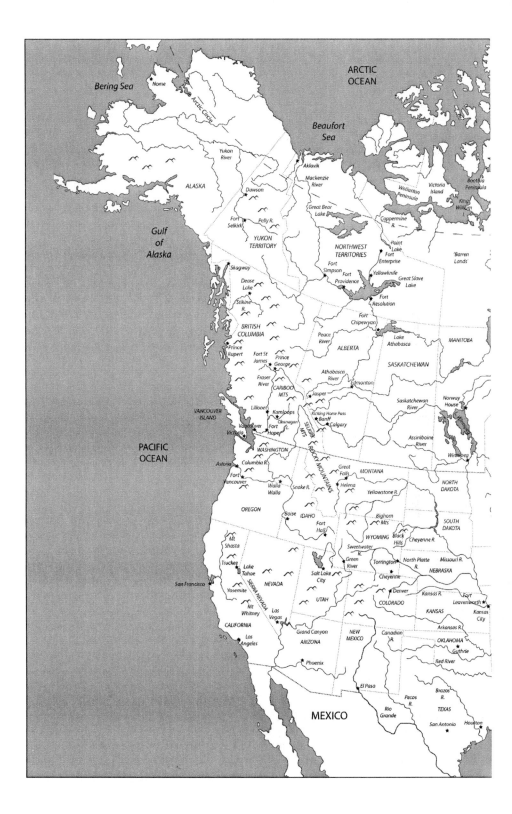

Acknowledgements

Many people have contributed to the inception and process of this book, which grew out of seeds planted in discussions with the late Susan Manning and Alex Murdoch of the University of Edinburgh. The project we were planning never came to fruition, but this book is partly the consequence of ideas exchanged at that time: my thanks to both. I am particularly grateful also to Fiona Graham, who helped to get the show on the road, and to all the following who provided comment, advice, encouragement, information, suggestions, books, companionship, contacts, opportunities and dinner along the way: Mark Abley, Arthur Blue, John Burnett, Ann Colley, Chris Dixon, Edinburgh Central Library, Sally Harrower, Teri Hedgpeth, Jeremy Johnston, Diana Lary, Caroline McCracken-Flesher, John Mackenzie, Irving Massey, Paul Matthews, National Library of Scotland, Lauren Perry, Faith Pullin, Bruce Richardson, Wyoming Humanities Council.

Part of Chapter 7 was published in a different form in the *Journal of Stevenson Studies*, vol. 8, 2011.

Contents

© Jenni Calder, 2013

Edinburgh University Press Ltd
22 George Square, Edinburgh EH8 9LF
www.euppublishing.com

Typeset in Sabon by
3btype.com, and
printed and bound in Great Britain by
CPI Group (UK) Ltd, Croydon CR0 4YY

A CIP record for this book is available from the British Library

ISBN 978 0 7486 4739 2 (hardback)
ISBN 978 0 7486 4738 5 (paperback)
ISBN 978 0 7486 4740 8 (webready PDF)
ISBN 978 0 7486 8217 1 (epub)

Lost in the Backwoods

Scots and the North American Wilderness

Jenni Calder

EDINBURGH
University Press

they encountered what Johnson described as an 'epidemick' of migration.[3] At Armadale in Sleat, two weeks after the *Hector*'s surviving passengers (there had been many deaths at sea) disembarked at Pictou, Boswell and Johnson were taking part 'with much activity, [in] a dance … [which they call] *America*'. Boswell described how the couples whirled in circles 'till all are in motion'. The dance, Boswell explained, 'seems intended to shew how emigration catches, till a whole neighbourhood is set afloat'.[4]

Johnson was exercised by conflicting versions of North American settlement. In one, 'whole neighbourhoods' transplant themselves and 'departure from their native country is no longer exile'. They gain land and a better climate (Johnson claimed) and carry with them 'their language, their opinions, their popular songs, and hereditary merriment: they change nothing but the place of their abode; and of that change they perceive the benefit'. But an alternative story takes them to a wilderness 'where the first years must be spent in toil, to clear the ground which is afterwards to be tilled', and where 'the whole effect of their undertaking is only more fatigue and equal scarcity'.[5] The reality was probably an amalgam of both accounts. For most emigrants, wilderness and toil were unavoidable and the benefits a long time coming. But language, custom and song were profoundly sustaining. Cultural traditions were tools for survival that were as important as practical skills, many of which could only be learnt along the way as new settlers struggled with the unfamiliar and the unforeseen.

Around the time the Pictou emigrants set foot in Nova Scotia, Daniel Boone was leading a group of colonists through the Cumberland Gap to establish a foothold west of the Appalachians. He had explored the area some years earlier with a Scottish Indian trader called John Finley. They were attacked by a band of Shawnees, Cherokees and Delawares, and Boone's son and another young lad were captured and tortured to death. The expedition turned back, but this was only a temporary pause in the movement west, in which Scots and Ulster Scots were prominent, making their way along what became known as the Wilderness Road to settle in the newly opened territory. Meanwhile, in December 1773, Europeans dressed as Mohawks boarded three East India Company ships waiting in Boston harbour to discharge their cargo of tea. They heaved opened tea chests overboard into the harbour waters. The Boston 'tea party' triggered similar actions in Atlantic ports throughout the colonies. It was a defining moment in anti-British feeling, which led to open hostility and the signing of the Declaration of Independence in 1776.

The American Revolutionary War would have reverberating consequences for Scots in North America and at home. In that year on a Vermont homestead a son was born to Simon and Isabella Fraser, who in 1773 had left Strathglass, near Inverness. Simon Fraser fought for the British and did not survive the war, and the family was forced to leave Vermont and start again on the British side of the border. The son, also Simon, would stamp his identity on the map of Canada.

There had been a Scottish presence in North America for more than a century before the Revolutionary War, and Scots made a striking contribution to the conception of the United States of America. But in the last quarter of the eighteenth century, for reasons emanating from both sides of the Atlantic, the nature and pace of Scottish emigration changed. The main focus of this book is the late eighteenth and nineteenth centuries, during which there was a huge, though fluctuating, migration of Scots to North America. Not all remained. Some were sojourning merchants or explorers or speculators, others came as visitors in search of information or adventure. There were those who sought out the wilderness, and others who were dismayed to confront it. Few were able to escape it, although sometimes the wilderness they encountered was created by those who had gone before.

The vision of an apparently unpopulated country contained both promise and threat. Much of the promise rested in freedom from constraint and the possibility of land ownership, themselves incentives for commitment and hard graft. Virgin soil suggested not only productivity but control. The hand that wielded the axe, the foot that drove the spade into the earth, would reap the benefit. For some – though perhaps not for those striving to make the soil productive – wilderness offered a spiritual connection to the natural world and closeness to God. The threat took many different forms, from the very real dangers of extremes of climate, to marauding beasts and marauding humanity (both native and incomer), to the less tangible menace of unconquered terrain. Unknown territory was potentially the habitat of all of humanity's subconscious fears. Deeply planted in European culture was the notion of the sinister forest, a place of moral anarchy and dark deeds. But in the nineteenth century in both Scotland and North America there was growing confidence that civilisation could take possession of wild places and render them submissive to human need. The belief that anything was possible drove many Scots; it also created new forms of wilderness and fresh scope for unrestrained action.

Some of those who made their way to North America vanished in the pioneering process, many were lost before they began, others gave up. Wilderness could make heroes out of settlers; it could also encourage villainy and barbarity. But all who came from Scotland brought with them a reputation, not always deserved, for endurance and enterprise, for godliness and thrift. Thousands had a grounding in hard times, which served them well when they came face to face with wild country of a scale and an intensity that even the bleakest Highland glen could not suggest. Thousands believed not only that hardship was what life offered, but that the prospect and experience of hardship brought moral strength.

The legacy of the wilderness experience has helped to shape the character of both Canada and the United States, and is expressed in the work of many writers. Twentieth-century and twenty-first-century interpretations keep these experiences alive and plant them more firmly in the national consciousness, on both sides of the Atlantic. They remind us of the impact of wilderness in historical contexts and highlight its continuing relevance.

In the early 1860s, Susan Moir, from an Aberdeen family, settled with her mother, stepfather and sister in a makeshift shack at Fort Hope on British Columbia's Fraser River. One day she looked up from berry-picking and saw:

> a solitary horseman, the most picturesque figure I had ever seen. He rode a superb chestnut horse, satiny and well-groomed, untired and full of life in spite of the dust, heat and long journey. He himself wore a beautifully embroidered buckskin shirt with tags and fringes, buckskin pants, embroidered leggings and soft cowboy hat.

This was Angus McDonald leading a Hudson's Bay Company pack-train from Fort Colville on the Columbia River, east of where Alexander Ross endured his lonely sojourn half a century earlier. Born in 1816 in Torridon in Wester Ross, McDonald had been in the company's employment since the age of twenty-one. He was a strikingly tall, dark, black-eyed figure – it was no wonder that the teenage Susan was impressed. He spoke several native languages as well as French, English and his own native Gaelic, and had been married for many years to Catherine, of mixed Nez Perce and French Canadian descent. He was, he said later, taken completely by surprise to see a white girl on the trail as 'he had lived so long without seeing anyone except Indians'.[6] By 'anyone' we must assume he meant 'any woman', as many of the Hudson's Bay Company employees were Scots. He lifted his hat and rode on.

In the following three decades both sides of the Canadian–United States border saw the construction of railways, vital for political cohesion and economic development. The railway became a symbol of man's conquest of some of the world's most hostile terrain. Much of the imagination, skill, boldness and cunning required was supplied by men such as James Jerome Hill, George Stephen, Donald Smith and J. S. Kennedy, all from Scotland or of Scottish descent. The railways reinvigorated settlement, heralding the end of the 'wild frontier', though arguably encouraging new aspects of wildness. As in Scotland, they brought people closer to wilderness and enabled them to encounter it as spectators. They did not, however, necessarily make much impact on the lives of those who continued to take up land in wild places; like the Doig family, who in the 1890s arrived in Montana from Dundee and struggled among unyielding mountains, where: 'over time the altitude and climate added up pitilessly, and even after a generation or so of trying the valley, a settling family might take account and find that the most plentiful things around them still were sagebrush and wind'.[7] For isolated home-steaders the locomotive's whistle expressed simultaneously both civilisation and loneliness.

Between the doggedly resigned Alexander Ross, the romantic figure of Angus McDonald and the susceptible young girl on a remote mountain trail, the railway titans and the Doigs who stepped off the train at Helena to continue by wagon into the Big Belt Mountains, there are thousands of North American Scots with a wide variety of attributes and attitudes whose wilderness encounters are part of Scottish and North American history. *Lost in the Backwoods* engages with some of them; there is much territory yet to be explored.

NOTES

1. Alexander Ross, *Adventures of the First Settlers on the Oregon or Columbia River* (London: Smith, Elder, 1849), p. 146.
2. Alexander Ross, letter to Henrietta Rankine, No. 01.051822, *Transactions*, Manitoba Historical Society.
3. Samuel Johnson, in Samuel Johnson and James Boswell, *A Journey to the Western Isles of Scotland* (Mineola: Dover [1775] 2008), p. 70.
4. Boswell, *A Journey to the Western Isles*, p. 308.
5. Johnson, *A Journey to the Western Isles*, p. 70.
6. Margaret A. Ormsby (ed.), *A Pioneer Gentlewoman in British Columbia. The Recollections of Susan Allison* (Vancouver: University of British Columbia Press, [1976] 1991), p. 10.
7. Ivan Doig, *This House of Sky. Landscapes of the Western Mind* (London: Harcourt, [1978] 1992), p. 22.

1

Scotland's Hard Country

It seemed a hard country, this of Appin, for people to care about as much as Alan did.

R. L. Stevenson, *Kidnapped*

Any place in which a person feels stripped of guidance, lost, and perplexed may be called a wilderness.

Roderick Nash, *Wilderness and the American Mind*

The burgh of Stirling was once a frontier town. It stands at what was for centuries the lowest crossing point of the River Forth, which has its source on the slopes of Ben Lomond and winds its way east to open out into a broad firth spilling into the North Sea. For centuries, boats from continental Europe made their way upriver. Stirling Castle, visible for miles around, was a focus of kingship and power, and from its height spreads a vista that encompasses a crowded scenario of Scotland's past. To the west and north is the Highland Line, an arc of mountains reaching round from Ben Lomond to Ben Vorlich. To the east are the gentler Ochil Hills, outliers of the more massive mountains looking over their shoulders. Below, the Forth flows through carse land and city, and on through what was the crucible of Scotland's nineteenth-century industrial and commercial success.

Stirling was a transition point between Lowland Scotland, by the mid-eighteenth century already developing rapidly as farmland was improved and industry expanding, and the barren, untamed Highlands. 'Forth bridles the wild Highlandman' is a traditional saying; wishful thinking, as Highlanders moved with ease on land and water. But for the English and Lowland Scots alike, and for many of the soldiers who periodically garrisoned the castle, the Highlands were wild country inhabited by warlike people, who dressed oddly and spoke a barbaric language. They felt more comfortable with the existence of a barrier, however inadequate, between them and the alien territory that stretched from the Grampians in the east to the Outer Hebrides in the west, and from Cape Wrath in the north to the Mull of Kintyre in the south. Roads were almost non-existent, and for those not indigenous to the glens and mountains access was perceived as virtually impossible.

WRITING THE HIGHLANDS: NEW ROADS

In Neil Munro's novel *The New Road* (1914), set in the 1720s, Aeneas
Macmaster, brought up on the shores of Loch Fyne in the southern
Highlands, is fascinated by Bleau's 1655 *Atlas Scotia*. It shows the Scottish
Highlands 'without a line to cut its rough ferocity'. Aeneas saw on the map:

> The mountains heaped like billows of the sea, the ranging bens, the glens
> with rivers coiling in them; great inland lochs and forests. He saw high-
> sounding names like Athole, Badenoch, and Brae Lochaber, Lorn and Spey;
> they moved him like a story. All his days they had been known to him, but
> mistily and more as things of fable than of actual nature – lands of the fancy
> only, like the lands of Ossian, figuring in winter songs and tales of old
> revenge.[1]

From earliest imaginings, wild landscape has been part of the narrative of
Scotland, shaping its mythology and imprinting its history. It affected the
way Scots themselves were characterised: the Romans built the Antonine Wall
to keep the savages at bay, and even Lowland Scots in more recent times were
often depicted as uncouth and belligerent. The Borders were notoriously
beyond the law until well into the seventeenth century. In the eighteenth
century no amount of urban sophistication and gentility could mask an
awareness of wild country and wild people beyond the Highland Line, and
a consequent nervousness. In nineteenth-century Scottish cities there was a
lingering sense of threat. It was not just an urban underclass that haunted
the streets, but past eruptions of a violence that seemed intimately connected
with a hostile and unforgiving landscape.

Wilderness, whether natural or manmade, is where humanity seems
diminished. The habitat of native Highlanders may have been wild, but it
was not a wasteland. The lochs, the rivers and the sea, the riverside straths
and the green hillsides, had sustained them for thousands of years and
nourished a rich culture. Far from being diminished by their environment,
they drew strength from it. But when travellers from the south first penetrated the Scottish Highlands, they recoiled from the overwhelming bleak
melancholy of much of what they saw. They approached their journeying in
the same spirit as explorers. 'A journey to the Scottish Western Isles was [in
the seventeenth and eighteenth centuries] looked upon as one of the most
formidable feats of travel which an explorer could undertake.'[2] The
introduction to the 1820 *Steamboat Companion* commented that in the
previous century:

> our southern neighbours regarded the north of Scotland as the land of
> barbarism and misrule; and looked upon a visit to the Scottish lakes, and
> Highland districts, as little short of a journey to the source of the Nile; and

considered a perambulation through our country of Alpine wonders, as an undertaking not less hazardous than that of penetrating the savage wilds of Africa.[3]

And like explorers in the New World or in Africa (Alexander Mackenzie was exploring the far northwest of what would become Canada between 1789 and 1793, and Mungo Park was making his way up the Niger in the 1790s) these travellers often expected to find native inhabitants who were savage and primitive: 'almost as barbarous as cannibals', wrote Richard Franck in 1656, and a century later a view of Highlanders as being rather less than human was not uncommon.[4]

In 1724, in the wake of the failed Jacobite uprisings of 1715 and 1719, General George Wade was appointed Commander-in-Chief North Britain and he embarked on a road-building project intended to bring the Highlands within reach of government. Over the next fifteen years he oversaw the construction of 240 miles of military roads and forty bridges, linking Inverness in the north, the Highlands' largest urban centre, with the southern Highlands. Captain Edward Burt was with General Wade in Scotland and published a series of letters describing his experiences. Burt did not venture far off such beaten tracks as there were without a guide. He made excursions from Inverness on horseback, his guide on foot. On one of these trips through a 'most horrible' landscape, a 'terrifying sight', his guide walked barefoot beside his horse, 'in dangerous places leading him by the bridle, winding about from side to side among the rocks, to such gaps where the horses could raise their feet high enough to mount the stones, or stride over them'.[5] On another expedition the path was so rocky that Burt had to dismount, and he commented tetchily, 'what vexes me most of all, they called it a road'.[6] Burt was no doubt wanting to impress his readers back in the south of England with his powers of endurance and so was not inclined to underplay the rigours of his journeys, but later eighteenth-century travellers echoed his response.

Munro's novel is an account of the building of Wade's road and its impact on the natives. Highlanders watched with apprehension and foreboding:

> They saw it used continually, so far as it was finished, by the redcoats and the Watches; standing, wrapped, themselves, in plaids, on thicket verges or the slopes of hills in mist, like figures of some other clime or age, they watched, with gloomy brows, dragoons pass cantering, four abreast, or companies of footmen, out of Ruthven Castle.

This alien activity was deeply disturbing: 'here, in Badenoch, the world

seemed coming to an end'.[7] What the Highlanders witnessed was a transformation of their habitat, a destruction of the natural environment which
was integral to their way of life. It was not just that the road brought
incursions into their country, but that its construction was itself a
threatening activity. If the redcoats viewed Highlanders as savages and
'cursed that barren tableland on which they were sequestered, prisoned in
by gloomy mountain walls', to the watching Highlanders 'the scene looked
scarcely human':

> Spread out half a mile along the red gash through the heath were vague
> forms moving in the crackling fire light, as in labours, and in tortures of
> perdition, iron clattered, block and tackle creaked, and through the night
> rose strange and melancholy cries.[8]

The contrast in perspective is stark. To the transplanted soldiers the
Highlands are a hostile wilderness, without the familiar comfort of green
fields and pleasant trees. To the natives, the building of the road is a vision
of hell. Like Native Americans observing – and trying to halt – the progress
of the wagon trains and the Iron Horse, they saw the road as destroying a
way of life. Its violation of the landscape was a terrible portent.

When the British army marched into the Highlands in 1746 to quell the
Jacobite Rising maps were few. The savage repercussions that followed the
defeat of Prince Charles Edward at Culloden may have been exacerbated by
a convenient dehumanising of the clansmen, but an additional factor was
the affinity of Highland people with the Highland landscape. The hunted
Jacobites could melt into the hills, follow undetected paths, negotiate precipitous heights, cross violently turbulent rivers. The frustration of a modern
army trying to deal with the natives of a barbaric and apparently collusive
landscape was intense. It was an unyielding territory that had made its
people 'hard and brave', in the words of Ninian Campbell, Aeneas
Macmaster's uncle.[9] An army disadvantaged by landscape and outwitted by
an invisible enemy is liable to over-react when the opportunity arises. There
are clear parallels with North America. The characterisation of Native
Americans and First Nations as savage owes much to their organic connection
with wild country: the menace lies in environment as much as in demeanour.

Neil Munro's Aeneas makes a journey from Inveraray on Loch Fyne to
Inverness. At their best, existing 'roads' were tracks, or the broader swathe
of drove roads; at their worst they were twisted paths barely negotiable by
sturdy Highland ponies. Munro bluntly states that beyond Stirling, roads
stopped: 'on the castle rock the sentinel at nightfall saw the mists go down
upon a distant land of bens and glens on which a cannon or a carriage
wheel had never yet intruded'.[10] Without cannons and carriages, the wild
Highlands would never be tamed. The new road would bring both, and also

enable trade that would introduce transforming commodities to a people perceived as primitive. Munro puts into the duke of Argyll's mouth the opinion that 'savage Hielandmen' would be more readily subjugated by luxuries than by dragoons. He believed 'that the spirit of the mountains could be pacified if once the people got a taste for something more than brose and tartan'.[11]

On horseback, Aeneas follows the track east to Loch Lomond, which takes him through the Rest and Be Thankful Pass, 'the wild abyss below Ben Arthur and Ben Ime'. This was the route from Inveraray to Lowland markets, and well travelled by drovers: 'the very rock of it was stripped by feet of men and beast'.[12] But then he follows a rougher track along Loch Lomondside to Tyndrum, where he joins the route of the Appin and Skye drovers who brought their cattle south. At the inn at Bridge of Orchy he meets his Uncle Ninian, whom he is to accompany to Inverness.

From Bridge of Orchy, Aeneas and Ninian continue on foot, and not wanting to draw attention to themselves – 'there's not a corrie opening on the moor that might not have a band of ruffians in it' – avoid the path and exchange their trousers for the kilt.[13] Ninian knows the territory, and leads the way through hidden glens and alongside unnamed lochs into Glen Etive. Up to this point the travellers had never been out of sight of signs of humanity for long. However wild the landscape, they had passed clachans and scattered houses, and had seen cultivated strips of land, cattle on the hill, and men and women going about their work. But now they were on 'a desert edge' and looking at the 'scowling mountains of Glen Coe'. To the east stretched Rannoch Moor, empty, sombre, ash-grey, pitted with black peat hags, described by Ninian as 'the bleakest place in Albyn':

> The end of it was lost in mist from which there jutted, like a skerry of the sea, Schiehallion. God-forgotten, man-forsworn, wild Rannoch, with the birds above it screaming, was, to Aeneas, the oddest thing, the eeriest in nature, he had ever seen. It charmed and repelled him. He thought no wonder that the tribes who dwelt beside it should be wild, and envious of Lowland meadows. The very sight of it, so bleak and monstrous, filled him with feelings of revolt against the snug and comfortable world.[14]

Rannoch Moor appears often in Scottish fiction and non-fiction as an epitome of wilderness landscape. There was a track through it, but in another of Munro's novels, *John Splendid* (1898), his hero gets lost on the desperately lonely and lifeless moor. The mist descends, and he walks with great difficulty 'upon the coarse barren soil, among rotten bog-grass, lichened stones, and fir-roots that thrust from the black peat-like skeletons of antiquity'. He reflects that such 'stricken' terrain, pitted with 'grey, cold, vagrant lochs', deserted by wildlife, must seem a nightmare to the stranger.[15]

Munro's description owes much to R. L. Stevenson's earlier account of Rannoch Moor in *Kidnapped* (1886), in which David Balfour's perception of the Highland landscape's unrelenting hostility is unequivocally confirmed. The moor is a wasteland:

> Much of it was under heather, much of the rest broken up with hags and bogs and peaty pools; some had been burnt black in a heath fire; and in another place, there was quite a forest of dead firs, standing like skeletons. A wearier looking desert, man never saw …[16]

Through this terrain, David Balfour and his Highlander guide and companion, Alan Breck, make their way on hands and knees, as the red-coats scour the heather in vain. *Kidnapped* is set around thirty years later than *The New Road* and more than a century after *John Splendid*, but the defeat of the Jacobite Rising and the consequent attempts to 'civilise' the Highlands had done nothing to diminish the ominous, in Stevenson's description almost gothic, savagery of parts of the landscape. For David, a Lowlander, it is the territory of nightmare, just as Munro suggests. But the hazards of wild country are not confined to the north. At the beginning of *Kidnapped* David takes the green drove road from the quiet village of his birth, apparently unaware of potential danger. Stevenson reminds us in his essay 'Pastoral' of the wild side of the drover's life:

> The drove roads lay apart from habitation; the drovers met in the wilderness, as to-day the deep-sea fishers meet off the banks in the solitude of the Atlantic; and in the one as in the other case rough habits and fist-law were the rule. Crimes were committed, sheep filched, and drovers robbed and beaten; most of which offences had a moorland burial and were never heard of in the courts of justice.[17]

The rough habits and rough justice of the Borders found a favourable environment in frontier territory on the other side of the Atlantic.

The desolation of Rannoch Moor and the sombre bleakness of Glencoe, inseparable from the resonance of the infamous massacre of 1699, remain. The author of a 1936 book for walkers predicted that there would eventually be a road across the moor east to west: it has never happened. It is still 'a great, bald, empty badland, the biggest, uninhabited wilderness in Britain', 'a wild, dreich, desolate place, devoid of people'.[18] Stevenson's David barely survives the moor, and twenty-first-century writer Robert Macfarlane, reminds us that in winter people still lose their lives there, 'harassed to death by the cold that settles upon it'. When Macfarlane himself crossed the moor on foot he noticed the tricks of distance played by the vast expanse of sameness:

So extensive was the space within which we were moving that when I glanced up at the mountains west of the Moor, to try to gauge the distance we had come, it seemed as though we had not advanced at all: that, like explorers walking against the spin of pack ice, our feet fell exactly where we had lifted them.[19]

Each of these accounts presages or echoes the experience of Scots in the North American wilderness. In the twentieth century, the Scottish landscape continued to be an environment for adventure, with stronger echoes of North American frontier tales. When John Buchan's Richard Hannay in *The Thirty-Nine Steps* (1915) is pursued through the wilds of Galloway, there is no escaping Stevenson. But also present are hints of the Wild West, of territory wild enough to hide in and where the rule of law is precarious. Twenty-five years later, Buchan would deliver a much bleaker narrative set in Canada's far north.

TRAVELLERS IN 'REGIONS MOUNTAINOUS AND WILD'

In 1769, Thomas Pennant, from Wales, made his first tour of Scotland, which took him through Perthshire and on to Deeside and Aberdeen before turning west along the Moray coast to Inverness. He continued north into Sutherland and Caithness. He returned along the west shore of Loch Ness to Fort Augustus and Fort William, and on through Glencoe. He experienced plenty of wild landscape, but was impressed by the roads, General Wade's legacy. Wade, he wrote, had:

forced his way through rocks supposed to have been unconquerable; many of them hang over the mighty lakes of the country, and formerly afforded no other road to the natives than the paths of sheep or goats, where even the Highlander crawled with difficulty, and kept himself from tumbling into the far adjacent water by clinging to the plants and bushes of the rock.

Where the rock was immune to the pick-axe, gunpowder was used to 'subdue' their 'obstinacy'. The road-builders laboured heroically to overcome the resistance of nature, sometimes 'suspended from above by ropes on the face of the horrible precipice'. Stubborn rock, steep mountainsides that afforded no foothold, treacherous bogs, tangled moors, were all 'at length constrained to yield to the perseverance of our troops'.[20] The message is clear and in tune with Enlightenment views of human potential: with skill and determination, the impediments of nature can be overcome.

Like so many travellers in the Highlands, Pennant is both impressed and alarmed by the landscape he traverses. The pass at Killiecrankie has a terrifying grandeur. The road through Glen Tilt he found 'the most dangerous and the most horrible I ever travelled: a narrow path, so rugged that our horses often were obliged to cross their legs, in order to pick a secure place for their feet'. Below them 'roared a black torrent, rolling through a bed of rock, solid in every part but where the Tilt had worn its ancient way'.[21] The approach to Braemar is 'a wild, black, moory, melancholy tract'. Yet he finds the Deeside mountains romantic and magnificent, and admires the view over 'immense and broken crags'. Pines grow out of the naked rock 'where one would think nature would have denied vegetation'.[22] On his southward journey from Inverness he is impressed by Glencoe's mountains, but the 'long day's journey' from the Black Mountain, Rannoch Moor again, was 'truly melancholy, almost one continued scene of dusky moors, without arable land, trees, houses, or living creatures, for numbers of miles'.[23]

Yet Pennant is struck by the scale and beauty of the landscape and makes repeated contrast with the squalor of Highland living conditions. He is genuinely shocked at the mean and meagre cottages he finds on Tayside, for example, which he terms 'the disgrace of North Britain, as its lakes and rivers are its glory'.[24] On Deeside, the roads and bridges are excellent, but the 'houses of the common people ... are shocking to humanity', appearing at a distance like mole hills.[25] This disjunction between natural beauty and human degradation disturbs Pennant. He is a man of his time, with a belief in humanity's capacity for controlling nature and improving what we would now call the quality of life. Roads and bridges represent progress, and humanity's ability to overcome natural barriers. They enable travellers to make their way in safety, and mean that the natural world is more accessible.

Pennant is aware that these benefits seem slow to trickle down to the inhabitants of these dramatic landscapes, and cannot disguise his relief when he heads south down Loch Lomondside, leaving behind the 'black barren dreary glens' populated by 'murderous Macgregors'. He is 'struck with rapture' when he leaves the wilds behind and enters cultivated country, 'well planted, and well inhabited'. Like early nineteenth-century Scots travelling through Scottish settlements in Upper Canada, he looks for signs that humanity has gained control of the wild. And yet he wonders if he will encounter among these 'softer scenes' the hospitality, 'the mountain virtue', he met with in harsher territory: 'for in the Highlands every house gave welcome to the traveller'.[26]

Highland hospitality is much commented on in the eighteenth and nineteenth centuries, and seems organic to wild territory. It stems from an understanding that survival in a difficult environment depends on collective effort and mutual support. It is often remarked that people who are deprived are more likely to share what little they have. The struggle for survival produces an intimate relationship with want and an empathy with those in need. Pennant is dismayed at homes that look like mole hills, but that very analogy underlines the connection between human survival and the environment. The Highland clachan, with homes built of stone and mud, roofed with turf and heather, and furnished with objects made from local materials, seems less of an imposition on the natural world than more sophisticated dwellings, filled increasingly with factory-made commodities. Similarly, North American native dwellings, made from animal skins, trees, mud or snow, are a minimal encroachment on the land.

Pennant made a second journey in 1772, this time island-hopping in the Hebrides. Impressed as he was by vistas of rocky islands, rugged hills, teeming wildlife, the power of the Corryvreckan whirlpool off the island of Jura, the mountains of Mull and Rhum, the charm of Canna, he was even more appalled than before at the destitution he encountered. He witnessed people 'worn down with poverty: their habitations scenes of misery'. The inmates of houses without windows or chimneys were 'lean, withered, dusky and smoke-dried', sometimes surviving on whatever shellfish they could glean from the shore.[27] They were people on the edge of defeat, their environment barely providing the means of sustenance. A century or so later, Scots in North America would comment on native destitution in much the same way.

Pennant ends the account of his second journey with a plea for support for the Highlands. It is not the natural environment that is his prime concern, but the people whom that environment no longer seems able to support. Speaking through the figure of an ancient warrior who appeared to him in a dream, he makes an appeal for Highlanders to be instructed in 'the science of rural economy'. Neglect and oppression is likely to 'force them into a distant land, and necessitate them to seek tranquillity by a measure which was once deemed the punishment of the most atrocious criminals'.[28] Pennant's belief that the harsh facts of nature could be overcome by the ingenuity of humankind did not prevent the departure of thousands for a 'distant land': it was already happening when he was making his Hebridean journeys. His second trip took place just a year before the departure of the *Hector* from Loch Broom, carrying 300 impoverished Scots to Nova Scotia, a journey that has become emblematic of Scottish transatlantic migration.

In this same year, 1773, two conspicuous figures entered the Highlands in an equally pioneering spirit. Dr Samuel Johnson was, of course, an Englishman; his companion, James Boswell, was a Scot, but a Lowlander, and even to a southern Scot 'the state of the mountains and the islands is equally unknown with that of Borneo or Sumatra: Of both they have only heard a little, and guess the rest'.[29] Prepared for a foreign territory and for some discomfort, the two men were nevertheless confident that there would be no danger in encountering either the landscape or its inhabitants. The people had been tamed, with a combination of ferocious reprisal after Culloden and the beginnings of agricultural and industrial development. Now there

were roads, maps and charts, and the influence of the English was bringing
'elegance and culture' beyond the Highland Line. In the event, both the
stark power of the wild landscape and the refinement of clan chieftains'
hospitality took the two gentlemen by surprise.

At the end of August, Boswell and Johnson set out from Inverness on
horseback, with two Highland guides on foot, following Wade's road along
the east shore of Loch Ness to Fort Augustus, and enjoying the scenery. The
road surface was 'so hard and level', wrote Johnson, that the horses needed
little guidance and their riders could look around them. He noted the contrast
between the 'horrid nakedness' of the rocks (naked nature made most
eighteenth-century commentators uncomfortable) and the more pleasing
wooded stretches.[30] But in his account he gives most attention to the loch
itself and speculation as to whether it can be true that it never freezes. He
concludes: 'Natural philosophy is now one of the favourite studies of the
Scottish nation, and Lough Ness well deserves to be diligently examined.'[31]
Johnson is reluctant to allow himself to be awed by nature; if men apply
themselves, they will reach understanding and, it is implied, control.

But there are moments when Johnson has to acknowledge the force of
natural phenomena. On their second day of travelling they made a detour
to view the Falls of Foyers. The scene, said Johnson, 'strikes the imagination
with all the gloom and grandeur of Siberian solitude'. (He had, of course,
never been to Siberia.) To reach the falls they had to clamber over 'very
rugged crags, till I began to wish that our curiosity might have been grati-
fied with less trouble and danger'. The falls themselves were 'of such
dreadful depth, that we were naturally inclined to turn aside our eyes'. But
the weather had been dry, so the volume of water was not great, and
Johnson had to imagine the effect of a thousand streams flowing into a
single channel, 'struggling for expansion in a narrow passage, exasperated
by rocks rising in their way, and at last discharging all their violence of waters
by a sudden fall through the horrid chasm'. His comment that 'nature never
gives everything at once' suggests that perhaps the environment was less
controllable than he liked to think, and he is clearly attracted by the
potential for violence.[32]

Boswell and Johnson continued their journey to the west coast, through
a landscape that was characterised by a dreary 'nakedness' and, even when
impressive, of little use. It presented 'a uniformity of barrenness' that could
'afford very little amusement to the traveller' and no stimulus to the
imagination. He argued that 'an eye accustomed to flowery pastures and
waving harvests is astonished and repelled by this wide extent of hopeless
sterility'. It could not be cultivated and had no intrinsic value. America's
Great Plains would provoke a similar response. Yet he believed that it was
important to experience wilderness:

Regions mountainous and wild, thinly inhabited, and little cultivated, make a great part of the earth, and he that has never seen them, must live unacquainted with much of the face of nature, and with one of the great scenes of human existence.[33]

Johnson was unlikely to succumb to visions of the sublime, but on the way to Glenshiel they stopped to rest the horses and he had a moment of epiphany. He sat by a burn 'in the midst of savage solitude' (though he was not alone) and pondered the nature of wilderness:

the imaginations excited by the view of an unknown and untravelled wilderness are not such as arise in the artificial solitude of parks and gardens, a flattering notion of self-sufficiency, a placid indulgence of voluntary delusions, a secure expansion of the fancy, or a cool concentration of the mental powers. The phantoms which haunt a desert are want, misery, and danger; the evils of dereliction rush upon the thoughts; man is made unwillingly acquainted with his own weakness, and meditation shows him only how little he can sustain, and how little he can perform.

Confronted with the 'real thing', the contrived environment of 'parks and gardens' seems not only tame, but delusional, encouraging a false idea of security. Sitting in a remote glen he found almost no trace of human habitation, and he speculated on how easy it would be for someone 'unprovided with provisions and ignorant of the country' to lose his way and perish. Yet, he adds, again evoking distant wild places, 'what are these hillocks to the ridges of Taurus, or these spots of wildness to the deserts of America?'[34]

'America' indicates a scale and intensity of wilderness beyond any experience that Scotland could offer. Yet Johnson's emphasis on isolation and the lack of human presence has little to do with the height of mountains or the extent of emptiness. When in *Kidnapped* David Balfour believes himself marooned on the tiny island of Erraid – 'I had never seen a place so desert and desolate' – it is solitude above all that undermines his spirit. 'I had become in no way used to the horrid solitude of the isle, but still looked around me on all sides (like a man that was hunted) between fear and hope that I might see some human creature coming.'[35] Every move he makes on Erraid is a contest with granite, heather and bogs – the landscape resists him, and he resists the landscape. But his head is 'half turned with loneliness' and 'the horror I had whenever I was quite alone with dead rocks, and fowls, and the rain, and the cold sea'.[36] The horror returns on Ben Alder when the feverish David lies in Cluny's Cage, a place that to him is redolent of primitive savagery: 'a black, abiding horror – a horror of the place I was in, and the bed I lay in, and the plaids on the wall, and the voices, and the fire, and myself'.[37] On Ben Alder he is not alone, but he is unable to connect with the Highland environment. In the North American wilderness the sheer strangeness, the extreme distance from the familiar, could undermine a grip on reality.

Samuel Johnson found it difficult to reconcile wilderness, a hostile environment in which a man could die of exposure and starvation, with progressive, civilised and enlightened humanity. It bothered him that Britain contained places so elementally hostile, which the majority of its inhabitants would never experience. He had to admit that there were times when nature had, and might always have, the upper hand. It was a delight and a relief when he met, as he did on Raasay and Skye, clan chieftains who welcomed him with sophistication, good food, wine and brandy, and congenial entertainment. He was much more interested in people than in scenery, and felt comfortably at home in these pockets of the unwild. And they seemed a validation of human potential: wilderness did not negate the possibility of civilised living.

The Gaels themselves did not underestimate the severity of their environment, but at the same time celebrated its regenerative life. Poets such as Rob Donn Mackay (1714–78) of Sutherland and Duncan Bàn Macintyre (1724–1812) of Glenorchy express an intimacy with landscape which is domestic rather than romantic. Mountains and glens are experienced as part of daily life. They are not tame, but neither are they a source of menace or of the sublime. Duncan Bàn Macintyre's engagement with the deer on the slopes of Ben Doran, in his most famous poem 'The Praise of Ben Doran', expresses an affinity with their wildness. His 'Song of the Misty Corrie' evokes a scene very different from the brooding barrenness that makes strangers in the Highlands so uneasy. The corrie is 'soft, dappled, blooming', full of wild flowers. He highlights some of the same features that strike the stranger, but to rather different effect:

> Around each spring that is in the region
> is a sombre brow of green water-cress,
> a clump of sorrel at the base of boulders,
> and sandy gravel, ground fine and white:
> the water seethes without heat, and gurgles,
> bubbling from base of the water-fall,
> generous streams with their plaits of greensward
> running in torrent and spiral swirls.[38]

John Macrae from Kintail emigrated to North Carolina in 1774. A resigned but uneasy exile 'in the shade of the wood that is there for all time' and beset by the cries of 'wolves and wild beasts' he remembers the Old Country not as wilderness but as a place of plenty.

> At onset of autumn we'd be of good cheer,
> the deer in the forest, the salmon in stream;[39]

In the nineteenth century and after, the attachment of Highlanders to homeland was often sentimentalised. The cosy and picturesque depiction of Highland life clashed with the destruction of traditional values resulting from the devastation of war and the efforts of clan chiefs and landowners to modernise. It helped make change more palatable – at least for those not directly affected by it. Some of those who left the Highlands did so with the hope that in the New World they would be able to maintain a traditional way of life which was under threat in Scotland. But they could not take the landscape with them, and their culture, organic to their demanding environment, was cut off from its origins. Retaining the language and the music became a way of maintaining a connection with their native wilderness.

OSSIAN AND AFTER: 'SCENERY OF A FAIRY DREAM'?

Pennant, Boswell and Johnson were in the Highlands less than thirty years after the defeat of the Jacobites in 1746. They had little, if any, awareness of Gaelic culture or curiosity about the language. The Highlands were safe, or safer, but in spite of new roads and attempts at improvement the landscape had not been tamed and, indeed, its wildness was enhanced by a lingering atmosphere of violence and the demeaning consequences of defeat. That lurking violence would feed into eighteenth- and nineteenth-century attempts to reinterpret the Highlands. The landscape's human history, of course, went much further back than the half-century of Jacobite risings, but no 1770s traveller in the Highlands could have been unaware of the events of 1745–6. They would almost certainly have also been aware of the figure of Ossian, who thanks to James Macpherson appeared, or re-appeared, in 1760.

Macpherson, born in Badenoch in 1736, was one of several Gaels with an interest in recording the Gaelic oral tradition. Drawing on this tradition he produced versions of Gaelic ballads in English that brought the Highland landscape and an heroic past to an enthusiastic audience, while at the same time sparking a long-continuing debate about the authenticity of his material. Those who responded with such excitement to Macpherson's stirring evocations were largely unaware that there was a living Gaelic literature in which wild landscape was a quotidian environment rather than the arena of grand actions and inflated emotions. Johnson was impressed neither by the poems themselves nor by Macpherson's claims of their authentic origins, but many others lapped up the potent combination of heroic tale and romantic landscape. Nearly half a century later, Walter Scott would tap into the vein with his own epic verse narratives, which began to appear in 1805.

In his poetry Scott evokes Border and Highland landscapes and draws a mythic past out of mountains, lochs and rivers. Although eighteenth-century travellers often included historical background in their commentary, and Macpherson's Ossian tales are inseparable from the landscape, Scott was the first to project landscape as history, to demonstrate that Scotland's story could not be told without connecting to the natural environment. In his poetry and later his fiction, wild country repeatedly defines not just a way of life but a narrative of the past. By making a connection with nature, he was making a connection with a continuum of history.

By the time Scott was becoming acquainted with the Highlands, the contrast between agricultural improvement and industrial exploitation in the Lowlands, and the terrain beyond the Highland Line was more striking than it was in Pennant's day. When Scott published *The Lay of the Last Minstrel* (1805) and *Marmion* (1808), a second phase of Highland road building was under way, planned and supervised by Thomas Telford. Telford, a shepherd's son from Langholm in the Borders, built roads, bridges and canals that made a lasting imprint on the Highland landscape. But Scott was writing about a much earlier period, when an exotic Highland wilderness was untouched by modern communications. *The Lady of the Lake* (1810), set in the Trossachs in the time of James V, depicts an 'enchanted land', a vibrant landscape of mountains, lochs and sunsets presented as the environment of both romance and conflict:

> So wondrous wild, the whole might seem
> The scenery of a fairy dream.[40]

The impact on the contemporary imagination would be huge. The lochs and mountains of the Trossachs, a compact and contained area, were a short distance from Stirling and quickly became one of the earliest tourist destinations in the Highlands. Carriages came from Edinburgh and Glasgow, and steamers plied the Forth to deliver the curious and the excited to a glorious but no longer menacing wildness.

When Scott came to write *Waverley* (1814), his first novel, he was looking back only a few decades rather than centuries, but still evoked a time when to the incomer the Highlands were an impenetrable wilderness. Edward Waverley enters Highland territory under the guidance of clansman Evan Dhu. They follow a steep and rugged path and look down at a burn far below them.

> A few slanting beams of the sun, which was now setting, reached the water
> in its darksome bed, and shewed it partially, chafed by an hundred rocks,

and broken by an hundred falls. The descent from the path to the stream was a mere precipice, with here and there projecting fragments of granite, or a scathed tree, which had warped its twisted roots into the fissures of the rock.[41]

For Waverley the fact that only a native can detect a trail through the mountains adds to the romance of the experience. Evan Dhu seems to find his way 'by instinct, without the hesitation of a moment'.[42] Waverley is totally in his hands, just as David Balfour in Stevenson's *Kidnapped* is totally dependent on Alan Breck, and Aeneas in Munro's *The New Road* would be hopelessly lost without Ninian Campbell – and this in spite of the fact that Aeneas is, just, a Highlander. It is the nature of the territory that enforces this dependence and makes emphatic the division between Highland and Lowland. Lowlanders have no need for the wilderness skills that are essential to survival in the Highlands. The ability of Highlanders not only to find their way but to vanish in the landscape is highlighted by all three writers.

Scott's *Rob Roy* (1818) returns to the territory of *The Lady of the Lake*. Like Edward Waverley, *Rob Roy*'s Frank Osbaldistone sees romance in the Highland hills. Travelling north from Glasgow with Bailie Nicol Jarvie, his first impression is of 'hopeless barrenness', but when they cross the actual and symbolic dividing line of the River Forth, he enters a moonlit landscape which instantly appeals to his imagination.[43] Frank and the Bailie spend the night in the Clachan of Aberfoyle, a collection of meagrely furnished hovels, but this does not dampen Frank's enthusiastic response to the natural surroundings. The next morning he emerges from 'the smoky, smothering atmosphere of the Highland hut' into a stunning scene of 'natural romance and beauty'. The loch, 'an enchanting sheet of water', glitters in the sunshine. All around are high hills 'waving with natural forests of birch and oak'. Like Samuel Johnson, Frank communes with nature on his own and finds that the sun and wind in the trees 'gave to the depth of solitude a sort of life and vivacity'. The suggestion that solitude lends a particular resonance to humanity's relationship with nature comes up repeatedly in late eighteenth- and early nineteenth-century responses, and is echoed in descriptions of North American landscape. (Solitude is positive, conducive to appreciative contemplation, while isolation implies uncertainty and fear of the unknown.) Scott, through the eyes of Frank, reflects that 'man alone seemed to be placed in a state of inferiority, in a scene where all the ordinary features of nature were raised and exalted'.[44] The natural environment, at least in its grander manifestations, puts humanity in its place, changing the perspective in which individuals operate. Solitude diminishes the individual even more, yet, as some North American pioneers would find, it also enhances a sense of freedom.

But this changed perspective applies only to those unfamiliar with the landscape. To Frank, the loch and the surrounding hills are benign and unthreatening, and there is a thrill in succumbing to their romantic appeal. Later that day, as he and the Bailie make their way deeper into the mountains with a troop of English soldiers, they experience the terrain rather differently. Following a zigzagging 'broken track' they are negotiating the 'precipitous face of a slaty grey rock' when they become aware that they are being watched.[45] A group of 'mountaineers' emerges from the landscape as if they have grown out of it, which in a sense they have. Their leader is a woman, Helen MacGregor, the wife of Rob Roy, and Scott's description of her reinforces her affinity with the wild country to which she belongs. Her face is 'imprinted with deep lines by exposure to rough weather' and her features are 'strong, harsh and expressive'.[46] This is no conventional romantic female, but a woman formed by the hard country she inhabits. In the ensuing skirmish the Highlanders have an easy victory. They know the terrain and make it work to their advantage.

Later in the novel Rob Roy himself is captured by the soldiers, but escapes by diving into the River Forth. He chooses a spot where 'the river was rendered inaccessible by the steepness of its banks, or the thickets of alders, poplars, and birch, which, overhanging its banks, prevented the approach of horsemen'.[47] The natives have the advantage, not only because they are bred to the terrain, but because the incomers are burdened by unsuitable equipment and tactics. Fenimore Cooper's Leatherstocking Tales and many later North American adventure narratives would illustrate similar circumstances. At the time of the action of *Rob Roy*, Wade's roads were not yet built, but although they were intended to improve the mobility of the military, off-road mounted troopers were still disadvantaged. Stevenson and Munro would also demonstrate the importance of being able to travel, like Cooper's Natty Bumppo, through wild country on foot.

At the end of the novel, Frank and the Bailie make their way south towards Loch Lomond, which to Frank formed 'one of the most surprising, beautiful, and sublime spectacles in nature'. Leaving Rob Roy picturesquely poised on a rock 'conspicuous by his long gun, waving tartans, and the single plume in his cap' (an image suggestive of a feather-bonneted Indian on a badland skyline), they are rowed down the loch by clansmen chanting in Gaelic. Frank almost succumbs to the romance.

> I felt something soothing in this magnificent scenery with which I was surrounded; and thought, in the enthusiasm of the moment, that had my faith been that of Rome, I could have consented to live and die a lonely hermit in one of the romantic and beautiful islands amongst which our boat glided.[48]

The Bailie, however, reflects rather differently on the scene. As a Glasgow merchant he recognises a commercial opportunity. The loch, he believes, could be drained, ploughed and planted, thus putting to productive use 'many a thousand acre, from whilk no man could get earthly gude e'now, unless it were a gedd [pike], or a dish of perch now and then'.[49] He adds that sufficient water should be left to enable barges to carry coal between Dumbarton and Glenfalloch. Scenery for its own sake is a luxury that a progressive Scotland cannot afford. (In twenty-first-century Scotland scenery is an economic necessity.)

Loch Lomond, with its head in the Highlands and its foot just thirty miles from Glasgow, a city already surging towards its position as an industrial and commercial giant, irresistibly beckoned. It is charged with ambivalence. Travellers commented on its rugged beauty, yet often expressed a sense of relief that, heading south, they were leaving behind an alien wilderness. For Thomas Pennant, Loch Lomond was the 'most beautiful of the Caledonian lakes', but as he left it behind he followed the River Leven to the Firth of Clyde.[50] He described the Vale of Leven as 'unspeakably beautiful' and he was immensely cheered by the sight of 'bleacheries, plantations and villas'. 'Nothing,' he wrote, 'can equal the contrast in this day's journey, between the black barren dreary glens of the morning ride, and the soft scenes of the evening.'[51]

There is considerable irony in Scott's responsibility for transforming perceptions of the Highlands and encouraging a flood of travellers and tourists. Through characters such as Edward Waverley and Frank Osbaldistone, Englishmen with susceptible imaginations, he gives free rein to the romantic appeal of Highland scenery. Yet at the same time he provides a strikingly empathetic picture of the life that landscape sustained, and its combination of poverty, harshness, courage and generosity. Most of all, it is the intimate relationship between Highland landscape, Highland humanity and Highland culture that Scott emphasises; many later novelists of the Highlands tried to do the same.

The country that Scott knew best was the Borders where he spent much of his childhood and built Abbotsford, his home of later years. The Borders also feature in his poetry and fiction. *Redgauntlet* (1824) reminds us of an environment very different from the grandeur of the mountains. In that novel most of the action takes place on the Solway estuary, a territory of quicksands, mists and unpredictable tides that is hard to define. His hero, Darsie Latimer, an Edinburgh law student, approaches the Solway through barren, desolate countryside. It is as foreign to him as the Highlands are to Waverley. On the far side is Cumberland, which by contrast is 'crossed and intersected by ten thousand lines of trees growing in hedge-rows, shaded with groves and woods of considerable extent, animated by hamlets and villas, from which thin clouds of smoke already gave signs of human life and industry'.[52] *Redgauntlet* is concerned with the aftermath of the Jacobite Rising of 1745–6, and the barren quicksands are haunted by an atmosphere of primitive violence as well as uncertainty.

When Darsie reaches the Solway the sun is setting and the sky is like 'a huge battlemented and turreted wall of crimson and black clouds, which appeared like an immense Gothic fortress'.[53] The tide is out, and on the sands are mounted men galloping up and down spearing salmon, which in Darsie's eyes is a strange activity that enhances the gothic character of the scene. But the quicksands are dangerous and Darsie ignorant, and when he wanders too close to the now incoming tide he is rescued by one of the horseman, who turns out to be a key figure in the drama that unfolds. Like Edward Waverley and Frank Osbaldistone he has no understanding of the forces of nature. And just as the road builders cannot subdue the mountains, no amount of neat hedgerows or tidy hamlets will make the quicksands less sinister. It is notable in Scott that, although his message is that the old ways of the clans are, and should be, in the past and that the future lies with industry and improvement, there are aspects of the landscape that will never be conquered.

It is exactly this acknowledgement that enhances the romantic appeal of wild scenery. Human ingenuity can, perhaps, drain and plough up Loch Lomond; it can certainly build roads, soon to be followed by railways, but the landscape, Scott strongly implies with a confidence that is hard to share now, will survive. Where Scott's message becomes ambivalent is whether the way of life organic to that landscape can also survive. Rob Roy is an anachronism, not just because he operates outwith the law, but because his life, like that of the natives of North America as the frontier drew to a close, is embedded in a relationship with the land that cannot endure. Yet that relationship, and the culture it had sustained for hundreds of years, was immensely valuable. Part of Scott's motive for writing was to record a way of life that was passing, if not already passed, and he writes with regret about what has been lost – and, of course, through his words he regenerated the past and the environment of the past in an unparalleled fashion. On the other side of the Atlantic, James Fenimore Cooper would attempt something similar, as the frontier made its rapid progress westward and change followed hot on its heels.

TOURISTS: 'THEY FILL EVERY CONVEYANCE AND EVERY INN'

Over a period of about half a century, a succession of books brought Scotland's Highland landscape to readers all over Britain and in Europe and North America. If Scott fired the imagination, Pennant and other travellers helped through detailed observation and comments on roads and inns and amenities – or lack of them – to reassure potential tourists that this wild territory could be experienced in safety and reasonable comfort. At about the same time, and increasingly in the nineteenth century, Scots were travelling to North America and publishing accounts of their experiences. In Scotland, increasing numbers set forth to see for themselves the variations on the wilderness theme that Scotland offered: the grim, the bleak, the exotic, the magnificent, the romantic, the sublime. Steam transformed travel, first by water, then by rail. When in 1840 Lord Cockburn made a steamer trip to Iona and Staffa he commented on the numbers of mainly English travellers:

> They fill every conveyance, and every inn, attracted by scenery, curiosity, superfluous time and wealth, and the fascination of Scott, while, attracted by grouse, the mansion-houses of half our poor devils of Highland lairds are occupied by rich and titled Southrons.[54]

The Crinan Canal, opened in 1801, and the Caledonian Canal, opened 1822, made the west coast and the north more accessible, and steamers plying on Loch Lomond, for example, allowed people comfortable contact with the Highland landscape. Bailie Nicol Jarvie's vision had not come to pass, but another kind of industry, tourism, had taken hold.

By the 1840s, as Cockburn indicates, there was a new factor in the magnetic mix that drew visitors to the Highland landscape: sport. Fishing, grouse shooting and deer stalking became synonymous with the moors and mountains, and the wildlife they sustained became more important than the human. These recreational activities and the infrastructure that supported them would have a profound effect on notions of wilderness. They continued the displacement of the population, intensified the landscape's emptiness and provoked bitter comment: 'Why should we emigrate?' asked Donald Macdonald of Back of Keppoch. 'There is plenty of waste land around us; for what is extensive deer-forest in the heart of the most fertile part of our land but waste land?'[55]

Although the tourist intrusion on the wilderness was happening in Scott's lifetime, it was a combination of the railways and royal enthusiasm that completed the transformation of attitudes to the Highland landscape and the experience of it. In 1842, Queen Victoria made her first visit to Scotland and her first expedition across the Highland Line. Everything delighted her: the mountains, the waterfalls, wild Glen Ogle (which reminded Victoria of the Khyber Pass, which she had seen only in pictures), Loch Earn and Loch Tay, Gaelic boat songs, bagpipes, Highland hospitality. Prince Albert also enjoyed the landscape and the stag shooting, 'one of the most fatiguing, but ... most interesting of pursuits' as he described it in a letter. It involved being 'constantly on the alert', staying downwind and 'crawling on hands and knees ... dressed entirely in grey'.[56] (At around the same time as Albert was hunting deer in the Highlands there were Scots in North America pursuing bigger and more dangerous game – see Chapter 4.) As if to authenticate her experience, Victoria was reading Scott's *The Lady of the Lake*.

Two years later she and Albert were back, and during a stay at Blair Atholl made an expedition on ponies up the Hill of Tulloch, which afforded a splendid view of Glen Tilt (the same glen that had so dismayed Pennant), Blair Castle and the surrounding hills. It was, Victoria wrote in her diary, 'the most delightful, most romantic ride and walk I ever had'.[57] A third Scottish visit, in 1847, took them along the west coast and sealed her relationship with the Highlands. She and Albert determined to acquire a home there. Victoria's enthusiasm and the extension of the railway beyond Perth (the line to Inverness was completed in 1863) unleashed a flood of tourists to the Highlands. Hotels and holiday homes were built, and shops and other facilities emerged to supply visitors with their holiday and sporting needs. The landscape was tramped as never before, as visitors not only made their way to scenic spots and spent days on the hill after deer and grouse, but played golf, tennis and bowls on spaces given over to these activities.

CHANGE: 'LITTLE WOULD BE LEFT OF THE OLDEN TIME'

In the early years of the nineteenth century, Elizabeth Grant was a young girl whose family, the Grants of Rothiemurchus, divided their time between London and Speyside. Her response to the Highland landscape has an engaging enthusiasm tempered by practicality. 'I am sure I have backwoods tastes,' she wrote, commenting on her liking for the unsophisticated and using a word borrowed from the other side of the Atlantic.[58] She loved life 'in the rough' and spent hours roaming the countryside, sharing a pony with siblings and cousins, watching eagles, gathering cranberries, and always aware of both 'the bare rocky crags of the Grampians' and the human activity that belonged to the landscape: a primitive sawmill, the miller's hut beside 'a cleared field with a slender crop of oats', a peat stack, a grazing cow, with over all 'the wild charm of nature, mountain scenery in mountain solitude beautiful under every aspect of the sky'.[59] The young Elizabeth was used to life in London and Edinburgh, but relished the unfettered contact with the natural world that Rothiemurchus allowed her. At the same time, she recognised that life was changing. For those with the means, 'improvement' was the aspiration, and she understood that there would be consequences for the woods and hills she so much enjoyed. Whenever she returned to her Rothiemurchus home she found signs of change, the farmsteading and laundry moved further from the house, a new lawn, trees cut down. Her Aunt Frere had a gloomy vision of the future, prophesying that the distinctive character of Highland life would disappear: 'manners would change, the highlands would become like the rest of the world, all that made life most charming there would fade away, little would be left of the olden time, and life would become as uninteresting as in other little remarkable places'.[60] Beyond the immediate vicinity of the house the forest and the lochs, the hills, the Spey and the burns that fed it, remained unchanged, yet there is an underlying anxiety that the natural world may not be as robust as it once seemed. Similar feelings would be expressed by those who valued the North American wilderness.

Neil Munro looked back at the Highlands of the 1720s, and described a vast wild area with a few small commercial hubs at its margins. His Highland characters view the new road being driven through this territory with mixed feelings. It is a military road, engineered and built by soldiers to make it easier to control the volatile tribal people who live beyond the Highland Line, but it also opens the way to faster communications and easier trade, encouraging the duke of Argyll's belief that commerce is more likely than conquest to tame the clans. Scott's Bailie Nicol Jarvie takes a similar attitude: wilderness is of no value unless it can be made productive. Stevenson sets *Kidnapped* thirty years after General Wade's road building and shows us a Lowlander nearly overcome by the grim hostility of wild country. At the same time, Alan Breck, his Highland hero, has a canny understanding of the terrain and what is needed to survive. The native attuned to the environment outwits the English soldiers. But hanging over this, and hanging over Scott's novels also, is the knowledge that the Jacobites, who relied heavily on Highland support, lost, and the erosion of traditional Highland life and of the landscape, which had begun decades before 1746, accelerated. The Highland environment, for social, economic and political reasons, could no longer sustain a way of life that had once been almost entirely self-sufficient.

People from the south were attracted both by wild landscape and the idea that 'wild' people shared their island, that it was not necessary to cross an ocean to encounter true wilderness or exotic savages. The eighteenth-century traveller was impressed by the grandeur, fascinated by the relationship between life and landscape, and appalled by poverty that was in no way picturesque. The scale of Highland mountains and the power of Highland rivers were thrillingly elemental and untamed, yet their wildness was viewed with circumspection. At a time when Enlightenment attitudes encouraged a belief that humanity could control its own destiny, to be faced with the grim intractability of naked rock and sterile moor was disturbing. Scenery without development potential was of limited value.

A later generation would respond to the romance of the Highland land-scape as something of essential worth in itself, something undiminished by conquest and resistant to human interference. An intrinsic part of the romance lay in the landscape's separateness and inviolability. But romance becomes comfortable only when its source presents no real danger. When the wild Highland landscape no longer contained the threat of wild Highland people, all either tamed or departed, when a queen in a crinoline could scale a mountain without risk, when thousands could steam through the glens by rail or water, an illusion of benign connection with nature became possible. But for most people it remained an illusion, bolstered by images drained of all danger. In earlier times those who reported from beyond the Highland Line knew better.

In 1843, the infant Osgood Mackenzie, born in France, was brought home to Easter Ross. The family travelled on the newly opened railway to Aberdeen and by steamboat to Inverness. The Mackenzies were lairds with homes at Conon near Dingwall on the east coast and at Gairloch on the west coast. Making the journey between them was difficult, as the recently constructed road stopped at the southern end of Loch Maree, a loch lined by mountains and often too stormy for small boats. A generation earlier, the journey was even more challenging, with rough tracks negotiated on foot and goods carried on pack ponies. Without roads, there were no wheeled vehicles. There were no bridges either: rivers had to be forded, with children sometimes carried across by men on stilts. The two successive husbands of the landlady of the inn at Kinlochewe were drowned 'in trying to get people across this wild river [Kinlochewe River] on horseback when it was in flood'.[61] At the end of the 1840s a road was built along the loch, a project promoted by Osgood Mackenzie's mother. It was the time of the potato famine, and there were large areas of starvation and destitution in the Highlands. The road building was a 'work fare' scheme, with those who worked being paid in 'miserable doles' of maize meal.[62] Mary Mackenzie insisted on paying the men a proper wage. Out of the famine, which sent hundreds of families to North America, came 'about the only thing which could possibly open up the country'. Osgood remembered 'the first wheeled vehicle, a carrier's cart, that ever came to Gairloch, and the excitement it caused!'[63] By that time, wheeled vehicles were crossing the Rocky Mountains in large numbers, against all odds and all predictions. Among those who made that journey were many Scots.

NOTES

1. Neil Munro, *The New Road* (Edinburgh: Blackwood, [1914] 1958), p. 47.
2. Donald J. Macleod, Introduction, Martin Martin, *A Description of the Western Isles of Scotland* (Stirling: Eneas Mackay, 1934), p. 19.

3. *Steamboat Companion*, in Bray, *Hebrides*, p. 206.
4. P. Hume Brown, *Early Travellers in Scotland* (Edinburgh: David Douglas, 1891), p. 202.
5. Edward Burt, *Letters from a Gentleman in the North of Scotland*, in A. J. Youngson (ed.), *Beyond the Highland Line* (London: Collins, 1974), p. 73.
6. Ibid., p. 74.
7. N. Munro, *The New Road*, p. 114.
8. Ibid., p. 115.
9. Ibid., p. 224.
10. Ibid., p. 45.
11. Ibid., p. 16.
12. Ibid., p. 55.
13. Ibid., p. 68.
14. Ibid., p. 88.
15. Neil Munro, *John Splendid* (Edinburgh: B&W, [1898] 1994), p. 262.
16. Robert Louis Stevenson, *Kidnapped* (Edinburgh: Canongate [1886] 1989), p. 141.
17. Robert Louis Stevenson, 'Pastoral', *Memories and Portraits* (Glasgow: Richard Drew [1887] 1990), p. 66.
18. Ian Nimmo, *Walking with Murder* (Edinburgh: Birlinn, 2005), p. 149.
19. Robert Macfarlane, *The Wild Places* (London: Granta Books, 2007), p. 74.
20. Thomas Pennant, *Tour of Scotland 1769* (Perth: Melven Press, [1771] 1970), p. 214.
21. Ibid., p. 108.
22. Ibid., p. 109.
23. Ibid., p. 213.
24. Ibid., p. 84.
25. Ibid., p. 117.
26. Ibid., p. 226.
27. Thomas Pennant, *The Voyage to the Hebrides*, in Bray, *Hebrides*, p. 75.
28. Ibid., p. 87.
29. Johnson, *A Journey to the Western Isles*, p. 64.
30. Ibid., p. 20.
31. Ibid., p. 21.
32. Ibid., pp. 22–3.
33. Ibid., p. 27.
34. Ibid., p. 28.
35. Stevenson, *Kidnapped*, p. 80.
36. Ibid., p. 85.
37. Ibid., p. 151.
38. Derick Thomson, *Gaelic Poetry in the Eighteenth Century* (Aberdeen: Association of Scottish Literary Studies, 1993), p. 81.
39. Thomson, *Gaelic Poetry*, p. 197.

40. Walter Scott, *The Lady of the Lake* (London: Adam & Charles Black, 1904), p. 7.
41. Walter Scott, *Waverley* (Oxford: Oxford University Press, [1814] 1986), p. 76.
42. Ibid., p. 78.
43. Walter Scott, *Rob Roy* (Edinburgh: Collins, [1817] 1953), p. 309.
44. Ibid., p. 338.
45. Ibid., p. 343.
46. Ibid., p. 344.
47. Ibid., p. 373.
48. Ibid., p. 405.
49. Ibid., p. 406.
50. Pennant, *Tour of Scotland*, p. 223.
51. Ibid., p. 226.
52. Walter Scott, *Redgauntlet* (London: Penguin, [1824] 2000), p. 41.
53. Ibid., p. 20.
54. Henry Cockburn, *Circuit Journeys* (Hawick: Byway Books, [1888] 1983), p. 51.
55. Malcolm MacLean and Christopher Carrell, *As an Fhearann* (Edinburgh, Stornoway and Glasgow: Mainstream, An Lanntair Gallery and Third Eye Centre, 1986), p. 41.
56. David Duff, *Queen Victoria's Highland Journals* (Exeter and London: Webb & Bower and Michael Joseph, 1983), p. 30.
57. Ibid., p. 43.
58. Elizabeth Grant, *Memoirs of a Highland Lady* (Edinburgh: Canongate, [1898] 1988), vol. I, p. 34.
59. Ibid., p. 223.
60. Ibid., p. 98.
61. Osgood Mackenzie, *A Hundred Years in the Highlands* (London: Edward Arnold, 1921), p. 10.
62. Ibid., p. 30.
63. Ibid., p. 31.

2

The Never-ending Forest

We are now in America
At the edge of the never-ending forest

Gaelic lullaby, anon.

There are trees to cut down, roots to grub up, the ground to plow, corn, indigo, tobacco, to plant.

William Mylne, *Travels in the Colonies*

When on 15 September 1773 the brig *Hector* dropped anchor in Pictou Harbour, Nova Scotia, her ill and exhausted passengers reached the end of a punishing transatlantic voyage. On the nine-week crossing from Scotland's west coast they had lost many of their number: several adults and eighteen of the seventy children on board had died of dysentery or smallpox. Yet they were buoyed by the promise of homes and provisions awaiting them, and an established community that would help to support them.

The story of the *Hector* and her passengers has become emblematic of an emigration narrative evoking reluctant departure from Scotland and disappointment in the New World. The people of the *Hector* responded to a vision of a fresh start in a land of opportunity which was being strenuously promoted by those for whom North America offered prospects for large-scale economic gain. For the land speculators success depended on settlement; often those who invested in large tracts of North America had little notion of the nature of the land they were buying, and even less of what would be required to settle and develop it. They needed people, and over a period of around 200 years Scotland was intermittently seen as a land of surplus population.

The *Hector* had sailed from Loch Broom in July, with 200 men, women and children on board. They came from the Loch Broom area, from Assynt further north, from Dornoch and Beauly in Easter Ross, and a few from the Lowlands. They were driven by poverty and changes in land use which made it increasingly difficult for tenant families to survive. Thomas Pennant had been shocked at what he saw in Assynt: 'I never saw a country that seemed to have been so torn and convulsed.' But he added: 'This tract seems the residence of sloth; the people almost torpid with idleness, and most wretched.'[1] Easter Ross was more cultivated, but the pressures on the tenantry were considerable, especially in the wake of 1772 which saw widespread famine. John Ross, the emigration agent recruiting for the *Hector*, energetically took advantage of deprivation, but despite his efforts it was late in the season when the *Hector* departed. Storms and adverse winds delayed her further. When she finally entered the Gulf of St Lawrence her passengers were running short of food.

Although most of those on board were Highlanders, used to hardship and to wild country, even if, contrary to Pennant's observations, they had been fit on departure by the time they disembarked they were not in good shape. When they set eyes on what had been promised to them as a settled township they were dismayed. Before them were massed trees, some as much as 200 feet high, punctuated here and there by clearings and occasional cabins. There were no homes waiting for them, no supplies in readiness and it was too late in the season for planting the crops vital for survival. True, land had been surveyed and marked out on their behalf, and the man responsible, Robert Patterson, agent of the Philadelphia Company which had acquired the land, guided them to it. There were no paths through the dense trees, scant daylight penetrated and the leap of imagination required to see the uncleared land sown with crops and populated with the beasts familiar to them in Scotland defeated the newly arrived immigrants. Robert Patterson noted their dismay: 'never did there seem to be offered to men such an utter mockery'.[2] For many of them, trees of any kind were a novelty; for all of them trees of this size and this impenetrability, and all the detritus of the forest, the deadfalls, the tangled branches, the stubborn roots, were inconceivable. Robert MacDougall, whose Gaelic *Emigrant's Guide to North America* was published in 1841, advised emigrants not to bring with them axes from Scotland, 'for Scottish smiths do not know how to make one that would be of any use'.[3] Any intending emigrant reflecting on that advice would have been challenged to imagine the enormity of what it implied.

Many of the *Hector*'s emigrants turned their backs on the forest. They drifted away to look for employment in more established communities, following a blazed trail through the trees to Truro, for example, forty miles away. But some stayed in the township of Pictou. They survived their first winter in hastily constructed lean-tos. The *Hector* returned with provisions, but her erstwhile passengers were told that they were not entitled to them unless they settled on the forbidding land allocated. As so often in Scottish experience, opportunity was embedded in a tangle of strings attached.

Local Mi'kmaq and the few existing settlers taught crucial survival skills to those who remained in the area. They learnt to hunt and fish, to make snowshoes and to walk with them, and to adopt the canoe as using the waterways was much easier than hacking a trail through the forest. The terrain took its toll on men and women already debilitated by their voyage, and not all survived. Thirteen years later, when the Reverend James MacGregor appeared out of the forest to take up his Pictou ministry, there was a Scottish Presbyterian community at Pictou, but he was as dismayed at what he saw as the *Hector*'s passengers had been:

> When I looked around the shores of the harbour I was greatly disappointed and cast down, for there was scarcely anything to be seen but woods growing down to the water's edge. Here and there a mean timber hut was visible in a small clearing, which appeared no bigger than a garden compared to the woods. Nowhere could I see two houses without some wood between them.[4]

James MacGregor, who had grown up near Loch Earn in Perthshire, spent the rest of his life ministering to an extensive and scattered parish, which entailed arduous journeys on foot and by canoe. He, too, had to learn to use snowshoes and negotiate his way, travelling alone, through almost impenetrable forest and across swollen rivers and treacherous swamps. Bolstered by his faith, he got on with the job: his response could be characterised as typically Scottish. He almost implies that he relished the discomfort, that the flinty nature of Presbyterian belief required difficult circumstances. He grew accustomed to overnighting under the trees – 'for there is no travelling in the woods at night when there is no road' – and to losing his way.[5] There were those who vanished into the woods and never reappeared. The experience of being cut off from the sky could bring acute disorientation: 'Persons, when once they get off the beaten track, get frightened and bewildered, and lose all presence of mind.'[6]

William Bell arrived as minister to the Scottish settlement of Perth, Upper Canada (now Ontario), in 1817, and grew accustomed to travelling many miles on foot and by canoe to preach to large open-air congregations who emerged from the backwoods to hear the word of God. He heard tales of those who vanished in the forest for days and weeks. If his concern was primarily to reclaim lost souls rather than bodies, his own travels were an ever-present reminder of how close to wilderness they all were. He believed it would take many years before the land was sufficiently productive to sustain a substantial population.

The story of the *Hector* is sometimes cited as a Scottish version of the *Mayflower*'s Pilgrim Fathers, but in fact it tells us something rather different. The seventeenth-century emigrants to New England were fleeing persecution, and one can argue parallels with the circumstances of deprivation that drove the *Hector*'s passengers to leave Scotland. But the Pilgrim Fathers ceased to be victims once they had made the decision to voyage to the New World.

They had taken their future into their own hands. The people of the *Hector* remained victims, let down by those who had taken advantage of their circumstances in Scotland, whatever heroism the retelling of their story lends them. They were victims of exploitation, and many of them were defeated also by the land itself. While the people of the *Mayflower* (with Native American help) drew on the abundance of their new home to give thanks for the success of their enterprise, the people of the *Hector* struggled to feed their families. Today, Pictou celebrates its Scottish founding fathers, but there was little to celebrate in those first years when the forest was a constant threat.

There is a painting in Edinburgh's Museum of Scotland which epitomises a certain kind of Scottish stoicism in the face of displacement to the forested wilderness. 'Coronach in the Backwoods' by George Simson, 1859, shows a Highland family in a cleared patch of Canadian forest. The wife sits with an infant in her arms, apparently weeping. On the ground is a letter, we assume a letter from home with bad news. Beside her stands her husband, very upright and looking straight out of the canvas, playing a coronach, a lament, on the pipes. A collie dog sits looking mournful, but equally stoical. The shape of a log cabin can just be made out behind them, and beyond is the forest, dense, dark and threatening. The man's axe, symbol of the huge effort involved in clearing the trees and building shelter, leans on his left. The painting plays on sentimental notions of exile, while at the same time combining both strength and vulnerability. The playing of the pipes was an act of defiance as well as consolation, an expression of faith in a tradition that did not in any practical way advance the battle against the forest. Yet Scottish identity is here presented as a tool of survival.

It is probable that George Simson was never in Canada, and that his emigrant family emerged from a combination of travellers' tales and imagination. Yet it encapsulates the severity of displacement and a powerful attachment to the homeland, as well as fortitude. Scots at home, especially those encouraging emigration, were keen to promote the heroism of the pioneer, while also emphasising the Scottish connection. Simson's log cabin and axe do not transform his Highlanders into Canadians, but symbolise the robust determination of Scots. In reality, the Scottish emigrant family's native land was almost always lost to them, whatever efforts they made to retain their language and their music. Their chances of preserving direct links, of letters continuing to be exchanged over the generations, were slim.

In the Canadian context, despite the story of the *Hector*, the emigrant Scot most often represents the successful conquest of the wild. In North America generally, Scots were valued as settlers. They were believed to be tough, resilient, accustomed to hardship and sustained by religious conviction.

From 1763, when the end of the French and Indian wars secured British North America, Scots were to be found everywhere, as settlers, soldiers, fur traders, entrepreneurs, explorers. For almost all of them, wilderness was part of the experience. Wilderness was what the colonies signified, but wilderness could mean many different things. It suggested vast tracts of land rich in vegetation and wildlife, and empty of all but a transient and sparse native population. It was promoted as land for the taking, virgin soil full of potential for anyone with the grit and determination to develop it. But it also meant wasteland, deserts hot and cold, mountains of a size inconceivable even to Highland Scots, extremes of weather, vast turbulent rivers, ice-bound seas and treacherous coastlines, swamps and quicksands. It meant death by starvation, cold, drought, drowning, violence of all kinds. It meant elemental confrontations not just with landscape and climate, wild beasts and wild people, but with themselves. Wilderness was freighted with mythology and symbolism, as wasteland which threatened and undermined humanity, but also where faith could be strengthened. It was where in Scotland members of the early Celtic church could cultivate a connection with God, and where in North America survival could be interpreted as proof of God's mercy. It was where men and women could lose their minds, where desperation could drive them to murder in order to survive and to eat human flesh. And the North American wilderness was where being Scottish had meaning and resonance beyond the confines of Scotland's wild terrain and its particular history.

BACKWOODS: 'INURED TO A STORMY CLIMATE AND SCANTY FARE'

In Catherine Parr Traill's story *Lost in the Backwoods* (1852), Duncan Maxwell, a Highland soldier who fought at Quebec in 1759, marries a French Canadian woman and settles on the shore of Lake Ontario. He is 'accustomed to brave all sorts of hardships in a wild country, himself a mountaineer, inured to a stormy climate and scanty fare from his earliest youth'.[7] He and his brother-in-law take up adjoining land claims and get to work: 'what toil, what privation they endured for the first two years!' Pierre, the Frenchman, is volatile and optimistic, while Duncan is 'stern, steady, persevering, cautious'.[8] Gradually over the years they make a success of their farms, and their families increase.

But Traill's story is not about a Scotsman, a Frenchman and their success-ful pioneering. It is about their children, Hector and Catharine Maxwell, aged fourteen and twelve, and their cousin Louis Perron, also fourteen. One summer's day the three of them set out to search for straying cattle, equipped with baskets for gathering wild fruit, a tin pot for water, an axe in case Hector spots a useful tree, and Louis' *couteau de chasse*. We learn later that Louis also has a pocketful of bits and pieces – rusty nails, lengths of twine, strips of leather – that he has scavenged. The itemising of equipment is significant.

A few hours' walking takes the children into unfamiliar territory, and they soon realise they have lost all sense of their direction home. But, though vexed and anxious, they prepare to spend the night in the wild. With his axe Hector lops off branches to make a shelter, while Catharine uses Louis' knife to cut ferns for a bed. The next day Louis finds partridge eggs. They search for a flint and with some difficulty make a fire over which they boil the eggs in the tin pot. Later, Louis fashions a larger vessel out of bark, native-fashion.

Over the next few days the children attempt to find their way home, only to become increasingly disorientated. They find a lake which they cannot identify, streams which may or may not lead in the right direction, rocky hills, swamps, thick woods and lush clearings. They are fearful of getting doubly lost, of missing their way back to their shelter. If they stray too far, sensible Hector believes, they could become 'involved in the mazes of that dark forest and perish'.[9] On one of their forays, they follow a deer track into a valley:

> The utter loneliness of the path, the grotesque shadows of the trees that stretched in long array across the steep banks on either side, taking now this, now that wild and fanciful shape, awakened strange feelings of dread in the mind of these poor forlorn wanderers; like most persons bred up in solitude, their imaginations were strongly tinctured with superstitious fears. Here, then, in the lonely wilderness, far from their beloved parents and social hearth, with no visible arm to protect them from danger, none to encourage or cheer them, they started with terror-blanched cheeks at every fitful breeze that rustled the leaves or waved the branches above them.[10]

There are real dangers in the forest as well as imaginary ones. There are wolves, bears, possibly hostile natives, as well as all the hazards of wild terrain and extremes of weather. Benighted in the woods, they hear the 'long wild cry' of a wolf and then see 'with speechless horror' the gaunt outline of 'the terrible beast … its head raised, its neck stretched outward, and ears erect, as if to catch the echo that gave back those dismal sounds'.[11]

But the children are of pioneer stock, and have a fund of common sense and practical skills. It is summer, there are wild strawberries and whortle-berries, and the boys kill birds and small animals with stones. They fish with a hook made by Louis from a bit of tin from his pocket. They make a more permanent shelter, and have every expectation of being found, sooner or later, by their families. But they are not found, and winter approaches.

They have the foresight to lay in food stores and make warmer clothes out of animal skins.

Hector, Catharine and Louis spend three years lost in the backwoods. During that time they rescue a Mohawk girl from warring Ojibways who have already slaughtered her family. She joins the youngsters' household, and contributes her own native skills to their battle for survival. She can hunt with bow and arrow, fish, prepare animal skins, make snowshoes and effortlessly handle a canoe. The boys acknowledge her superiority in these matters, but remind themselves that in other areas, spinning and knitting, milking cows, and the multifarious domestic tasks that were required of pioneer white women, she would be clueless. And it was the pioneering white children who saved her life. All three are concerned at her lack of Christian faith, which they set out to rectify.

Throughout the narrative there is stress on the contrasting characters of the two boys. Hector is prudent, steady, focused, while Louis is inventive and quick-thinking, but reckless. Catharine – and it is perhaps no accident that she bears the name of her creator – is practical and industrious, taking her domestic duties seriously. The key to their success is their pioneer upbringing:

> Early accustomed to the hardships incidental to the lives of the settlers in the bush, these young people had learned to bear with patience and cheerfulness privations that would have crushed the spirits of children more delicately nurtured. They had known every degree of hunger and nakedness: during the first few years of their lives they had often been compelled to subsist for days and weeks upon roots and herbs, wild fruits, and game which their fathers had learned to entrap, to decoy, and to shoot.

The boys had learnt to make traps and they could shoot (they lament their lack of a rifle) and use a bow; 'they could pitch a stone or fling a wooden dart at partridge, hare, and squirrel with almost unerring aim'. 'This useful and practical knowledge,' Traill adds, '... enabled them to face with fortitude the privations of a life so precarious as that to which they were now exposed.'[12]

The wilderness, though, is not only a territory of threat and privation. The landscape is often beautiful, and Traill suggests that the youngsters' appreciation of the picturesque is due in part to their Highland origins. Hector and Catharine had 'insensibly imbibed a love of the grand and picturesque, by listening with untiring interest to their father's animated and enthusiastic descriptions of his Highland home, and the wild mountainous scenery that surrounded it'.[13] Wandering 'by wild cliffy banks, beset with huge boulders of red and gray granite and water-worn limestone', past flowering shrubs, silver birch, bilberries and cranberries, the youngsters are 'delighted with the picturesque path' and gaze 'with curiosity and interest on the lonely but lovely landscape before them'.[14] The wilderness is not barren but full of bounty, which Traill details with some particularity, often giving scientific names to plants and at one point referring readers to a display of Canadian partridge in London's British Museum (a clue as to the intended readership of the book). But without knowledge and skill, the bounty is of little use.

The story of three years in the backwoods is both an adventure story – the culminating episode has Catharine captured by Ojibway and rescued in a manner that echoes Fenimore Cooper – and a manual of survival. In the acknowledged tradition of *Robinson Crusoe* (the story's original title was *The Canadian Crusoes*) it is full of useful information and encouragement to resourcefulness. Character and background play their part, but trial and error and luck are also factors. Godliness is equally important; the youngster's faith sustains them. And when eventually Hector Maxwell and Indiana, as they call their Mohawk companion (her original name is overlooked), become man and wife, the Mohawk girl has been baptised. There is no question but that she will embrace the role of pioneer wife and all that goes with it. She will be absorbed into the society of the incomers, a solution clearly approved by her creator. She may not forget her native skills, but there will no longer be the need to engage with the wilderness as her own family had done. Her change of identity is not questioned, nor is the demise of her way of life. Catharine and Louis are married on the same day, and all four go on to live happy and prosperous lives. This is their reward for being true to both their Scottish and their pioneer heritage.

In choosing to write about children, and for children, and in particular about children removed from the adult world, Traill is able to explore a (relatively) uncorrupted confrontation with nature. Although the three have some differences of approach, they do not compete. Survival depends on collaboration and mutual support. The children's innocence underlines the message that the experience of hardship has moral as well as practical advantages. It brings an appreciation of safety and comfort, of family and community. Its testing qualities not only improve survival skills, but enrich a moral strength. Delicate nurturing is no preparation for life or faith, although the sympathetic appreciation of nature is also a moral asset.

The whole point of surviving the wilderness is to move on to a more civilised existence, while retaining the moral and practical lessons of hardship. Emphasising the passing of an era, Traill tells us that the log cabins once inhabited by the Maxwell and Perron families have 'fallen to decay' and 'no trace or record remains of the first breakers of the bush'. With their lost children finally recovered, Duncan Maxwell and Pierre Perron and their families move on to another settlement near Montreal to join Highlanders already established there, and their Lake Ontario home is now 'a green waste' beside 'the smooth turnpike road that leads from Cobourg to Cold Springs'.[15] A road has replaced the tentative forest trails, but we are reminded that wilderness is not far away. If there is some ambivalence here, and regret at the obsolescence of the pioneer spirit, there is also the suggestion, which recurs in North American pioneering narratives, that an heroic experience of wilderness is hard-wired into the Canadian and US national narratives.

Henry Thoreau, writing in the 1840s and 1850s, stressed the need to engage directly with the wild, asserting not only the 'beneficence of Nature' but the belief that succumbing to its influence was important: 'it is a surprising and memorable, as well as valuable experience, to be lost in the woods any time'.[16] Daily life should not eliminate risk, for danger is an essential part of an elemental connection with the real world:

> Men come tamely home at night only from the next field or street, where their household echoes haunt, and their life pines because it breathes its own breath over again; their shadows morning and evening reach farther than their daily steps. We should come home from far, from adventures, and perils, and discoveries every day, with new experience and character.[17]

The New World offered an opportunity of 'new experiences', less available in the eroded Old World. Thoreau's wilderness at Walden Pond was on the doorstep of a long-established community, but he was able to make expeditions to more demanding terrain, in Maine, for example, and emphasised the need to respond to the wild and see it as a resource both practical and spiritual. John Muir would echo and enlarge on this embrace of the natural world.

Those for whom the engagement with nature was a matter of survival might, if they could pause long enough from their labours, have considered such transcendentalism an irrelevant luxury. Like Cooper, Thoreau (and Muir) contributed to the mythologising of wild landscape and an argument that America's frontier had an intrinsic value beyond space for settlement and exploitation. In addition to its spiritual and regenerative power, it was a breeding ground for heroes. Something similar was occurring in Scotland. The wild landscape remained, and remains, as a continual prompt for the invention, if not the reality, of an heroic past. There are suggestive parallels between the emergence of the kilted Highlander as a romantic hero and that of the buckskin-clad frontiersman.

ROUGHING IT: 'THE COARSE HARD LIFE OF THE AXEMAN'

Catherine and Susanna Strickland were English sisters who both married former soldiers from Orkney, Thomas Traill and John Moodie. In the 1830s, both couples emigrated to Upper Canada. The sisters each wrote books about the pioneering experience. Catherine's *Lost in the Backwoods* is set in the area near Cobourg, on Lake Ontario, where John and Susanna Moodie took over a farm in 1832. The land was already cleared, so the Moodies escaped the most backbreaking effort of settlement; nevertheless, making a success of farming was a very demanding and often dispiriting task. Later, they moved on to a new land grant slightly further north, near where Catherine and Thomas Traill were already settled. The Moodies named their new home 'Melsetter', the name of a village on the island of Hoy in Orkney.

The books Susanna Moodie wrote about her experiences, *Roughing it in the Bush* (1852) and *Life in the Clearings Versus the Bush* (1853), have become classics of pioneering in Canada. Her sister Catherine was more prolific in her output, writing manuals for emigrants and many stories for children, including *The Young Emigrants* (1826) published before Catherine had set foot in British North America. Between them, they provide a striking and extensive account of settlement in the wild. Moodie stresses the hardships and tribulations, particularly for those unused to strenuous physical effort. For them 'the coarse, hard life of the axeman' was not to be recommended.[18] Traill was more upbeat. 'In Canada persevering energy and industry, with sobriety, will overcome all obstacles,' she confidently states in her *Female Emigrants' Guide* (1854), and *Lost in the Backwoods* illustrates exactly that. But she does acknowledge the challenge that lies ahead of the settler: 'The giants of the forest are not brought down without much severe toil; and many hardships must be endured in a backwoodsman's life, especially by the wife and children.'[19]

The axe in Simson's painting 'Coronach in the Backwoods', and that Hector Maxwell providentially carries with him when he and his sister and cousin set out on what they think is a day's excursion, is a prominent symbol of pioneer effort and success. Without this essential tool the battle to conquer the forested wilderness could not begin. The luckless arrivals at Pictou in 1773 had to acquire axes and learn how to use them. In poetry written by Scottish emigrants the axe is often celebrated; 'In Western Woods' by John Macfarlane from Abington, Lanarkshire, is an example:

> In western woods an exile
>   In dreamy musing stands,
> The gleaming axe uplifted,
>   And stayed with steady hands.[20]

If 'dreamy musing' does not quite suggest pioneer industry, the uplifted axe and steady hands are a perfectly arrested symbol. John MacCorkindale from Islay, in Upper Canada in the 1850s, conveys a more purposeful and expressive image:

When I set out with my axe
to fell the trees
the work was hard, but it was heartening
to see their tops bending,
then causing a tremor all around,
falling in the direction I thought best.[21]

John Mortimer, born in Cape Breton in 1858 of parents from Aberdeenshire, evokes the heroism of the toiler in the forest more than a hundred years after Scots began arriving in Canada in significant numbers. The title of his poem, 'The Felling of the Forest', itself suggests the magnitude of the task:

Once more I swing
The glittering axe, and hear its echoes ring
Through the deep solitude; with toil once more
Is reared the rude hut by the river's shore.[22]

The axe is inseparable from the hands that hold it and the arms that swing it. Although settlers often cooperated in the building of shelter, the axe itself can be wielded by one man only. It is a solitary weapon against the vastness of the forest. (In Jan Troell's 1972 film, *The Emigrants*, based on the novels by Vilhelm Moberg, a story of Swedish emigration which has much in common with the Scottish experience, hero Carl-Oscar makes his solitary march through the forest with his axe on his shoulder and marks his claim with a single blow to a tree. Later he is alerted to the arrival of a new settler when he hears the sound of an axe coming from a nearby claim.) The axe also represents labour itself and the moral worth of purposeful activity. In contrast, for James Fenimore Cooper's pioneer hero, Natty Bumppo, there is no nobility in the axe. Driven west by encroaching settlement he laments: 'They scourge the very 'arth with their axes … It was a grievous journey that I made, a grievous toil to pass through the falling timber and to breathe the thick air of smoky clearings.'[23]

'Dark', 'interminable', 'never-ending', 'sombre', 'dreary', the Gaelic '*gruamach*' (gloomy): these are the adjectives most often used to describe the North American forest and they resonate with a primeval fear of the forest as a source of threat. For John McClean, in Nova Scotia in the first half of the nineteenth century, the landscape is both alien and sterile: 'I am alone in the gloomy forest; my thoughts are restless, I cannot sing; I found this place contrary to nature, every talent that was in my head has departed.'[24] Such a bleakly dislocating effect counters efforts both to adapt and to recreate old ways in a new environment. The wilderness appears to undermine the connections of culture and identity which were such important tools of survival. To Susanna Moodie the forest is an expanse of dreary uniformity, 'a stern array of rugged trunks, a tangled maze of scrubby underbrush, carpeted winter and summer with a thin layer of withered buff leaves'.[25] With each stretch of forest indistinguishable from the next, the effect is discouraging and debilitating rather than alarming. John Lorne Campbell visited Nova Scotia in 1932, and drove through dense forest interrupted by an occasional farmhouse. Some of the farms seemed abandoned, with trees reclaiming the once cleared land: 'The forest seemed to be alive and to hold the country in its grip, intense, malignant, ever ready to reclaim as its own the land that had once been torn from it.'[26] The forest is threatening, but humanity's encroachment is an assault.

TRAVELLERS: 'THE PATHLESS WILDERNESS'

Many Scots who had no intention of transplanting themselves permanently were nevertheless sufficiently attracted to North America to make often lengthy visits. One of these was John Howison, who spent two and a half years in Upper Canada. In his book, *Sketches of Upper Canada* (1821), he described the experience of 'solitary wanderings in the pathless wilderness'. He goes on:

> The sombre forests standing erect in impenetrable strength, and stretching their boughs into the deep, cold, blue sky; the stars rising in solemn and unobtrusive grandeur; the stupendous galaxies moving in solemn silence through the immensity of space; the moss clothing the trunks of the trees in phosphoric brightness and the roar of distant cataracts swelling and diminishing upon the ear.[27]

He is impressed by the 'magnitude and beauty' of the trees, and the sheer scale of the Ontario landscape and of the labour involved in taming it. But the forest is also ominous:

> Occasional gusts of wind swept through the forests with deep and dismal murmurs, and my imagination magnified the sound of one horse's feet into that made by a whole troop. The indistinct murmur of voices seemed to rise among the cadences of the breaking waves; and I often looked around me, almost expecting to see crowds of the spirits of Indian warriors issuing from the woods in solemn procession, mourning the subjection of their territories, and the extinction of their tribes, and breathing curses upon Europeans.'[28]

An awareness of the forest as territory of potentially hostile natives is never far away, although often without this sympathetic acknowledgement of the subjection of the indigenous population. The first natives encountered by most Scots settling along the Atlantic coast and the northeastern interior were Iroquoian and Algonquian peoples whose natural habitat was wood-land. The forests and the rivers that ran through them provided their food and all their resources for survival. In *Lost in the Backwoods*, Hector and Louis have learnt their forest skills from the First Nations, and many early settlers owed their survival to native assistance. The 'pathless wilderness' of the settlers was a landscape that any native could read. The prints of deer, the sounds of birds, the disturbance of vegetation, all spoke to those indigenous to this environment.

This is conveyed vividly in Cooper's novels. Natty Bumppo succeeds as hunter, pathfinder and protector because he is, like the Indians, and like Walter Scott's Highlanders, a product of the wild. Natty and the natives belong in the wilderness; the settlers are intruders. The axe represents intrusion as much as it does conquest of the wild. It also suggests perman-ence; natives are peripatetic, and never had a need to fell large quantities of trees, although wood provided shelter and the material for household goods, weapons and – most important – canoes. Their lives left the forest intact.

For the intruding Europeans the forest seems to be only just kept at bay. Clearing the bush was a constant activity, necessary to keep routes open and prevent homes and crops from being swallowed up. There was no let-up in the intense labour of maintaining enough land to feed a family with some surplus to sell. A natural clearing was a blessing – it opened up the sky and let in the sunlight. It might be a place for making camp, or even of recreation, a picnic perhaps, or just a pause for rest from hunting or berry-picking. But for most pioneers in the forest the axe was essential.

The notion of clearing the land was not alien to the Scottish crofters arriving in North America. Many would have cleared stones and boulders to make way for crops of potatoes or oats. In Scotland's Highlands and Islands the preparation of land for planting had never been easy. But this did not make the trees any less daunting, and for many Scots clearance had an additional level of meaning. For generations clearing the land had meant the removal of natural obstacles to survival. From the late eighteenth century, clearance more often meant the removal of human beings, themselves seen as obstacles to productive development. Over a century and a half, thousands of displaced men, women and children arrived in a land that they then had to clear, to transform wilderness into homes and communities, while the homes they had left were transformed into a kind of wilderness. But they, the victims of clearance, were themselves complicit, and in some cases active, in clearing those human beings for whom the wilderness was a source of material and cultural sustenance.

But there is no room in the face of the onward tramp of civilisation for a sentimental attachment to life close to nature or to the lives of those who lived close to nature. As in the Scottish Highlands, the primitive, however attractive and however integral to both the demands and the romance of landscape, must give way. By the end of Cooper's Leatherstocking novels Natty Bumppo is an anachronism, like Fergus MacIvor in Scott's *Waverley*, and like a recurrent hero of the Western who faces with dismay the arrival of the machine gun and motor car.

For many Scots in North America the forest was not only gloomy and ominous, it was also sinister and depressive. Once in the forest, you are trapped. William Fraser, who in 1846 settled in Illinois but then moved on to Oregon, wrote:

> Every step I take through this country
> Is in the dark forest that pervades it.

He goes on to lament the fact that:

> We can't see heather growing on the mountain top
> Or pure, clear stream currents.[29]

There was considerable ambivalence in some Scottish comment on the United States, arising less from nostalgia than from a sense of disappointment. In 1819, Eneas Mackenzie published *An Historical, Topographical, and Descriptive View of the United States of America*, intended as a guide to the prospective settler. He talks up American potential – 'in her plains and forests an industrious, enterprising, and intelligent population are daily creating new and extensive communities' – but a contradictory thread runs through his commentary.[30] America, he feels, attracts the dregs of Europe, and has become 'the receptacle for speculators and fortune-hunters, for adventurers and base and demoralized characters of every shade and description'.[31] The new Americans are often lazy, careless and dissipated – a far cry from the stalwart axe-wielding pioneer. In the remoter areas he finds people with 'a disconsolate wildness in their countenances, and an indolence and inactivity in their whole behaviour'.[32] He condemns slavery, both for its inhumanity and because it encourages white people to do very little themselves. It offends a Calvinist ethic in more ways than one.

Mackenzie's observations suggest that wilderness breeds wildness, and that although pioneering endeavour in the United States is often spectacularly successful, if it fails the consequences are a particularly degraded kind of marginal existence. Through the century many comment on the forms of degeneracy that result when Europeans are removed from 'civilised' society, and when natives are cut off from their sustaining wild environment. But Mackenzie is also alert to success. He cites Ohio as an example of a territory that was transformed in a couple of decades from a 'wilderness frequented by savages' to a society of incomers which in a seven-month period in 1811 sent 800 boats down the Ohio River 'laden with the productions and manufactures of this country'.[33] Cincinnati was clamouring for tradesmen of all kinds, and many Scots responded to the call. But while cities such as Cincinnati and Pittsburgh were growing at frightening speed, the backwoods remained, the axe was still a vital tool, and the potential for losing direction – in many different senses – remained. This, of course, was part of the excitement of the New World: the alliance of rapid industrialisation with untamed territory that continued to demand traditional pioneering skills.

Thomas Hamilton from Glasgow, a former soldier and neighbour of Walter Scott at Abbotsford, visited the United States some years after Mackenzie, in 1831, with the intention of writing about his travels. The consequent book, published two years later, was not complimentary to the young republic. He commented on a frontier population 'thinly scattered through regions of interminable forest'.[34] He travelled by steamboat down the Ohio and Mississippi rivers, which gave him a leisurely opportunity to observe the Mississippi backwoods, 'dreary and pestilential solitudes, untrodden save by the foot of the Indian'. The wilderness landscape was both 'dismal' and 'impressive', the dark rolling waters of the river as disheartening as the oppression of the forest.[35] The scattering of log huts did nothing to relieve the daunting prospect. The knowledge that the wilderness offered refuge to criminals and to 'men of broken characters, hopes, and fortunes, who fly not from justice, but contempt' heightened the sense of demoralisation, which in turn rendered the backwoods sinister as well as ominous.[36] There is no suggestion of the heroic in Hamilton's depiction of the backwoods settler, or of promise in virgin land. William Richard Grahame was visiting the United States from Scotland at around the same time as Hamilton. He was looking for land to purchase and was disappointed in what he saw. He, too, steamed down the Ohio through a 'wilderness of forests, flats and swamps', and noted the scattering of crudely constructed shacks and the rough attempts at cultivation.[37]

Some years later, Alexander Muir, a lawyer from Aberdeen, went to Canada to visit family who had settled there. Although he did not detect a degenerate influence, the realities of the wild were sharply brought home. He travelled up the Ottawa River from its confluence with the St Lawrence. During a stay in a settlement near the river, where he found many Scots, he visited the home of fellow Scot and local MP, Archibald Petrie, 'a neat framewood cottage' with a veranda and set in grounds 'laid out with much taste'.[38] At the end of a pleasant meal in congenial and civilised company, he set off for his lodging through dense forest and the encroaching dusk. The howling of wolves and the awareness of bears in the vicinity added to his alarm. He made it back, but the experience underlined the error of assuming that refinement banished danger, and it no doubt influenced his account of what was meant by the 'bush':

> an interminable forest of the loftiest trees you could imagine, from 50 to 150 feet and in some places you may travel days nay weeks or months before coming upon a clearance or human dwelling, hence the great danger of going into the bush without a guide and a compass.[39]

The backwoods meant not just oppressive battalions of trees, but a particularly intense isolation, where distance was magnified by enclosure.

By the early nineteenth century, enough was known in Scotland about the New World for the forested wilderness no longer to come as a surprise to the emigrant. The Scottish press took a great interest in transatlantic prospects, and commercial links ensured a stream of information. In addition, there were the travellers, like Mackenzie and Hamilton, who wrote of their experiences, and a rash of emigrant guides, some providing detailed advice on how to travel and what to take. The predominant message was that the emigrant who arrived with nothing (as thousands did) was going to have a hard time; and that making a new life in the New World entailed hard work, perseverance and a measure of luck. The forest trails, if they existed at all, were not paved with gold.

Playing a key role in settlement were the land companies, which acquired vast acreages as land grants on condition that they brought in settlers to develop them. The Philadelphia Company, which brought the *Hector*'s emigrants to Pictou, was one of the earlier ventures. Leading figures in the company were the Reverend John Witherspoon from Paisley, and John Pagan from Glasgow. Throughout the history of North American settlement, wilderness attracted the land speculators, who seized opportunities for selling on land or of exploiting its resources (see Chapter 6). Scots were prominent in North American land speculation, many without setting foot in the territory seen as the source of potential wealth.

JOHN GALT IN WANCHANCY NEIGHBOURHOODS

Half a century after Witherspoon and Pagan enticed Highland emigrants to Nova Scotia, the Canada Company was formed, which acquired the Huron Tract, over a million acres between lakes Huron and Ontario in Upper Canada. Secretary of the company was John Galt. Galt, born in Irvine, Ayrshire, had had a mixed career by the time he set sail for North America in 1825, but latterly he had become known as a novelist, publishing four works of fiction in quick succession: *Annals of the Parish* and *The Provost* in 1822, and *The Entail* and *Ringan Gilhaize* in 1823. Galt had grown up in Greenock, where his father was involved in the West India trade, and his first job was in the Greenock customs house, which gave him early exposure to trans-atlantic connections. Canada was a beguiling prospect.

The Canada Company intended to do things thoroughly, and sent five commissioners, including Galt, to inspect the territory they hoped to acquire. They sailed to New York, and took a steamboat up the Hudson River, crossing Lake Ontario to York, not yet the city of Toronto. From there they headed west into the forested interior. The deal was clinched and the following year Galt was back to select a site for a town to be called Guelph (named for George IV, whose family name was Gwelf). For Galt, conquering the wilderness meant building towns, with all the infrastructure and amenities that that implied. There were plenty of Scottish examples to inspire him, from the industrial village of New Lanark to Edinburgh's New Town, both late eighteenth-century ventures, but both, however challenging, very different propositions from laying foundations in the forest. As Galt made his way through the forest on foot, much to his vexation he got lost. 'I was excessively angry,' he commented, 'for such an accident is no trifle in the woods.'[40] Perhaps as a gesture of reasserting control, he and his companions felled a maple tree on the chosen site, a moment he describes in his autobiography: 'The tree fell with a crash of accumulating thunder, as if ancient Nature were alarmed at the entrance of social man into her innocent solitudes with his sorrows, his follies and his crimes.'[41]

But Galt had already discovered that the 'solitudes' of the wilderness were not so innocent. Solitude in the backwoods could mean death, and the dispelling of solitude, the creation of a substantial community, would inevitably alarm 'ancient Nature' a great deal more than the crash of a single tree. And there was some prescience, or hindsight, in Galt's comment, as in the eyes of some, Guelph, or at least Galt's aspirations for Guelph, was itself a folly.

Galt was enthusiastic and vigorous in his development of the town, and spent generously on roads, bridges, mills, even a ballroom, to create what he considered to be necessary amenities. His aim was to create a place of 'superior character' even if the first settlers were 'not of that rank of life to make such things important'.[42] He himself would preside over a flourishing and cultured community. Like many others, he saw the wilderness as providing space for a role denied him in the Old World. It was an opportunity to find himself; in the process, he spent the Canada Company's money freely. To recoup their outlay the company had to bring people in to take up land grants, but in ten years only half of its million acres had been settled. After two years Galt was called back to London to face the consequences. Unable to convince the company that his ambitions for Guelph were justified, Galt was relieved of his position as superintendent. He had for many years been in a financially precarious position and the loss of his job brought imprisonment for debt in London's King's Bench prison. It was there that Galt turned his North American experience to more productive use, writing his novel *Lawrie Todd, or Settlers in the Woods*, published in 1830.

It is the 1790s, and Lawrie Todd's involvement in radical politics necessitates a hasty departure from Scotland, with the aim of making a new life in the youthful United States of America. After two false starts, in New York City and New Jersey, he sets off with his family to take up a 50-acre land grant near Utica. He is heading for a 'newly located town' called Babelmandel, reluctant to go 'too far into the wilderness, lest I should pass the reach of education, and expose my children to the hazards of ignorance, – a matter of deepest concernment to those who think of settling in the bush'.[43] Lawrie, who by this time has suffered the deaths of his wife and one of his children, has no heroic illusions about the pioneering life: both his pragmatism and his concern for his children's education can be seen as characteristically Scottish.

However, the family cannot escape the wilderness, and as they leave behind first Schenectady on the Hudson and then Utica further west, they enter a landscape that is almost gothic in aspect, marked by human activity yet without the comforting signs of productive life. The road becomes 'a mere blazed trail' through a terrain of 'tree stumps and cradle heaps, mud-holes and miry swards'. They pass 'hundreds on hundreds of vast and ponderous trees covering the ground for acres, like the mighty slain in a field of battle, all to be removed, yea, obliterated, before the solitary settler can raise a meal of potatoes'. Lawrie is deeply dismayed as he contemplates 'seemingly ... the most hopeless task which the industry of man can struggle with'.[44] The puny effort to tame the trees only emphasises the power of the wild and adds to the menace of the woods.

Galt describes in detail the task of gaining a foothold in the forest: the felling of trees; the logging and burning; the construction of a log cabin and its rebuilding when first they are flooded out, then burnt out by a forest fire. His second wife dies, his son gets into trouble. At the same time, the relentless sequence of disaster is almost a fulfilment of expectation, the classic Scottish assumption that a goal easily attained has little worth. When Lawrie returns to Scotland, it is with a sense of achievement, for in the end he conquers the forest and can make his reappearance in his native land as a successful man. He travels in a cabin, rather than among 'the caravan of human cattle' who shared his departure.[45] His heart lifts when he looks out from the coach making its way from Edinburgh to Dalkeith on a road superior to those in America. He sees a 'fine, open, and cleared country ... not a tree to be seen'.[46] Here is a land where humanity is in control.

The novel was a great success, which encouraged Galt to return to the North American theme for a second time, with *Bogle Corbet or The Emigrants* (1831). After an unsuccessful venture in the Caribbean and pushed by economic circumstances and family difficulties, Bogle Corbet decides to emigrate to Upper Canada. Before he and his family depart they are warned against the wilderness. 'The hardships of the woods are no' wholesome,' says his adviser, who suggests that they settle in an established town rather than take on 'the awesome solitude of the wild woods, and the wanchancy neighbourhood of bears and trees'.[47] But, as Lawrie Todd found, wilderness is almost inescapable.

As the Corbet family sails up the St Lawrence they look out at narrow strips of settlement backed by a vast wild hinterland. With a stop in Montreal to purchase supplies, especially axes, they make their way onward by road, with the turbulent St Lawrence on one side and unending forest on the other. They reach York, and continue on to somewhere near Hamilton. Galt has taken his hero into territory he knows well, for Guelph is not far away. One of their party is a weaver from Glasgow, who comments 'there's a wide difference ... between the Gorbals and this wild country, which was all ta'en from the Indians, who have the best right to the land, if anybody has a right'.[48] This is an unusual acknowledgement of the original inhabitants of the forest.

Bogle acquires a farm and helps to found a new town, Stockwell, believing that his leadership has been essential to the immigrant community's success. Galt has a message for the intending immigrant. Carving a livelihood out of virgin forest is dispiritingly hard work, a task for the determined and energetic which demands skill and experience. He criticises the lack of support available from the colonial government, and stresses that a town, implying a cohesive community, makes more sense than scattered settlement. Collaboration and collective effort will achieve more and help to expel the gloom experienced by those who embark on a solitary struggle in the forest at a distance from neighbours. Dispersal in the forest is a form of banishment. Bogle follows his own advice, and unlike Lawrie Todd, sticks it out, remaining in his new country and contributing to its development.

The novel, though, did not repeat the success of *Lawrie Todd*. It is certainly more didactic in tone, content and structure, which may be part of the reason, but perhaps it was also because Bogle Corbet was a true immigrant. Lawrie has his adventure and, in traditional adventure story fashion, returns to 'normality'. Bogle adapts to a new world and is lost to the old. And he pays a heavy price. Whatever the satisfaction of survival and partial success in the wild, it is a grim tale of hardship and sacrifice, not calculated to enthuse those contemplating a new life in a new land. Although some Scottish readers may have relished a tale where hardship has its own value, and ultimately brings rewards, publishing success depended on a much wider appeal.

'THE LONG FIGHT WITH THE FOREST'

Glengarry County, along the upper St Lawrence, was settled by Highlanders in the 1780s. When John Howison visited forty years later he was not impressed. The settlers were still living in primitive log cabins, and had made little effort to transform the wilderness into a civilised community. Ralph Connor, who grew up in Glengarry, was rather more upbeat in his depiction of pioneer life, although he does not downplay what he calls 'the long fight with the forest'.[49] In *Glengarry School Days* (1902) he describes a community of scattered log houses and barns in small clearings carved out from the dark green forest. The children, accustomed to the distance between the homesteads and the encroachment of the woods, make their way home from school along blazed paths that take them through pines, balsam, spruce and silver birch. Connor evokes the 'brittle Highland courage toughened to endurance' which he sees as characteristic of the pioneer Scots, who have a 'self-respect born of victory over nature's grimmest of terrors'.[50] The forest may be grim, but the tone of his writing is celebratory rather than gloomy. The 'persevering energy' identified by Catherine Parr Traill has achieved a community that has a church and a school, and has maintained a Highland identity and Highland traditions. 'They come of a race that sees things through,' says Connor of the Glengarry pioneers, echoing Traill's belief in Scottish grit and guts.[51]

A century or so later, even in those areas of Ontario, Quebec, New Brunswick and Nova Scotia that had been massively logged out, the forest retained its quality of sinister intrusion. Margaret Atwood (of partly Scottish descent) in her novel *Surfacing* (1972) takes her heroine back to the bush where she spent her childhood. She is searching for her vanished father, who had deliberately tried to recreate the experience of the first settlers 'who arrived when there was nothing but forest'.[52] Surrounding the abandoned cabin is a jungle, with tree trunks and leaves forming 'a solid interlocking fence, green, green-grey, grey-brown' which has to be hacked through.[53] The heroine remembers a manual she read as a child, *How to Stay Alive in the Bush*: 'it wasn't until then I realized it was in fact possible to lose your way'.[54] She wonders if her father, living alone in the cabin, could have lost his mind: 'Bushed, the trappers call it when you stay in the forest by yourself too long.'[55]

The insidious effect of wilderness on four young urbanites is a key feature of the novel. Apart from the heroine herself, they have no backwoods experience and no survival skills. They have no connection with a pioneer heritage. The heroine makes a vain effort to return to the wild, eventually, against all her principles, submitting to rescue. But there is no longer a bold perception of hardship having worth for its own sake. Wilderness is a source of confusion and disorientation, not a test of moral and practical achievement.

D. R. MacDonald's novel, *Cape Breton Road* (2001), quite specifically evokes a Scottish experience of Cape Breton, although Innis Corbett, his central character, has grown up in Boston and has almost lost touch with his Scottish heritage. (The name's echo of John Galt's character is perhaps deliberate.) When Innis returns to Cape Breton he has his own, very modern, idea of how to exploit the backwoods, but it entails the deployment of traditional skills. At first, Innis sees the woods as a place in which to hide, an environment in which he can disappear. Gradually, he learns to understand the trees, to observe and use their features 'to braid an invisible tether … that would lead you back to where you wanted to return'. But he gets over-confident, and suddenly he is lost:

> The sun he'd kept on his left shoulder had gone, absorbed into a sky cold as milk, and the wind he'd remembered as east, east on his face, had dodged somehow around, leaping at him in different directions, confusing him in showers of dry leaves. Small clearings of light in deep spruce and fir and stripped hardwoods mocked him as he plunged first toward one, then another.[56]

The landmarks he had noted vanish or change shape. Baffled by deer trails leading in different directions, scared by sounds he cannot interpret and by a sinister 'flick of fur', he is a 'city boy without a city',[57] and he remembers the story of another refugee from the city, a woman who loses her way and is found at last by Mounties and a tracker dog. But Innis has good reason not to attract the attention of the Mounties, or to be 'taken out of here by a dog and kindly rescuers'. When at last he identifies a familiar tree and finds the blaze he cut into its trunk, it is 'like seeing his name carved there'.[58]

Innis gets a job clearing a path through the woods, for which prowess with an axe is essential. It is a test of his manhood.

> He stepped away as the trunk gave out a tentative crack, shifted slightly above his blade, and then plunged with gathering force, striking the debris around it like an enormous switch. He stood panting amid vibrations of dry branches, the dust of dead needles and bark. Around him lay trees already tumbled, busted deadfalls, splintered trunks, spikes of broken branches you could barely climb through.[59]

Here is wilderness depicted as a challenge to individual endeavour. The forest constantly regenerates and there is still a need to cut down trees. Innis is drawn to the pioneer heritage, and to the physicality of getting to grips with wilderness, but for him remoteness and isolation present an opportunity that escaped the first Cape Breton settlers: he grows cannabis. Deep in the trees he finds a clearing ringed by birch and maple. He needs to use not an axe but a pick:

He chopped through mats of sod and stubborn roots, worked soil clean of stones … When the reddish clay was as fine as he could make it with a trowel, he prodded each plant free of its pot, nesting carefully the white net of roots into its hole.[60]

In the end Innis *is* lost, as he has been, in a sense, from the beginning. In a stolen Cadillac, escaping the Mounties, he tries to find his way through the Everlasting Barrens, where the trees are dense but stunted, 'branches curled and huddled, roots twisted into the soil'.[61] Whatever human activity there might once have been has long since vanished. It is getting dark. Innis is determined not to be 'fooled any more by roads that went nowhere', but then out of the darkness a moose looms and instead of fleeing the approaching car turns on it.[62] The Cadillac in a ditch, Innis struggles on foot, totally disorientated by the tangled trees, blinded by the stars, stumbling and tripping, impelled by a vision of safety but also by confused pictures of his disturbed past. His attempts to re-enact pioneer skills are of no use to him now. Wilderness now seems to deprive him of the individuality his 'pioneering' bestowed. In fact, the novel suggests that losing your way in the twentieth century is a greater challenge than it was for the first settlers. There is, in a sense, more at stake.

The Cape Breton road goes nowhere and our last sight of Innis Corbett leaves him still lost in the backwoods. It is no longer possible, as it was for Catherine Parr Traill, to enter the wilderness in a state of innocence or to expect from it some form of redemption. Margaret Atwood's *Surfacing* contains the same message. Modern life suggests that although the wilderness is still there, the very act of entering it brings contamination. The direct and intimate contact with unsullied wildness, as described by John Muir (see Chapter 8) is beyond our reach, because we, literally and metaphorically, carry too much with us. A pocketful of oatmeal, tea and bread, which sustained Muir, is not sufficient for the modern traveller in the wild. While Hector, Catharine and Louis set about building a shelter and foraging for food, Innis is desperately seeking a telephone. His cannabis planting has entailed moving through the woods on foot; he has used an axe, learnt to observe trees and plants and the movements of wild animals; he has re-encountered the Gaelic of his forebears. But when he steals a car he breaks faith with Cape Breton's Scottish legacy, or tries to, and has nothing adequate to put in its place.

In 1788, the Reverend James MacGregor would have turned his back on Pictou if he had been able. 'Nothing but necessity kept me there,' he wrote, 'for I durst not think of encountering the dangerous road to Halifax again, and there was no vessel in Pictou to take me away.'[63] For most Scots, once arrived in the New World there was no return journey. But for MacGregor, at least, there were the rewards of ministering to a flock who needed and valued his presence. And there were other rewards. The never-ending forest was a place of beauty as well as danger, of fascinating variety as well as gloom. Autumn especially brought an intensity of colour and contrast – 'nothing can be compared to its effulgent grandeur', he wrote:

> Two or three frosty nights, in the decline of autumn, transform the boundless verdure of a whole empire into every possible tint of brilliant scarlet, rich violet, every shade of blue and brown, vivid crimson, and glittering yellow. The stern, exorable fir trees alone maintain their eternal somber green. All others in mountains or in valleys burst into the most glorious vegetable beauty, and exhibit the most splendid and most enchanting panorama on earth.[64]

As Catherine Parr Traill makes clear, adversity did not dull a response to the attractions of the natural world. Her young heroes' appreciation of nature's beauty as well as bounty contributes to their survival, and their ordeal equips them for a stable and productive future. Becoming lost in the backwoods was not defeat, but ultimately a conquest. They have re-enacted the experience of their pioneering parents and proved their worth. They have demonstrated their credentials, as pioneers, as citizens, and as the rightful inheritors of a colonised territory. Margaret Atwood's heroine is not able to recreate this, nor is D. R. MacDonald's Innis Corbet: the wilderness is still there, but they cannot disentangle themselves or it from modern life or from the contradictory legacy of settlement.

NOTES

1. Thomas Pennant, *A Voyage to the Hebrides*, in Youngson (ed.), *Beyond the Highland Line*, p. 191.
2. In Donald MacKay, *Scotland Farewell: The People of the Hector* (Toronto: Natural Heritage/Natural History Inc., 1996), p. 138.
3. Robert MacDougall, *The Emigrant's Guide to North America*, ed. Elizabeth Thompson (Toronto: Natural Heritage Books, [1841] 1998), p. 14.
4. In MacKay, *Scotland Farewell*, pp. 169–70.
5. Ibid., p. 174.
6. Susanna Moodie, *Life in the Clearings* (London: Richard Bentley, 1855), p. 175.
7. Catherine Parr Traill, *Lost in the Backwoods* (Whitefish: Kessinger, [1852] n.d.), p. 4.
8. Ibid., p. 5.

9. Ibid., p. 44.
10. Ibid., p. 39.
11. Ibid., p. 41.
12. Ibid., p. 22.
13. Ibid., p. 36.
14. Ibid., p. 66.
15. Ibid., p. 166.
16. Henry David Thoreau, 'Walden', in *The Portable Thoreau*, ed. Carl Bode (New York: Viking 1964), p. 420.
17. Ibid., p. 456.
18. Moodie, *Life in the Clearings*, p. 1.
19. Catherine Parr Traill, *The Female Emigrant's Guide and Hints on Canadian Housekeeping* (Toronto: Maclear, 1854), p. 49.
20. D. Clark, *Selections from Scottish Canadian Poets* (Toronto: Caledonian Society of Toronto, 1909), p. 239.
21. Margaret MacDonnel, *The Emigrant Experience: Songs of the Highland Emigrants in North America* (Toronto: University of Toronto Press, 1982), p. 145.
22. Clark, *Scottish Canadian Poets*, p. 198.
23. James Fenimore Cooper, *The Prairie*, (New York: New American Library, [1827] 1964), p. 78.
24. John Lorne Campbell, *Songs Remembered in Exile* (Edinburgh: Birlinn, [1990] 1999), p. 20.
25. Ibid., p. 19.
26. Susanna Moodie, *Roughing it in the Bush* (London: Virago, [1852] 1986), pp. 215–16.
27. John Howison, *Sketches of Upper Canada* (Edinburgh: Oliver & Boyd, 1825), pp. 180–1.
28. Ibid., p. 143.
29. In Michael Newton, *We're Indians Sure Enough* (Alexandria: Saorsa Media, 2001), pp. 180–1.
30. Eneas Mackenzie, *An Historical, Topographical, and Descriptive View of the United States of America* (Newcastle, 1819), p. 26.
31. Ibid., p. 371.
32. Ibid., p. 212.
33. Ibid., p. 398.
34. Thomas Hamilton, *Men and Manners in America* (Edinburgh: Blackwood, 1833), vol. II, p. 95.
35. Ibid., p. 191.
36. Ibid., p. 187.
37. Fred B. Grahame, *The Diary of William Richard Grahame in the United States and Canada 1831–1833* (Dundas: Magra Publishing, 1989), p. 26.
38. George Mackenzie (ed.), *Aberdeen to Ottawa. The Diary of Alexander Muir* (Aberdeen: Aberdeen University Press, 1990), p. 45.

39. Ibid., p. 46.
40. John Galt, *Autobiography of John Galt* (London: Cochrane & McCrone, 1833), p. 57.
41. Ibid., p. 59.
42. Ibid., p. 62.
43. John Galt, *Lawrie Todd, or Settlers in the Woods* (London: Richard Bentley, 1830), p. 84.
44. Ibid., p. 87.
45. Ibid., p. 300.
46. Ibid., p. 303.
47. John Galt, *Bogle Corbet* (London: Colburn & Bentley, 1831), vol. II, p. 195.
48. Ibid., vol. III, p. 46.
49. Ralph Connor, *Glengarry School Days* (Toronto: Westminster Co., 1902), p. 26.
50. Ibid., p. 26.
51. Ibid., p. 333.
52. Margaret Atwood, *Surfacing* (London: Virago, 1979), p. 59.
53. Ibid., p. 49.
54. Ibid., p. 48.
55. Ibid., p. 60.
56. D. R. MacDonald, *Cape Breton Road* (London: Chatto & Windus, 2001), p. 43.
57. Ibid., p. 44.
58. Ibid., p. 46.
59. Ibid., p. 63.
60. Ibid., p. 132.
61. Ibid., p. 283.
62. Ibid., p. 285.
63. In Mackay, *Scotland Farewell*, p. 171.
64. Ibid., p. 174.

3

Desperate Undertakings

The canoes were in danger of sinking or being broken to pieces; it was a desperate undertaking.

Simon Fraser, *Journal*

I could almost fancy at times that I have never been anything but an inhabitant of these wilds.

John Richardson, letter (quoted in Robert Johnson, *Sir John Richardson*)

At the time the people of the *Hector* arrived in Nova Scotia, in September 1773, the vast hinterland of the northern part of the American continent was territory known only to scattered bands of First Nations and a very few Europeans. But it had long since been identified as a source of wealth. That wealth came predominantly from the trade in furs, a product of the wild which necessitated engagement with the most extreme conditions.

The Hudson's Bay Company (HBC) was formed in 1670 to exploit the apparently insatiable European demand for fur, especially beaver. Two years later the company constructed an outpost, Moose Factory, on Hudson Bay, accessible by ship only during the summer months. Rupert's Land, the vast area of about 1.5 million square miles north and west of the St Lawrence River and the Great Lakes, was granted to the company. But increasingly in the eighteenth century fur traders and trappers were operating independently and without regulation, until in 1768 they received formal permission to engage in the trade. In 1779, independent traders came together to form the North West Company (NWC), based in Montreal and run by Scots. Scots also came to dominate the Hudson's Bay Company.

The gathering of furs depended on the ability of individuals to penetrate deep into uncharted territory and make amicable contact with aboriginal peoples, who trapped and traded the furs for a range of commodities offered by the companies: knives, axes, guns and ammunition, kettles, blankets and – though officially discouraged – liquor. The demand for furs drove the company's men further and further into the wild in their search for new sources of beaver. Underpinning this search was the need to survey and map routes for conveying the furs to the St Lawrence or Hudson Bay, from where they could be shipped to Europe. Towards the end of the eighteenth century there was a parallel search. Beyond the Pacific shore there was another potential market for the products of the North American wilderness, but to reach it required a transcontinental route, by sea – the Northwest Passage – or by land, using the river system.

ALEXANDER MACKENZIE: 'INSANE DETERMINATION'?

Towards the end of June 1789 one large and two small canoes were making their way uncertainly through the waters of Great Slave Lake. The party was led by a twenty-five-year-old Scot called Alexander Mackenzie who was hoping to locate the outlet of a great river which would take them to the Pacific Ocean, but was not at all sure where he might find it. Great Slave Lake is a large and confusing expanse of water lying in the vast stretch of the American continent now known as Canada's Northwest Territories. Mackenzie negotiated swamps and mudflats in his search, and on 29 June, at the far western point of the lake, he found what he was looking for, a wide and strong current pouring out of the lake to the west.

Four weeks earlier Mackenzie's party of five *voyageurs* (two with their wives), a Chipewyan guide called English Chief and his two wives, and two younger natives, had left Fort Chipewyan, an NWC trading post on the western shore of Lake Athabasca. Their three canoes were packed with supplies and provisions, guns, ammunition, tents, fishing nets, and a range of goods for use as gifts or for trade. The first weeks of their journey, following the Slave River between the two lakes, were plagued by bad weather, ice, driftwood, rapids, mosquitoes and blackfly. All the party were accustomed to extremes of terrain and climate, and were judged to have the necessary stamina and experience for the journey they were undertaking.

Some twenty years earlier Samuel Hearne had been instructed by the Hudson's Bay Company to seek a passage west from Hudson Bay across the Barren Lands, and eventually, in 1771, had reached the Coppermine River which flows into the Arctic Ocean at Coronation Gulf. It was a grim and often desperate journey and brought little benefit as it was clear there was no practical route west. But the fur trade's search for access to the north and west continued, and impelled Mackenzie's expedition of 1789.

Alexander Mackenzie was born in 1764 in Stornoway on the island of Lewis, and grew up in nearby Melbost. His father, Kenneth, had fought the Jacobites in 1745–6. In around 1774, after the death of his wife, Kenneth Mackenzie and his son left Scotland for the American colonies, then on the brink of war. Kenneth and his brother John, already settled in the colonies, were both Loyalists, and with the outbreak of war joined the King's Royal

Regiment of New York. It seems that Kenneth died as a prisoner of war. Alexander was sent to safety in Montreal, where at the age of fifteen he began work with a small company of fur traders, Gregory, Macleod & Co. He quickly proved his abilities and after only five years was made a partner in the firm, assigned first to Churchill River, then to Fort Athabasca. By this time Gregory, Macleod & Co. had merged with the NWC. Alexander Mackenzie was twenty-four years old.

Involvement in the fur trade required a range of practical skills, most of which could only be learned on the job and with the assistance of those accustomed to dealing with the particular demands of wilderness and an extreme climate. Adaptability and a readiness to learn, from experience as well as from others, were crucial. Most NWC expeditions were a mixed band of Scots, French Canadian *voyageurs*, First Nations and Métis. They needed to be able to construct and repair birch bark canoes, to paddle and navigate in often extraordinarily difficult conditions, to build dwellings and trading posts, to make, use and repair snowshoes, to hunt and to butcher, to pack and carry heavy loads. But practical skills were not enough. Qualities of leadership and diplomacy were crucial. Without the ability to establish good relations with the First Nations, to maintain morale in the face of savage weather, hostile terrain and near starvation, to assess the possible and accept the impossible, the fur trade and the exploration that underpinned it could not have happened.

Mackenzie's canoes were loaded with 5 tons of goods in 90-lb packages. Each man could carry a 90-lb load, some could carry two. Each canoe was crewed by a guide, a steersman and eight paddlers. When a portage was necessary, as it often was, it took six men to carry the canoe. The men were expected to keep going for up to twenty hours a day, with a few minutes rest every two hours, and they would often continue for two or three weeks without a rest day. The recognition that it was vital to sustain momentum impelled them onwards: this is a common factor in all the first-hand accounts of such travel. Faced with an obstacle, raging rapids or a sheer cliff face, the first response was to find a way to keep going. This determination, dogged, obsessive even – Scottish Canadian writer Hugh MacLennan refers to Mackenzie's 'insane determination' – was crucial to the fur-trading enterprise.[1] Equally important was a responsiveness to aboriginal experience, which equipped the traders with survival skills and helped to establish good relations with the natives on whom the trade depended.

The journey following the river that would be named for him disappointingly took Mackenzie to the Beaufort Sea, not the Pacific. MacLennan commented: 'nothing was more in the life-style of the Highlander than Alexander Mackenzie's feat in searching for the Northwest Passage in a canoe. After an achievement of incredible boldness and endurance, what,

after all, did this Highlander find but nothing?'[2] MacLennan's suggestion
that heroic failure was typically Highland reflects the shadow of Culloden
and the mythology of romantic defeat, but nevertheless highlights a tenacity
seen as characteristically Scottish. It played a part in sending Alexander
Mackenzie on a second attempt to find a river route to the Pacific.

This time he left Fort Chipewyan on 10 October 1792, and entered the
Peace River, with the intention of wintering near the confluence of the
Peace and Smoky rivers. For two months they lived in tents while more
permanent quarters were built. It was bitterly cold, the frost 'so severe that
the axes of the woodmen became almost as brittle as glass'.[3] It was a
difficult winter, with numbers of the local First Nations and his own men
becoming sick. Mackenzie did his best to act as doctor, but found it hard to
deal with the inaction imposed by winter conditions. The isolation and
confinement were oppressive. When the time came in the spring to prepare
for the onward journey, there were problems recruiting native guides, on
whom Mackenzie acknowledged his dependence although he confessed he
had little trust in them. In a letter to his cousin Roderick Mackenzie, also
an HBC employee, he expressed his despondency and indecision. 'I was
never so undecided in my intentions as this year,' he wrote. 'I hardly know
what I am about.'[4]

However, on 9 May a 25-foot canoe loaded with 3,000 lb of goods and
supplies set off. There were ten men: Mackenzie, his second-in-command
Alexander McKay, six French *voyageurs*, and two natives to act as hunters
and interpreters. The canoe was overloaded and very soon sprung a leak. A
pause was necessary to re-seal it with pine resin (this was a recurrent task
on all river journeys). They followed the Peace River west through 'the most
beautiful scenery I had ever beheld', but conditions became increasingly
hazardous.[5] In the Peace River Canyon, they came on rapids roaring between
steep river banks. The canoe had to be unloaded and towed through the
rapids, with the baggage carried along the precipitous rock cliffs. The towing
line broke and the canoe was nearly lost, leaving the men alarmed and
demoralised. Mackenzie was forced to call a halt: 'it would not only have
been unavailing but imprudent to have proposed any further progress at
present, particularly as the river above us, as far as we could see, was a white
sheet of foaming water'.[6] Some of the men wanted to give up and turn back,
but Mackenzie ignored their protests. He did, however, accept that to continue
by water was not practical. The next part of their journey was by land, porta-
ging with exhausting effort the canoe and all their goods over a mountain.

By the end of May they thought they were through the worst, only to
find that ahead of them lay another chain of mountains. Their name, the
Ominous Mountains, suggests their effect. The party arrived at the juncture
of the Finlay and Parsnip rivers, which join to form the Peace River.

Mackenzie took every opportunity to question any natives he encountered about topography and routes, and in deciding which direction to take he followed native advice. They headed south on the Parsnip River, expecting to find a route across the Continental Divide to another great river, which Mackenzie believed had to be the Columbia. But soon they again encountered fierce rapids, and again the men protested. Mackenzie's account of this episode reveals his self-confidence and the extent of his authority.

> The rush of water was so powerful, that we were the greatest part of the afternoon in getting two or three miles – a very tardy and mortifying progress, and which, with the voyage, was openly execrated by many of those who were engaged in it: and the inexpressible toil these people had endured, as well as the dangers they had encountered, required some degree of consideration; I therefore employed those arguments which were the best calculated to calm their immediate discontents, as well as to encourage their future hopes, though, at the same time I delivered my sentiments in such a manner as to convince them that I was determined to proceed.[7]

Mackenzie portrays himself as distinct from his men – 'these people' – and less susceptible to the rigours of the journey. He is unquestionably their leader, responsible for taking decisions and ensuring that they are accepted and implemented. But although his account throughout his journal emphasises his own role and status, it also makes it clear that an expedition into such extremes of wilderness required unity of purpose and mutual dependence. Mackenzie needed men with the will and the stamina to endure 'inexpressible toil' and live with the daily possibility of death.

They continued upriver. Extremes of weather added to their troubles, intensely cold one day, very hot and thick with mosquitoes the next. They met a band of Sekanis from whom Mackenzie hoped to learn about a possible route to the sea, but he suspected 'the fidelity' of his interpreter and felt that information was being withheld. Having persuaded his men of the need to carry on, in his journal he expressed doubts. 'In my present state of information, to proceed further up the river was considered as a fruitless waste of toilsome exertion; and to return unsuccessful, after all our labour, sufferings, and dangers was an idea too painful to indulge.'[8] He carried on. Pride clearly played its part in impelling him forward, perhaps intensified by the disappointment of his first expedition.

They left the Parsnip River and portaged along a 'beaten path leading over a low ridge of land'.[9] They had crossed the Continental Divide. On James Creek, which Mackenzie named the 'Bad River' because of its particularly alarming rapids, the canoe was holed and nearly lost. When the steersman panicked, Mackenzie again quickly exerted his authority:

My peremptory commands superseded the effects of his fear, and they all held fast to the wreck; to which fortunate resolution we owed our safety as we should otherwise have been dashed against the rocks by the force of the water, or driven over the cascades.[10]

The men, brave as they were, needed Mackenzie's leadership to keep a grip on their courage. Safely on land, they were rewarded with a 'hearty meal' and 'rum enough to raise their spirits'. Mackenzie delivered another pep talk, assuring them that the experience 'would enable us to pursue our voyage with greater security', and urging 'the honour of conquering disasters, and the disgrace that would attend them on their return home, without having attained the object of the expedition'. He went on to praise their 'courage and resolution'.[11]

On 18 June they reached the Fraser River, believing it to be the Columbia. Two days later the battered canoe was in such a bad state they had to build another. Natives advised that the river was not navigable and would lead them far to the south. Reluctantly, Mackenzie decided to backtrack, despite his recognition that this could damage morale, and take an overland route west. They cached the canoe and all but essential supplies, and carried their loads of pemmican, rice, guns and ammunition. Mackenzie also carried the 'troublesome addition' of his telescope.[12] Much of the route, following the West Road River, was on existing native trails but on occasion Mackenzie had to beat a path through the dense undergrowth. Two weeks later the party descended into the Bella Coola gorge, and another two days brought them, on 22 July, to the head of a salt water inlet. Mackenzie was satisfied he had reached the Pacific Ocean and recorded the fact by inscribing on a rock: 'Alex Mackenzie from Canada by land 22nd July 1793'. Honour was satisfied, and they set off on the return journey. It took just over a month to get back to Fort Fork.

Alexander Mackenzie reached the Pacific Ocean, making his party the first to cross the continent north of Mexico. He highlighted the endurance of his men, and in doing so drew attention to his own achievement:

Their toils and dangers, their solicitudes and sufferings, have not been exaggerated in my description. On the contrary, in many instances language has failed me in the attempt to describe them. I received, however, the reward of my labours, for they were crowned with success.[13]

He had done what the NWC had asked of him. He had journeyed from the edge of the fur-trading empire to the Pacific Ocean, but in doing so had established that the route to the west coast was not practicable for trade. Men could cross the Rocky Mountain wilderness, but the river and mountain challenges would make the transport of trade goods impossible.

Mackenzie was twenty-nine years old. He had extended knowledge of a vast tract of land, to the north and west of Lake Athabasca. He had demonstrated that men could overcome unimagined obstacles with a combination of skill, courage and determination, and he had shown extraordinary qualities of leadership and diplomacy. His journals, published in 1801, would inform and inspire others, and for a period he was celebrated and lionised. The year following publication he was knighted. Although Mackenzie's journals were prepared for publication by an editor, William Combe, who may have improved or embellished the original, it is clear that Mackenzie was more than happy to present himself to the public as an heroic figure. There was, however, in his later life a sense of disappointment and disillusion. His plans for opening up Pacific trade and reorganising the fur trade generally came to nothing; it would be others who made possible the penetration of the fur trade west of the Rockies

From 1805 Mackenzie was based mainly in Britain, although he continued to work, without much success, to develop trade via the Pacific coast. He was, according to his biographer Roy Daniells, 'never the same man after the intense and continuous effort of the great journeys'.[14] In 1812 he married Geddes Mackenzie and took over her family's estate of Avoch in Scotland's Black Isle. Eight years later he died suddenly, possibly of Bright's Disease which may have been the legacy of those extraordinary journeys.

SIMON FRASER: 'SURROUNDED WITH DANGERS AND DIFFICULTIES'

In the period of savage reprisal after the battle of Culloden, William Fraser's house in Strathglass was burnt down by the duke of Cumberland. One of Fraser's nine sons, John, would fight with General Wolfe at Quebec in 1759. He remained in North America and settled in Montreal. Another son, Simon, in 1773 sailed to New York with his wife Isabella Grant and their children, continuing up the Hudson to Albany. They moved on to Bennington, Vermont, where in 1776 on their modestly successful farm their eighth and youngest child, Simon, was born. It was the year which saw, after a period of sporadic fighting, the signing of the Declaration of Independence. But the Fraser family were, like the Mackenzies, Loyalists. Simon Fraser senior fought for the British with General Burgoyne, who was defeated at Saratoga with disastrous consequences for the British. Fraser was captured and died in captivity in 1779, again echoing Kenneth Mackenzie's fate. The Fraser family possessions were confiscated by the victorious Americans and life was made very difficult for them. Five years after her husband's death, Isabella sold the farm and went to Upper Canada where she and her children settled in Glengarry County. The Fraser family had a double legacy of repression, threaded with irony. Their first home was destroyed by the British army, and they were forced to leave their second home because of their allegiance to the British army.

The family were related to Simon McTavish, who held a controlling interest in the North West Company, and two of Isabella's brothers were in the fur trade. These connections helped sixteen-year-old Simon Fraser to employment as an NWC apprentice. It was the year before Mackenzie's journey to the Pacific. Within a decade Fraser had acquired considerable experience in the field and had become an NWC partner. The pressure to expand the fur trade continued as rivalry between the 'Nor'Westers' and the Hudson's Bay Company intensified. There was a need for more trading posts at a greater distance from Montreal to open up trading possibilities in the deep wilderness. Expansion was spearheaded by Scots. In 1797, James Finlay, whose brother John had been with Mackenzie in 1792, explored the Peace, Finlay and Parsnip rivers. Three years later, Duncan McGillivray, from Inverness, penetrated west into the foothills of the Rockies and up the Saskatchewan. Each advance at this time was crowded with Scottish names.

There remained two formidable barriers, the vast territory of the Barren Lands between Hudson Bay and the Beaufort Sea, and the Rocky Mountains. Mackenzie had failed to find a commercially viable route to the Pacific, but there were beaver west of the Rockies and it was inevitable that the fur trade would reach out for them. In 1805, the year Mackenzie returned to the United Kingdom, Simon Fraser was instructed to establish trading posts in what would become British Columbia. He set off up the Peace River with twenty men, including John Stuart and James McDougall. The first task was to set up a base at Rocky Mountain Portage at the eastern end of the Peace River Canyon. Leaving Stuart in charge of the new trading post, Fraser continued up the Peace, Parsnip and Pack rivers and at Trout Lake (present-day McLeod Lake) built Fort McLeod, the first permanent European settlement west of the Rockies. Fraser named the territory New Caledonia. More forts were built: Fort St James on Stuart Lake; Fort Fraser on Fraser Lake; and Fort George (now Prince George) at the confluence of the Fraser and Nechako rivers, thus consolidating an NWC foothold. It was at Fort George that Simon Fraser prepared for the 1808 expedition for which he is best remembered.

Fraser has been described as a man of strength, determination, honesty and ambition, but also as 'illiterate, ill-bred, bickering, fault-finding ... of jealous disposition'.[15] There was no questioning his fortitude and his skill. He was of 'inconquerable will and energy', and, if somewhat eccentric, he was 'honourable in his dealings ... a man typical of his age and calling. An heroic spirit truly, if cast in the not altogether heroic mould of a fur trader. He stands there a commanding figure.'[16] He shared with Mackenzie the ability to respond rapidly to dangerous and unforeseen situations. This combination of quick thinking and practical intelligence was crucial to survival in the uncharted wilderness. And like Mackenzie, he had a perceptive understanding of the skills, knowledge and willingness to collaborate of the First Nations people they worked with. At the same time, both men regarded natives as savages: unreliable, infantile, unpredictable and potentially hostile.

On 28 May 1808, Simon Fraser and his party set off from Fort George down the Fraser River and immediately encountered dangerous currents, high winds and whirlpools. Caught in an 'immense body of water passing through this narrow space in a turbulent manner, forming innumerable gulphs [sic] and cascades, and making a tremendous noise', the first canoe was slammed against a projecting rock.[17] In Fraser's view 'to continue on the water would be certain destruction', but portage was impossible. They were forced to hack steps out of the rock so they could haul the unloaded canoes through the water: 'failure of the line or a false step of one of the men might have hurled the whole of us into eternity'.[18] Local natives advised them to take an overland route, but Fraser was adamant in his rejection of this alternative: 'going to the sea by an indirect way was not the object of the undertaking. I therefore would not deviate and continued our route according to my original intention.'[19]

Progress over the next few days was slow and painful, as they negotiated precipices, ravines and loose stones which made it difficult to keep their footing. Shoes wore out in a day, feet were blistered and full of thorns. Dragging the canoes and carrying heavy loads sapped their strength. Yet it seemed Fraser and his men were undeterred. 'Once engaged the die was cast … the crews cool and determined followed each other in awful silence.'[20]

It is perhaps not surprising that after two weeks of this Fraser was abandoned by his native guide and interpreter. A note of self-pity creeps into his account, alongside resignation:

> Here we are, in a strange Country, surrounded with dangers and difficulties, among numberless tribes of savages, who never saw the face of a white man. Our situation is critical and highly unpleasant; however, we shall endeavour to make the best of it; what cannot be cured, must be endured.[21]

In the midst of this he comments on native clothing, tools, weapons and customs, and also on physical skills and agility. 'We, who had not the advantages of their experience, were often in imminent danger.'[22] Finally, above present-day Lillooet, Fraser abandoned the canoes altogether and continued on foot. They returned to the water when they could, but that meant acquiring canoes from locals. Negotiating with First Nations communities as they made their way downriver was a delicate matter, which Fraser

handled astutely, mindful of rivalries between different bands and taking care
not to appear to favour any particular group. However, near the end of the
journey they encountered difficulties. At the mouth of the Fraser River, which
he now knew was not the Columbia as had at first been supposed, he was
harassed by local Cowichans and had to abandon his intention of exploring
the Strait of Georgia. He and his men beat a retreat upriver. Although no
lives were lost this was almost the last straw. Some of the men wanted to
head overland for Fort George and Fraser drew on all his powers to argue,
successfully, the necessity of sticking together. They made it back to the fort
on 6 August, but, like the journeys of Alexander Mackenzie, Simon Fraser's
achievement was of little benefit to the NWC. It demonstrated a negative,
that the Fraser River was not a navigable trade route to the Pacific Ocean.
The problem of transporting furs and maintaining trading posts remained.

More than twenty years later George Simpson, overseas governor of the
Hudson's Bay Company, which in 1821 had merged with the NWC, himself
made the journey down the Fraser River and confirmed that it was not, for
the purposes of the fur trade, navigable. He paid tribute to Simon Fraser's
achievement, which was, he said, 'an undertaking compared to which … the
much talked of and high sounding performances of his [sic] Majesty's recent
discovery expeditions in the Arctic regions, were excursions of pleasure'.[23]
These Arctic 'excursions' were indeed much in the public eye at the time, as
there had been a series of high-profile government-sponsored expeditions to
seek the Northwest Passage. The attempts of John Ross (1818), William
Parry (1819, 1821, 1824) and John Franklin (1819, 1825) to find a sea passage
to the Pacific did not succeed in their goal, but Simpson's barbed comment
was more a reflection on the nature of these expeditions than their lack of
success. The fur-trading expeditions were independently conceived and
resourced, and carried out by small groups who had experience of the
territory, proven survival skills and contacts with the native population. The
official expeditions were, by and large, without this understanding of the
environment or its people.

As with Alexander Mackenzie, Fraser's later career was almost inevitably
an anticlimax. He was for a while based at Fort Chipewyan, and in 1815
played a dubious role in the NWC's attempts to impede the settlement at
Red River (see Chapter 5), for which he was tried and acquitted in 1818. He
subsequently abandoned the wilderness to settle near Cornwall in Upper
Canada, a community established in 1784 by Loyalists from New York. He
married Catherine Macdonnell, had eight children, and farmed in relative
obscurity until his death in 1862. However, his imprint on the British
Columbian landscape is unavoidable. There are named after him a river,
lake, fort, bridge, highway, university and many streets.

ASTORIA: 'ALL THE PRIVATIONS HUMAN NATURE IS CAPABLE OF'

The North West Company was not alone in aspiring to gain a foothold on America's northwest coast. In the spring of 1804 an expedition led by Meriwether Lewis and William Clark (an Ulster Scot) set off from St Louis up the Missouri River to strike west and traverse the almost unknown territory that had come to the United States through the Louisiana Purchase the year before. Some eighteen months later, having crossed the Rockies, they followed the Columbia River to the Pacific shore. It took them another year to return. Very soon, the fur-trading potential of the area west of the Missouri was being explored by venturesome individuals, and in 1810 John Jacob Astor in New York launched the Pacific Fur Company with the intention of establishing a base at the mouth of the Columbia River. Many of the men he engaged for this operation were Scots well known for their Rupert's Land fur-trading expertise, among them David Stuart and his nephew Robert, Alexander McKay (who had accompanied Mackenzie on both his expeditions) and his son Tom, Donald Mackenzie (a cousin of Alexander Mackenzie), Duncan McDougall and Alexander Ross, all of Scottish Highland origins. Two Scottish Americans were recruited in St Louis, Greenock-born Ramsay Crooks and Robert McClellan, born in Pennsylvania of Scottish parentage. The latter was described by Alexander Ross as being an excellent shot and 'as brave as a lion'.[24] Crooks and McClellan had for several years operated as independent fur traders in the Upper Missouri. All of these men would play important roles in Astor's venture.

Astor, already successfully trading in opium and arms, was ruthlessly determined to extend his commercial empire, hoping to succeed where Mackenzie and Fraser had failed. His aim was to establish a trading post on the Pacific coast and pioneer trade routes by land and by sea. He was encouraged by President Thomas Jefferson, eager to consolidate an American presence in the northwest. 'All beyond the Mississippi,' Jefferson wrote to Astor, 'is ours exclusively, and it will be in our power to give our own traders great advantages over their foreign competitors.'[25] Wilderness and economic potential were inextricably linked.

Astor planned two expeditions to the Pacific, one party setting off from St Louis travelling overland, the other sailing from New York on the *Tonquin* to round Cape Horn and proceed up the Pacific coast. Both were perilous undertakings. The Stuarts, the McKays, Alexander Ross and Duncan McDougall sailed on the *Tonquin*, under Captain Jonathan Thorn, who was autocratic, unpredictable and the cause of many problems. The voyage was fraught, its inherent difficulties intensified by personal friction and open contention. Captain Thorn did not like the Scots and was particularly aggravated by the fact that they spoke Gaelic to each other, which he could not understand. Neither could he understand the French spoken by the *voyageurs* on board. Months at sea reached a climax when in the spring of 1811 they found themselves confronting the notoriously dangerous sandbanks and currents that guarded the entrance to the Columbia River. Despite stormy seas, Thorn insisted on two attempts to take soundings which resulted in the loss of ten members of the crew.

Eventually a channel was found into the river and landfall was made on the southern bank. The Astorians were faced, in the words of Alexander Ross, with 'gigantic trees of almost incredible size, many of them measuring 50 feet in girth, and so close together, and intermingled with huge rocks, as to make work of no ordinary labour to level and clear the ground'.[26] The work had to be done, however demanding and however unsuited the men were – some had never handled an axe before. It took two months to clear one acre and prepare a site for the building of a trading post. Meanwhile, Captain Thorn took the *Tonquin* up the coast with the aim of establishing trading contacts with local natives. It was the last the Astorians saw of the ship; all but one of those on board perished. It was learned later that they were attacked by natives on Vancouver Island. Among those killed was Alexander McKay.

While the fort was being constructed, forays were made into the interior to investigate trading potential, but the base was running out of supplies and the men were ill-prepared for the winter. Nevertheless, they marked the start of 1812 in style, as Duncan McDougall recorded:

> At sunrise, the drums beat to arms and the colours were hoisted. Three rounds of small arms and three discharges from the great guns were fired, after which all hands were treated to grog, bread, cheese and butter.[27]

They fired another salvo at sunset and danced until three in the morning. There may have been native women present, but men engaged in the fur trade were accustomed to dancing with each other, and there is little doubt that such celebrations, with or without a female presence, were a boost to morale.

In late October 1810, the overland expedition had set off up the Missouri River from St Louis and covered 450 miles before wintering at its confluence with the Nodaway. It was July the following year before they set off again, under the leadership of William Hunt. With him were Crooks, McClellan and Mackenzie, a Missouri trader called Joseph Miller, and more than fifty others, most of them French Canadians. It proved a desperate journey, across a seemingly endless prairie and formidable mountain ranges. By the time they reached the Wind River Range in present-day Wyoming they had travelled hundreds of miles over waterless terrain and had come near to starvation. There was, wrote Hunt, 'much suffering. Several persons were on the verge of losing courage.'[28]

They pressed on across the Great Divide to the Snake River where they were faced with a dilemma. Winter was approaching, the river was a maelstrom of rapids and boulders, there were mountains on all sides, and they were not sure which direction to take. Washington Irving, commissioned by J. J. Astor in 1838 to write an account of the Astorian venture, described their predicament:

> They were in the heart of an unknown wilderness, untraversed as yet by a white man. They were at a loss which route to take, and how far they were from the ultimate place of their destination, nor could they meet, in these uninhabited wilds, with any human being to give them information.[29]

Eventually Hunt decided to proceed downriver. With no provisions and a lack of game, they killed and ate their horses. 'They travelled painfully about fourteen miles a day,' Irving wrote. Snow and rain were falling. 'Their only sustenance was a scanty meal of horse flesh once in four and twenty hours.'[30] While on the march the Indian wife of their Métis guide gave birth. Irving commented: 'The mother looked as unconcerned as if nothing had happened to her; so easy is nature in her operations in the wilderness, when free from the enfeebling refinements of luxury, and the tamperings and appliances of art.'[31] Wild people were adapted to wild places, it seemed to Irving, and were able to endure conditions that defeated the civilised. The mother with her newborn child carried on without complaint while the white men 'crept feebly on, scarce dragging one limb after another'.[32] They ate the beaver skins they had collected and when the beaver ran out expected death. In the nick of time McClellan proved his reputation as a marksman by shooting a bighorn sheep.

They battled on to the Columbia River, and on 18 January 1812 an advance party, including McClellan and Mackenzie, reached Astoria, as the trading post near the river's mouth was now named. Four weeks later the main party arrived, though without Ramsay Crooks and another man, John Day, who 'reduced by famine and fatigue' had remained at the Snake River, where they survived the winter with the aid of friendly Walla Walla and eventually made it to Astoria.[33] Day, however, was unhinged by his ordeal and died within the year. (There are other tales of wilderness dementia. An HBC employee, William Stuart, who took part in a 1715 expedition into the Barren Lands, was reduced to lunacy by the experience.)

By the summer of 1812, with trading posts established in the interior, the Astorian venture appeared to be a going concern. It was time to report back to New York. The man given this responsibility was Robert Stuart. On 29 June, he set off with six men, including Ramsey Crooks and Robert McClellan. A month's travelling took them to the confluence of the Walla Walla and Columbia rivers, where the Columbia bends sharply north. They continued on to the Snake River. Advised by a Shoshone guide (who later stole Stuart's horse) they opted for a course to the south of Hunt's route west, but they were harassed by a band of Crow, who stole the remaining horses, and ran out of provisions. They were all weak, Crooks was ill, and the volatile McClellan stormed off on his own. They abandoned the southern route, but as a result it took them three exhausting weeks to gain only thirty miles east, and they still had not crossed the Continental Divide.

They caught up with McClellan, who had fared no better than the main party. They were all faint with hunger. Friendly Shoshone told them of a pass through the mountains, a broad sweep of plateau to the south of the Wind River Range, which took them across the Divide to the Sweetwater River. The most challenging part of the journey seemed to be over. But it was late in the season, and as they continued east game and water were scarce. There was a real prospect of starvation. According to Irving, one of the *voyageurs* proposed that they should draw lots to decide on who 'should die to save the rest'.[34] Stuart refused, and they struggled on.

They reached the North Platte River and passed a distinctive large lump of rock and decided to over-winter beside the river and within sight of equally distinctive red sandstone buttes. On a site more than 2,000 miles from their starting point, they built the first cabin in what would become the territory of Wyoming. But their encounters with Native Americans had not come to an end, and when threatening Arapaho made an appearance they decided to move on and make a second camp further east, near present-day Torrington. They celebrated the first day of 1813 eating buffalo and – their supply of tobacco exhausted – smoking a cut-up tobacco pouch.

In March they resumed their journey, in spite of blizzards, and finally reached Fort Osage on the Missouri, built three years earlier by the army fourteen miles upriver from what would become Independence, and housing the only garrison west of the Mississippi. Six more days took them to St Louis, having endured, Stuart wrote, 'all the privations human nature is capable of'.[35] From St Louis Stuart continued alone, on horseback across Missouri and Illinois and then by stagecoach to New York, where, a year after departing from Astoria, he delivered his despatches to J. J. Astor.

Robert Stuart successfully crossed the continent coast to coast from west to east, in itself a huge achievement. It was to have lasting significance. The route the Shoshone had told him of, through what would become known as South Pass, by mid-century had been travelled by thousands making their way to Oregon and California. The lump of rock by the North Platte would become known as Independence Rock and hundreds of overlanders would carve their names on it, while the striking sandstone outcrop near Stuart's first winter camp, later called Red Buttes, became an equally prominent landmark for those streaming west.

Less than a month after reaching New York, Robert Stuart married Betsy Sullivan in Manhattan's First Presbyterian Church. His involvement with the fur trade continued and took him eventually to Detroit. Unlike Alexander Mackenzie and Simon Fraser there is no sense of anticlimax in his later career, which saw him become state treasurer of Michigan, federal superintendent of Indian affairs, secretary of the Illinois and Michigan Canal Company, and owner of Detroit's first brick house. His encounter with the wilderness proved a training ground for a civic role in his adopted country. Ramsay Crooks, nearly overwhelmed by illness and hunger, was also successful in his later years, becoming president of the American Fur Company. At the time of his death in 1859 he was the last surviving member of the Stuart party. McClellan joined the Missouri Rangers and fought in the 1815 battle of the Sink Hole against Sauk chief Black Hawk, who continued to fight on behalf of the British although the war of 1812 was over. Later, McClellan opened a store in Cape Girardeau, Missouri.

TO THE ARCTIC: PUTTING 'A ROOF ON THE MAP OF CANADA'

By the early nineteenth century there was a rival to the beaver as a beacon of exploration in the northern wilderness, and again it was partly fashion that was the spur. Ships from Scottish ports – Aberdeen, Dundee and Leith – penetrated Arctic waters in the hunt for whales, the source of the commercially valuable raw materials blubber and baleen. Blubber produced oil used as a fuel and a lubricant; baleen was an essential material for the manufacture of corsets and crinolines. It was a whaler out of Whitby, Yorkshire, who initiated the decades of Arctic exploration that followed the end of the Napoleonic Wars.

In 1817, William Scoresby, who had been a pupil of Robert Jameson, professor of natural history at the University of Edinburgh, noted that the Arctic Ocean was unusually free of ice. When this information was communicated to Lord Melville, First Lord of the Admiralty – himself a Scot – he launched an expedition in search of the Northwest Passage. The *Isabella* and the *Alexander*, under the command of John Ross, son of a Church of Scotland minister from Stranraer in Wigtownshire, were to sail west and enter the Davis Strait, between Greenland and Baffin Island. With Ross was his nephew James Clark Ross, who would go on to establish the position of the magnetic North Pole and to become a pioneer of Antarctic exploration.

The *Isabella* and *Alexander* entered Lancaster Sound, north of Baffin Island, but there appeared to be no way through. It was late August, the threat of ice loomed, and Ross turned back. This initial foray into Arctic waters yielded little, but it was the beginning of several decades of vigorous and very costly activity in northern seas which generated a huge amount of public interest. It was not just the commercial potential of the Northwest Passage that attracted attention, but the ice-bound territory itself, which intrigued scientists and gripped the imagination. It was a new frontier, an ultimate and unsullied wilderness, and a challenge to the courage, ingenuity and determination of men. Scots were prominent among those who responded to that challenge.

In 1819, an ambitious, two-pronged expedition again entered the Arctic. The *Hecla* and the *Griper*, under the command of William Parry, sailed into Lancaster Sound. With him were James Clark Ross and Scottish surgeon-naturalist Alexander Fisher, who collected zoological and geological material. The other part of the expedition was land-based. Led by naval officer John Franklin, it set off from York Factory on Hudson Bay on a journey that would take them through some of North America's harshest territory to the Arctic coast. Key members of the expedition were John Richardson, Lieutenant George Back, Thomas Hood and John Hepburn, an ordinary seaman from East Lothian who had earlier served under Franklin. Dr John Richardson, born in Dumfries in 1787, was a Royal Navy surgeon who had served in the French and American wars. He had also been a pupil of Robert Jameson, an enthusiastic collector of rocks, minerals, fossils and fauna, and an inspirational teacher. Jameson persuaded former pupils and others, including William Scoresby and Alexander Fisher, to send him specimens from all over the world (Scoresby supplied him with a live polar bear). Jameson, presiding over an increasingly prestigious and important collection, played a significant part in expanding knowledge of the North American wilderness without ever leaving Scotland. John Richardson had considerable medical and wartime experience when he joined Franklin's first expedition at the age of thirty-two, and his training under Jameson was a good preparation for his role as surgeon-naturalist. Nothing, however, could have prepared him and his companions for what they would encounter in the Arctic wilderness.

Franklin's party sailed to York Factory on Hudson's Bay Company supply ships, but beyond that there was little cooperation from the company, which regarded government-sponsored exploration with some suspicion, and was preoccupied with the intensifying rivalry with the North West Company. The party left York Factory on 9 September; it took them nearly a month to reach Norway House at the northern end of Lake Winnipeg, following an established HBC route. They continued west to winter at Cumberland House. In January 1820, Franklin, Back and Hepburn set off on snowshoes up the Saskatchewan River, eventually reaching Fort Chipewyan on Lake Athabasca more than two months later. Richardson and Hood remained at Cumberland House until June, when they too made their way to Fort Chipewyan, a gruelling journey during which a leading voyageur was drowned in rapids on the Churchill River. At the fort, the four Orkneymen who were members of the party refused to go any further.

The remaining men headed north to Great Slave Lake, then followed the Yellowknife River and established Fort Enterprise on Winter Lake as their winter quarters, where they prepared for the most challenging part of their journey. They had brought from York Factory compasses, thermometers, a theodolite and other surveying and measuring instruments, as well as Bibles, prayer books, manuals on navigation and astronomy, and medical and natural history texts. They carried weapons and utensils: guns, pistols, ammunition and gunpowder, knives, daggers, axes, chisels, nails, fishing nets, kettles. They had blankets, beads, needles and cloth as gifts for natives. And they were well provisioned, with supplies brought from England and more purchased at Cumberland House and Fort Providence on Great Slave Lake. They had tea, sugar, flour, arrowroot, portable soup, chocolate, bacon, rice, three cases of preserved meat plus pemmican, dried reindeer tongues and dried moose, and three kegs of spirits. It was bitterly cold, with the trees being frozen so hard that attempts to fell them broke the axes. Collecting scarce firewood and hunting to supplement their provisions required constant effort. Some of the men were afflicted by snow blindness.

At Fort Enterprise they were joined by two Inuit interpreters, Augustus and Junius, and in June 1821 they were ready for departure. As well as all their gear and supplies, they were carrying four tents, two for the exclusive use of the officers (Franklin, Richardson, Back, Hood and Hepburn). Three heavily laden sledges were pulled by dogs and men, the men also carrying 40 lb of personal belongings. They headed due north and reached Point Lake in five days. A second trip had to be made to bring the three canoes.

They carried on to the Coppermine River. Like Mackenzie and Fraser, Franklin relied on First Nations information for guidance as to what lay ahead, and like them Richardson, who had begun his journal the previous August at Fort Enterprise, recorded a tendency to exaggerate the dangers. There was anxious anticipation of a stretch of the Coppermine known as Rocky Defile Rapid, which proved to be a 'narrow gloomy channel' with 'perpendicular rocky walls'. In spite of its perilous nature, Richardson concluded that 'although the grandeur of the scene was commensurate with their descriptions yet their habitual love of the marvellous had induced [the natives] to exaggerate the danger of passing it exceedingly'.[36] Richardson himself was never one for hyperbole. His journal is factual, measured and understated, and the value of his cool pragmatism would become increasingly apparent.

As they neared the mouth of the Coppermine River they came to Bloody Fall, where half a century earlier Samuel Hearne had witnessed the slaughter of a band of Inuit by Copper Indians. Franklin's party made their camp among scattered human bones. On 18 July they reached the Beaufort Sea. They began their exploration of the coast, but supplies were running low, the pemmican was mouldy and the hunting poor. By 9 August there remained only two bags of pemmican and some dried meat. 'The men began to apprehend the approach of absolute want. And we have for some days had to listen to the gloomy forebodings of the deer entirely quitting the coast in a few days.'[37] The need to fuel their strenuous labours day after day meant that the men had huge appetites, and food was equally important for morale. They were not impressed by the example of restraint set by their leaders. It was late in the season, there was no sign of game, and they made it clear that they did not want to carry on. On 21 August, they were down to half a bag of pemmican, and the decision was made to turn back.

On 4 September, they had 'a very scanty supper' of what remained of the pemmican, and then the weather deteriorated, with snow and gales.[38] On 6 September, Richardson recorded that they 'suffered much from the cold but more from hunger'. The next day they struggled on although 'in a very unfit condition'.[39] There was 30 cm of snow on the ground, and they had spent the night in the inadequate shelter of the tents with no fuel for a fire. Their garments stiffened with frost, they battled against high winds to pack up the tents and set off in the canoes through icy water. Franklin fainted from exhaustion. But at least they found game, and successfully bagged partridge, a few hares and a musk ox. This bounty did not last long, and when a few days later voyageur Pierre St Germain shared out meat he had saved from his ration the act was 'received with great thankfulness'. Richardson added: 'such an act of self-denial and kindness, being totally unexpected in a Canadian filled our eyes with tears'.[40]

But on 17 September they had nothing to eat except 'pieces of singed hide' and *tripe de roche*, lichen which they scraped off trees. This, Richardson said, 'would have satisfied us in ordinary times, but we were now exhausted by slender fare, and travel, and our appetites had become enormous'. Two days later 'the men were faint from hunger'.[41] They were on foot now, hoping to reach Point Lake, but then discovered that they were too far to the east and had to adjust their direction to make for the Coppermine River. On 23 September they dined on old shoes and some deer bones which they had found. Two days later their hunger was relieved when five small deer were shot, and the following day they at last reached Point Lake. But the men were now thoroughly demoralised, and Franklin and the other officers had to work hard to counter fragmented discipline. Richardson's comments are revealing:

The people ... had become careless and disobedient, they had ceased to dread punishment or hope for reward and it is a melancholy truth that gratitude for past favours or a sense of duty seldom influence the conduct of a Canadian voyageur. Although they beheld their officers suffering even in a greater degree than themselves, yet they considered the want of food as dissolving all ties between us, and they had not scrupled to steal from us part of the meat which had been allotted to us, with strict impartiality.[42]

The assumption was that naval discipline combined with leading by example should have held the men together. The leadership of Mackenzie and Fraser depended on an understanding of shared goals and shared effort. Although they too had their difficulties when their men resisted what was being asked of them, an appeal was made to their comradely sense of purpose rather than to a sense of duty. Richardson, admirable in so many ways and always asking more of himself than of his men, maintained a conventional distance between himself and those he led.

His demands on himself were put to the test when they faced the turbulent icy waters of the Coppermine. After an unsuccessful attempt to cross by raft, Richardson volunteered to swim across the river with a line to enable the raft to be hauled. But he was defeated by the paralysing effect of the water's extreme cold and was saved from death only by the men's quick action pulling him out of the river and wrapping him in a blanket to thaw out in front of a fire. Although he 'recovered tolerably', some five months later he was still feeling the effects. Richardson, who did not like to admit failure, explained that his severe debilitation had left him unable to resist 'degrees of cold that would have been disregarded whilst in health and vigour'.[43]

By this time the men's diet consisted mainly of *tripe de roche*, which brought bowel complaints, in turn causing further weakness. Richardson commented: 'The sensation of hunger is no longer felt by any of us, but we are scarcely able to converse upon any other subject than the pleasures of eating.'[44] On 6 October, two of the *voyageurs* collapsed and died, and Hood was very weak. It was decided that Franklin and most of the men would carry on to Fort Enterprise, while Richardson and Hepburn would remain with Hood and the bulk of the baggage. Franklin set off, but two of the men were too exhausted to continue and were sent back. One of them, an Iroquois called Michel, reappeared at the Richardson camp.

Weakness and bad weather kept Richardson, Hood and Hepburn in their beds, reading to each other from prayer books:

> They inspired us on each perusal with so strong a sense of the omnipresence of a beneficent God, that our situation, even in these wilds, appeared no longer destitute; and we conversed, not only with calmness, but with cheerfulness, detailing with unrestrained confidence the past events of our lives, and dwelling with hope on our future prospects.[45]

Prayer and the printed word were tools in their survival kit, the product, partly at least, of the Scottish regard for the Bible and literacy. It is clear that for Richardson religious faith was genuinely sustaining, without impeding practical necessity.

By 10 October, Thomas Hood was 'much affected with dimness of sight, giddiness, and other symptoms of extreme debility'.[46] Michel found, he said, the carcass of a wolf, part of which he brought to the camp. It was duly consumed. But Hood grew weaker and the effort to remain hopeful was almost beyond them. Resignation took over: 'we were no longer able to bear the contemplation of the horrors that surrounded us ... We were calm and resigned to our fate, not a murmur escaped us, and we were punctual and fervent in our addresses to the Supreme Being.'[47] On 20 October, Hood died, but not from starvation. He was shot in the back of the head when Richardson and Hepburn were at a distance from the camp. Suicide was a possibility, knowing that he was a drain on resources and that death was not far off, but Richardson suspected something more sinister. Over the next few days Michel's behaviour was increasingly erratic and threatening, and on several occasions he absented himself from the camp. Richardson and Hepburn feared for their lives.

On 23 October, Michel left camp, intending, he said, to gather *tripe de roche*. On his return Richardson:

> put an end to his life by shooting him through the head with a pistol. Had my own life alone been threatened I would not have purchased it by such a measure; but I considered myself as intrusted also with the protection of Hepburn's, a man, who, by his humane attentions and devotedness, had so endeared himself to me, that I felt more anxiety for his safety than for my own.[48]

Richardson had little doubt that Michel's absences from camp were to make a meal from what remained of the body of his companion, of which they had all already partaken. Whether Michel was responsible for murder cannot be certain.

The two survivors set off for Fort Enterprise. Hepburn had over the months demonstrated extraordinary courage and stamina, tirelessly searching for sustenance, and in this final stage of the journey physically supporting the weaker Richardson, who nearly did not make it, falling repeatedly and becoming so exhausted he could not stand. Each time he fell Hepburn, himself at the end of his strength, helped him to his feet. Richardson believed he owed his life to Hepburn, and both he and Franklin were generous in their commendations of him.

At dusk on 29 October, Richardson and Hepburn reached Fort Enterprise, but what they found appalled them. Most of the buildings had been hacked down and used for firewood. Franklin and his men were almost unrecognisable: 'The hollow and sepulchral sound of their voices, produced nearly as great a horror in us, as our emaciated appearance did on them.'[49] They had a meal of singed skins and soup made from pounded bones. On 1 November, two more of the *voyageurs* died. Hepburn's limbs had begun to swell.

Franklin's first expedition to the Arctic would have ended in unmitigated tragedy without the arrival, on 7 November, of dried meat sent by Akaicho, a Copper chief whose camp George Back had reached with a plea for assistance. Unable to control their hunger, the men ate too much and their stomachs swelled painfully. Akaicho's people cared for the starving men who, in their desperately diminished state, were astonished at the ease with which their rescuers carried logs and made a fire. But the fresh supplies could not last and it was imperative that the party moved on. On 15 November, they all left Fort Enterprise: 'The Indians treated us with the utmost tenderness, gave us their snowshoes and walked without themselves, keeping by our sides that they might lift us when we fell.'[50] The Indians prepared food and fed the struggling men 'as if we had been children, evincing a degree of humanity that would have done honour to the most civilized nation'.[51] It took them ten days to reach Akaicho's camp.

On 6 December, a party arrived from Fort Providence with dogs, but without the requested gifts that Franklin and Richardson intended for those who had shared their winter supplies and saved their lives. Akaicho accepted the lack of recompense philosophically, but on leaving his camp Richardson expressed his concern: 'We felt a deep sense of humiliation at being compelled to quit men capable of such liberal sentiments and humane feelings, in the beggarly manner in which we did.'[52] Four days took them to Fort Resolution, where HBC Chief Factor Robert McVicar, from Bowmore on Islay, who had been with the company since 1812, was in charge. It was 19 December 1821 and they would spend the rest of the winter there. While on their travels, the Hudson's Bay Company and the North West Company had joined forces, and a new chapter in the history of Canada's fur trade had begun, under the guidance of George Simpson.

Throughout his ordeal Richardson continued to collect specimens (although most had to be abandoned) and to sustain his role as doctor to the expedition, also treating members of the First Nations in need of help. He was the first in the northwest to record the effects of measles and whooping cough on natives who had never been exposed to these diseases, and he provided detailed accounts of the impact of malnutrition, hypo-thermia and exhaustion. As well as keeping his own journal, he contributed substantially to Franklin's official account of the expedition, providing valuable scientific information and assessing economic potential.

The death toll of the expedition was high. Richardson and Hepburn were the only survivors of their section, and they probably owed their lives to the consumption of human flesh as well as to their own extraordinary endurance and mutual support. There were long-term effects on health. The heroic Hepburn, who, championed by Franklin and Richardson, went on to have an interesting career in England and Australia, suffered from poor health for the rest of his life. But although the price paid was drastic, the expedition achieved a great deal. Nearly 600 miles of coastline were surveyed and mapped, climatic conditions recorded and knowledge of the Arctic shoreline was considerably advanced. As Leslie H. Neatby put it, Franklin 'had put a roof on the map of Canada, and given a definite shape to the North American continent'.[53] Without Richardson and Hepburn it is unlikely that Franklin would have survived.

JOHN RAE: 'A MAN EXACT AND TRUTHFUL'

Some twenty years later the Arctic wilderness killed Franklin and all the men who accompanied him on his final expedition. He had returned to the Arctic in 1825, Richardson and Thomas Drummond from Perth accompanying him. They explored the Arctic coast west of the Coppermine River and surveyed the area around Great Slave Lake, this time without any serious misadventure. They wintered at Fort Franklin on Great Bear Lake, where at Christmas and New Year a gathering of about fifty men, women and children, Scots, natives and Métis, including a piper and a fiddler, celebrated with music and dancing. But the Northwest Passage eluded them and subsequent expeditions, and in 1844 the Admiralty determined to make one more large-scale, well-equipped effort. Franklin, now fifty-nine, was appointed to lead it. In June the following year the expedition sailed from England in the *Erebus* and *Terror*. The ships were spotted by whalers in Baffin Bay, and then disappeared. A two-year absence in the Arctic was not unusual, and it took that long before a search expedition was mooted. It took another year to organise the search, by land and sea. The land search was undertaken by John Richardson, who took with him an HBC employee called John Rae.

Rae had grown up in Orkney and, like Richardson, had studied medicine at the University of Edinburgh. In 1833, at the age of twenty, he joined the Hudson's Bay Company as surgeon on the supply ship *Prince of Wales* and sailed to Hudson Bay, expecting to return to Orkney at the end of the season. He never made the return voyage. The ice closed in early that year, and the *Prince of Wales* was unable to make it out of Hudson Strait. Rae found himself stuck for the winter at Moose Factory in James Bay. Not one for inactivity, Rae at once made himself useful. He had had a rugged upbringing in an unforgiving climate, he understood weather and wildlife, could handle a boat and a gun, and was practical and self-reliant. George

Simpson recognised his abilities and offered him a job as surgeon and clerk at Moose Bay. Rae accepted.

Ten years later Simpson identified Rae as the man to complete the task of surveying the Arctic coast. During that time Rae had demonstrated his ability to adapt to extreme conditions and to learn from those with the necessary survival skills. He acknowledged as mentor a Cree called George Rivers, who taught him a great deal. Rae hunted, he travelled, alone as well as with others, became skilled in the use of snowshoes and sledges, and investigated the local wildlife. He exhibited a remarkable talent for self-sufficiency and calm endurance. On a hunting trip with George Rivers he plunged waist deep into a freezing pool to retrieve a canoe: 'there being no handy opportunity of changing clothes or drying myself, (it was freezing pretty hard), I was not quite comfortable'.[54] Rae had a singular gift for understatement.

Before undertaking the task set by Simpson, 'to complete the geography of the northern shore of America', Rae travelled on foot to Red River to learn surveying techniques.[55] Finding that the man appointed to instruct him was seriously ill he walked the 1,200 miles to Sault Ste Marie on Lake Superior, and on to Toronto to seek another instructor. While at Red River he met R. M. Ballantyne, then an HBC employee, later a best-selling novelist. Ballantyne described him:

> He was very muscular and active, full of animal spirits, and had a fine intellectual countenance. He was considered … to be one of the best snow-shoe walkers in the service, was also an excellent rifle-shot, and could stand an immense amount of fatigue.[56]

Letitia Hargrave, who knew Rae at York Factory where her husband was Chief Factor, was also impressed: 'He is a very good looking man & can walk 100 miles in 2 days.'[57] Norwegian explorer Vilhjalmur Stefansson would describe him as 'a man exact and truthful, and his methods of travel a generation ahead of his time'.[58]

Expectations were high. Although the main aim was to explore the Arctic coast east of Fury and Hecla Strait, Simpson stipulated a string of other duties. Rae was to collect botanical, zoological and geological specimens, measure temperatures and atmospheric pressure, record the state of the ice, winds and currents, and take soundings. He was also instructed to record Inuit customs and artefacts. All of this he did, sketching and describing in words what he observed, and collecting artefacts and specimens. His achievement as a collector has been acknowledged by subsequent scientists and ethnographers. At the time, it was taken for granted that these tasks were part of his role and part of the function of the Hudson's Bay Company.

It was July 1846 when Rae set off with twelve men by boat from Fort

Churchill to Repulse Bay further north on Hudson Bay, which became his base. The rest of the summer was spent in some initial exploration and in 'making every arrangement in our power for the preservation of life and health during the long and cold winter we had to encounter'.[59] They built a stone shelter and laid in supplies of food and fuel. Later, observing how effective snowhouses were at keeping in the heat, they built igloos. Through the winter, with the temperature dropping to 40° below freezing ('some few degrees more heat would have been preferable', was Rae's comment), Rae ensured that his men kept healthy, monitoring diet, sometimes reduced to one meal a day to save fuel as well as food, and prescribing enough exercise to keep fit without burning unnecessary energy.[60] On Christmas Day they ate a good dinner of venison and plum pudding with a modest allowance of brandy punch, but also played football. There was more football and another good dinner on New Year's Day.

Rae's preparations for the next season's work and his attention to detail were meticulous. He was also willing to experiment and improvise. None of this diminished the extremity of what he and his men encountered, but it did mean they were as well prepared as possible for the Arctic wilderness. Rae conveyed something of the experience:

> At one moment we sank nearly waist-deep in snow, at another we were up to our knees in salt water, and then again upon a piece of ice so slippery that, with our wet and frozen shoes it was impossible to keep from falling. Sometimes we had to crawl out of a hole on all fours like some strange-looking quadrupeds.[61]

Rae crossed what would be named Rae Isthmus to Committee Bay, and surveyed over 600 miles of unexplored coastline. It was a gruelling task which left the men 'much reduced in flesh' (Rae himself had to tighten his belt by 6 in) with several suffering from frostbite, but they all survived in reasonably good shape.[62] The striking feature of the expedition was that although the journey 'gave me harder work than anything I had previously experienced', they had lived largely off the land, without the encumbrance of large quantities of supplies from Churchill.[63] They had survived the winter as the Inuit did. While Rae and his men were investigating north and west of Committee Bay somewhere on the other side of Boothia Peninsula was what was left of Franklin's expedition.

On his return from Repulse Bay Rae carried on to London, where he reported directly to the HBC board. It was there that he met Richardson, who asked Rae to join him in the search for Franklin. Their first attempt took them down the Mackenzie River, east along the coast and inland to Great Bear Lake. They found no trace of Franklin, but took advantage of opportunities for further surveying and collecting. It was in many ways a productive partnership, but Rae was critical of Richardson and also of the Royal Navy men who made up the party. Rae felt that the sixty-year-old Richardson left most of the work to him, and he made some caustic comments in letters to George Simpson: 'My worthy Superior has an excellent appetite and has *filled out* amazingly since the *fatigues* of his journey from the Coppermine.'[64] The men were 'the most awkward, lazy and careless set I ever had anything to do with', which left Rae with even more to do.[65] Rae's letters are often spiked with sarcasm and reveal his impatience with those who ignored his advice or were slow to learn. In the summer of 1849 Richardson returned to England while Rae remained to continue the search.

That autumn he took up the post of Chief Factor of the Mackenzie River district, based at Fort Simpson, but he was not well suited to life as a fur trader, which he considered child's play. When the following year the call came to renew the Franklin search he was quick to respond. In the summer of 1851 he was with two men, two sledges and five dogs on the Wollaston Peninsula. As always he was travelling light: 'a pocket comb, a tooth brush, towel and a bit of coarse yellow soap … one flannel shirt (in addition to the shoes and socks absolutely requisite) besides my everyday suit'.[66] It was hard going, stony and fissured by deep ravines, and the fierce sun forced them to travel by night. They crossed to Victoria Island and journeyed on foot over rough ground that destroyed their moccasins and tore their feet. They found two pieces of wood, which Rae later speculated could be fragments of one of Franklin's ships. He had covered over a thousand miles in thirty-nine days, a remarkable achievement which was acknowledged by the award of the Royal Geographical Society's Founder's Gold Medal.

Rae's final Arctic expedition, in 1853, was intended to fill gaps in knowledge of the Arctic coast rather than continue the search for Franklin. He approached the task with his now well-recognised care and skill, but this recognition would soon fragment. With no expectation of locating traces of Franklin, Rae did in fact discover significant clues as to his fate, gleaning information and identifiable relics from Inuit. The Inuit told of coming on a party of emaciated men on King William Island dragging sledges and a boat, and later finding bodies and graves on the mainland. In his report Rae included the Inuit interpretation of what they had found, that 'from the mutilated state of many of the bodies and the contents of the kettles, it is evident that our wretched Countrymen had been driven to the last dread alternative, as a means of sustaining life'.[67] This sentence had explosive consequences. The British authorities and British society refused to believe that a British naval expedition could descend to consuming its dead.

Thousands of miles from the Arctic wilderness controversy raged among men and women (Franklin's widow fiercely resisted Rae's findings) who had no experience or understanding of Arctic conditions. Significantly,

Richardson, who had had his own encounter with cannibalism, supported Rae. Eventually, the value of Rae's information was accepted, and he and the two men with him received the reward which had been offered. It was the end of a remarkable career of Arctic exploration, but not of Rae's experience of the North American wilderness. Although he left the service of the Hudson's Bay Company, he returned to Canada and carried out survey work in preparation for a telegraph link from Red River through the Rockies to Vancouver Island. But the last twenty-five years of his life were spent in Orkney and London, where he wrote and lectured on Arctic travel, but he was never accepted by officialdom as the man of dedicated proficiency, independence and endurance that he was. There were numerous Franklin search expeditions. The leaders of all of them received knighthoods, except for Dr John Rae.

The far north of the American continent demanded adjustment to harsh conditions and an acceptance of often extreme privation. The contribution of Scots to the penetration of America's most hostile territory is unequalled, although their involvement was the result of accident as much as design, of opportunity as much as ability. John Rae's life and achievement is emblematic of this nexus. A rugged (but not underprivileged) childhood taught him resourcefulness as well as practical skills; a university education trained him as a scientist; his Orkney background made him aware of the opportunities offered by the Hudson's Bay Company; an accident of ice kept him in Hudson Bay where he caught the attention of George Simpson, an astute judge of men and their potential. His adaptability, even when compared with predecessors such as Mackenzie and Fraser, was striking, and his readiness to learn the survival skills of First Nations and Inuit peoples was unusual. Earlier explorers acknowledged a dependence on native knowledge, but it was laced with distrust and assumptions of superiority. Rae was able to move beyond the embrace of his white, Christian background and enter the wilderness in a spirit of pragmatic acquiescence to its demands. His journeys were not just forays into the unknown; they were part of life and experienced on their own terms. Self-reliance freed him from the constrictions of social and corporate infrastructures; although a highly regarded HBC employee there is no suggestion that either commercial gain or company loyalty were personal driving forces. Rae did not seek to conquer the climate or the terrain he travelled through. His aim was to understand how to live in the conditions they presented. He saw that humanity had a place in the far north, and that whatever the value of measurement and codification the lives of communities and individuals as shaped by the harshest of environments were valuable in themselves.

Each of the individuals involved in these experiences of extraordinary endurance is distinctive. They shared many qualities and there were some common factors in their backgrounds (although each was from a different part of Scotland), but there is no identikit intrepid Scot. In fact, it is their singularity and self-reliance that mark them out. Although a belief in human potential underlies their efforts, it was self-belief that propelled them, alongside a range of personal and commercial motives. Their lives subsequent to their great endeavours had varying degrees of success and disappointment. Only Robert Stuart, the Perthshire minister's son, went on to have a successful career in North America. Of the five, he is probably the least remembered and has left the smallest imprint on the map: South Pass is well known, but not Robert Stuart.

Extreme conditions could bring out the worst and the best in human nature. Arrogance fuelled the determination of Mackenzie and Fraser; at the same time they were persuasively diplomatic in their leadership role and in their dealings with indigenous communities. Extreme conditions could also impel men to extreme actions and could have long-term effects. Many died, a few, like Franklin, as popular heroes, but most Arctic deaths were messy and accidental, and a few were murderous. John Richardson, who ate human flesh and shot a man in cold blood, returned to Britain, was knighted and had an eminently respectable career as medical doctor and scientist. Like the others, Mackenzie and Fraser tested the capacity for perseverance, of themselves and their men, beyond imaginable limits, refusing to be deterred by overwhelming impediments. Mackenzie's achievement was acknowledged with a knighthood, but his later life was nevertheless coloured by anticlimax and frustration. Fraser had no such acknowledgement and lived out his life in Canada in relative obscurity.

Obscurity has, of course, been the legacy of most of the many hundreds of Scots, mainly Highlanders and Orkneymen, and sons of Scots who played a part in the exploration of North America's Arctic and Rocky Mountain wildernesses. The prominent fur traders have left their mark in archives and on maps (the fur trade is discussed further in Chapter 6), but most of those who made the trade's success possible have little presence except as recognisably Scottish names in records and journals. Among Scots who accompanied Rae on his expeditions were William Adamson, Charles Harrison, Halcrow Humphrey, George Kirkness and Daniel Wilson from Shetland; Orcadians James Clouston, John Corrigal (from Orphir where Rae grew up), George Flett, John Folster, William Hepburn and Edward Hutchison; and Highlanders Hector Mackenzie, Murdoch McLennan, Neil McLeod, Peter Matheson and Hector Morrison. These names may not appear on maps, but are nevertheless lastingly woven into North American history.

NOTES

1. Hugh MacLennan, *Scotchman's Return* (New York: Scribners, [1958] 1960), p. 7.
2. Ibid., p. 8.
3. Walter Sheppe (ed.), *First Man West. Alexander Mackenzie's Journal of His Voyage to the Pacific Coast of Canada in 1793* (Berkeley, CA: University of California Press, 1962), p. 61.
4. Ibid., pp. 77–8.
5. Ibid., p. 80.
6. Ibid., p. 96.
7. Ibid., p. 107.
8. Ibid., p. 120.
9. Ibid., p. 129.
10. Ibid., p. 132.
11. Ibid., p. 134.
12. Ibid., p. 188.
13. Ibid., pp. 276–7.
14. Roy Daniells, *Alexander Mackenzie and the North West* (London: Faber & Faber, 1969), p. 182.
15. In Lamb, Introduction, Simon Fraser, *The Letters and Journals of Simon Fraser*, ed. W. Kaye Lamb (Toronto: Dundum Press, 1960), p. 51.
16. Ibid., p. 52.
17. Fraser, *Journals*, p. 89.
18. Ibid., p. 90.
19. Ibid., p. 91.
20. Ibid., p. 97.
21. Ibid., p. 102.
22. Ibid., p. 117.
23. Lamb, Introduction, Fraser, *Journals*, p. 50.
24. Ross, *Adventures*, p. 178.
25. In Laton McCartney, *Across the Great Divide: Robert Stuart and the Discovery of the Oregon Trail* (Stroud: Sutton, 2003), p. 10.
26. Ross, *Adventures*, p. 71.
27. In McCartney, *Across the Great Divide*, pp. 109–10.
28. Ibid., p. 115.
29. Washington Irving, *Astoria: Adventure in the Pacific Northwest* (London: KPI, [1839] 1987), p. 237.
30. Ibid., p. 262.
31. Ibid., p. 263.
32. Ibid., p. 276.
33. Ibid., p. 297.
34. Ibid., p. 343.
35. In McCartney, *Across the Great Divide*, p. 265.

36. C. Stuart Houston, *Arctic Ordeal: The Journal of John Richardson* (Montreal and Gloucester: McGill-Queen's University Press and Alan Sutton, 1984), p. 70.
37. Ibid., p. 105.
38. Ibid., p. 125.
39. Ibid., p. 126.
40. Ibid., p. 133.
41. Ibid., p. 136.
42. Ibid., p. 140.
43. Ibid., p. 143.
44. Ibid., p. 144.
45. Ibid., p. 148.
46. Ibid., p. 150.
47. Ibid., p. 153.
48. Ibid., p. 156.
49. Ibid., p. 161.
50. Ibid., p. 165.
51. Ibid., p. 167.
52. Ibid., p. 179.
53. Leslie H. Neatby, *In Quest of the North West Passage* (London: Constable, 1958), p. 80.
54. Jenni Calder, in Ian Bunyan *et al.*, *No Ordinary Journey. John Rae, Arctic Explorer 1813–1893* (Edinburgh and Montreal: National Museums of Scotland and McGill-Queen's University Press, 1993), p. 46.
55. Calder, in Bunyan *et al.*, *No Ordinary Journey*, p. 48.
56. R. M. Ballantyne, *Hudson's Bay or Every-day Life in the Wilds of North America* (London: Nisbet, 1876), pp. 225–6.
57. Margaret Arnett Macleod (ed.), *The Letters of Letitia Hargrave* (Toronto: The Champlain Society, 1947), p. 211.
58. In Francis Spufford, *I May Be Some Time. Ice and the English Imagination* (London: Faber & Faber, 1996), p. 191.
59. John Rae, *Correspondence with the Hudson's Bay Company* (Hudson's Bay Record Society, 1953), p. 39.
60. Calder, in Bunyan *et al.*, *No Ordinary Journey*, p. 52.
61. Ibid., p. 53.
62. Ibid.
63. Rae, *Correspondence*, p. 45.
64. Ibid., p. 91.
65. Ibid., p. 83.
66. Ibid., p. 169.
67. Ibid., p. 276.

4

Glorious Independence

The glorious independence of man in a savage state.

Washington Irving, *A Tour on the Prairies*

Here was I, an obscure inhabitant of an obscure Scottish village, coasting the top of the world.

Isobel Hutchison, *North to the Rime-Ringed Sun*

In 1832, Washington Irving, son of an immigrant from Orkney, returned to the United States after a seventeen-year sojourn in Europe. He had visited Scotland in 1817, touring the Highlands, but was particularly keen to meet with the Edinburgh literati, especially Walter Scott whose narrative poems were doing so much to entice American visitors to Scotland. Irving did not visit his father's birthplace; he was much more interested in literary tourism and got no further north than the Trossachs of Scott's *Lady of the Lake*. His two-week tour also took him to Ayrshire to absorb the spirit of Robert Burns, and Abbotsford itself, where he was cordially received by Scott. He had, he wrote in a letter to his brother, visited some of 'the most remarkable and beautiful scenes in Scotland'.[1] But he had not strayed from the beaten track, and although he would soon be praising the courage and determination of the intrepid Scots who opened up the North American frontier, he had no direct experience of their rugged origins. For him, Scotland was a place of romance rather than a breeding ground of endurance.

When he went west, however, he portrayed Robert Stuart and his fellow Scots who crossed the formidable Rocky Mountains and the desolate plains as iconic adventurers. Before being approached by J. J. Astor to write an account of the Astorian episode, Irving had made a trip to the 'far west' in response to an invitation from Henry Ellsworth, a Connecticut lawyer who had been appointed US Commissioner of Indian Tribes in Arkansas and Oklahoma. Irving accompanied Ellsworth on a trip to Fort Gibson as secretary to the commission. He was hugely excited at the prospect: 'I should see those fine countries of the "far west", while still in a state of pristine wildness, and behold herds of buffaloes scouring their native prairies, before they are driven beyond the reach of a civilised tourist.'[2] He seemed unaware of the irony embedded in a role that was very much concerned with the country's inhabitants, by whom he was much impressed.

Scott had drawn an analogy between the aborigines of the Scottish Highlands and those of the New World. It is not surprising that in Irving's depiction of Native Americans there are hints of Scott's wild but pictures-que Highlanders. Irving relished 'the glorious independence of man in a savage state'. When he visited the Osage Agency he was particularly struck by a young Osage warrior 'of open, noble countenance and frank demeanour'. The young man sat astride his horse with rifle and blanket, 'ready at a moment's warning to rove the world'. Unencumbered by unnecessary possessions and 'artificial wants' the warrior 'possessed the great secret of personal freedom'. Irving clearly found this immensely attractive and enlarged on the impediments of civilisation: 'We of society are slaves, not so much to others as to ourselves; our superfluities are the chains that bind us, impeding every movement of our bodies and thwarting every impulse of our souls.'[3] Yet he was participating in the effort to destroy the traditional way of life of the Osage people.

The Highlands that Irving visited and read about were in a state of transition, and the sense of a vanishing heroic world was a large part of the attraction of Scott's work and Macpherson's Ossian epics. The year of Irving's western adventure, 1832, was the year of Scott's death, by which time his fiction as well as his poetry was widely available and immensely popular in America as well as Europe. Irving wrote his *Tour on the Prairies* on the eve of the great westward expansion that would open up the wilder-ness to thousands, and at the same time herald its demise. 'The slow and pausing steps of civilisation,' as Irving would write in his later account of the Astorian episode, would bring an end to an heroic age, just as 'progress' shouldered away the uncouth but romantic traditions of Gaeldom.[4] The noble savage could be described, fixed on paper and canvas by writers and artists, but could not survive. But for the incomer, the experience of wilderness was a useful education, enhancing a resourceful manliness and promoting qualities in tune with the foundation of the United States.

In this context the 1830s was a key decade. The territories between the Mississippi and the Missouri were beginning to fill. The era of the mountain men would soon draw to a close and the first wagon trains were crossing the Great Plains. In the northwest there were fur-trading posts west of the Rockies, and the far north, for all its grimness, was gradually ceasing to be *terra incognita*. The pressures on indigenous peoples were intensifying. But the vast North American landmass still offered plenty of unexplored territory, and the call of the wild rang across the Atlantic. In the same year that Irving thrilled to the promise of adventure in the west, William Drummond Stewart from Perthshire arrived in the United States eager to set foot in the wild terrain beyond the Missouri.

STEWART AND MURRAY: FREE MEN AMONG THE FREE

Stewart was the second son of the 5th baronet of Murthly Castle in Perthshire and had served in the Napoleonic Wars, fighting under Wellington at Waterloo. Approaching middle age, with a problematic personal life and not content with a peacetime existence that seemed to offer little scope for his talents, in 1833 he headed for St Louis, gateway to the West. He travelled from New York on horseback, following the westward progression of the frontier. He joined a pack train led by Ulster Scot Robert Campbell making for the annual rendezvous on Green River. This was his introduction to the rugged life of the mountain men, which he enthusiastically embraced, rubbing shoulders with legendary figures such as William Sublette, Jim Bridger, William Bonneville and Tom Fitzpatrick. He attended the next two rendezvous, and took every opportunity of exploring the neighbouring mountains.

On the westward trail in 1834 he fell in with fur trader Nathaniel Wyeth and accompanied him to Fort Vancouver, expansively presided over by Dr John McLoughlin, a Canadian-born Scot who had studied at the University of Glasgow. They were welcomed by a piper in full regalia. The following year at Fort Laramie Stewart met the party of missionary Marcus Whitman, on their way to establish a base on the Columbia River. He entertained them to tea. They sat on buffalo-hide chairs and consumed potted meat, cheese, pickles and marmalade and drank tea from proper cups and saucers. Stewart was very taken with Whitman's new wife Narcissa. Thirteen years later Marcus and Narcissa and eleven others were massacred by a Cayuse band at the Whitman mission at Waiilatpu. The Cayuse nation was ravaged by measles, brought by the whites and against which they had no immunity.

In 1837, Stewart recruited the artist Alfred Jacob Miller to accompany the train to that year's rendezvous on the Popo Agie River. Miller energetically sketched landscapes, Native Americans, mountain men and Stewart himself. These sketches he later transformed into large-scale oil paintings, some of which feature Stewart clad in buckskin and mounted on a white horse. On Stewart's return from this trip he learnt of the death of his elder brother, which made him heir to Murthly Castle. He returned to Scotland, but could not resist the continuing pull of the wild, and in 1843 was back in America to accompany Sublette to what was the last Rocky Mountain furtrappers' rendezvous.

Stewart loved the rugged, challenging, independent frontier existence and was happy to be depicted as a courageous and intrepid hero. But he also liked his comforts, and travelled with supplies of good food, wine and brandy (he was described as having a face red with drinking) which he liberally shared. George Frederick Ruxton, a young fur trapper, provided a semi-fictional account of two out-of-luck trappers meeting Stewart at Independence Rock. Stewart, he wrote, was:

> of middle height and stoutly built, [he] was clad in a white shooting-jacket, of cut unknown in mountain tailoring, and a pair of trousers of the well-known material called 'shepherd's plaid'; a broad-brimmed Panama shaded his face, which was ruddy with health and exercise; a belt round the waist supported a handsome bowie-knife, and a double-barrelled fowling-piece was *slung* across his shoulder.[5]

The trappers were baffled by this figure, and by his companion (Miller), a much younger man, elegantly dressed and riding on an English saddle. Stewart declined an offer to share the mountain men's meal of roasted snake and instead invited the two to join him for dinner. Two wagons drew up, and from them Stewart's black cook unloaded 'hams, tongues, tins of preserved meats, bottles of pickles, of porter, brandy, coffee, sugar, flour', along with equally unfamiliar 'pots and pans, knives, forks, spoons, plates'.[6] Before long 'steaming pots were lifted from the fire' and the mountain men were tucking in and washing down their unexpected meal with copious amounts of brandy. Stewart's hospitality did not end there. When he realised that the trappers were seriously in need he proceeded to re-equip them from his own stores, providing them with clothes, ammunition and 'two excellent Indian horses'.[7]

In Ruxton's eyes Stewart was an eccentric anomaly, a striking, generous but somewhat comic figure. In fact, Stewart's military experience enabled him to be a useful member of the expeditions he joined: there was no place for a passenger, even one of Stewart's largesse. And as there is no record of this meeting other than in Ruxton's account, it may be that the episode arises from tales of the eccentric Scot, of which there must have been many, rather than from an actual encounter. Ruxton's description of Stewart's appearance differs from Miller's depictions, and earlier in his tale Stewart is presented in a rather different light, where his prowess as a fighter is stressed: 'thar was old grit in him … and a hair of the black b'ar at that'.[8] (An unequivocally fictional reference to Stewart appears in George MacDonald Fraser's *Flashman and the Redskins* (1982), where Jim Bridger exclaims in admiration: 'wasn't he the prime coon, though?').[9]

The annual rendezvous were notoriously unrestrained, as men who had spent many solitary months in the wilderness made the most of access to liquor and native women. Stewart enthusiastically participated in these occasions. William Gray, a Presbyterian cabinetmaker who encountered

Stewart in 1836, clearly did not approve and commented sourly: 'His general conversation and appearance was that of a man with strong prejudices and equally strong appetites, which he had freely indulged, with only pecuniary restraint.'[10] Stewart was a showman – making his first appearance at the Green River rendezvous he donned tartan trews and a Panama hat – and the wilderness gave him ample opportunity for indulgence of all kinds. The rugged and unfettered environment highlighted his skills as well as his colourful boldness and his liberality. An exhilarating anarchy was the counterpart to the discipline necessary to survive in the wilderness.

Stewart left his own impressions of life in the Far West in two novels he wrote after his permanent return to Scotland. *Edward Warren* (1854) is largely autobiographical, while *Altowan, or Incidents of Life and Adventure in the Rocky Mountains* (1846) is a mélange of descriptive incident and romance based on Stewart's experiences and observations. In the introduction to the latter by J. Watson Webb the case is made for the authenticity of Stewart's portrayal of Indian life; in contrast, according to Webb, Fenimore Cooper's novels provided a 'nursery picture'.[11] Stewart does indeed describe in detail Blackfoot dress, equipment, encampments and habits. He shows us buffalo and bear hunts and Crow attacks. But all is illuminated by a rich glow of heroism and noble savagery. His Indians are 'perfect in proportion, full in muscle':

> the best models of Greek sculpture had sprung into life in these wilds; and nobleness of expression, freedom of action, and grace of attitude, could be marked in every part of the savage group ... their own energies of character, seemed to command the elements of which they were the emblems; and their uncontrolled freedom of motion, spoke a language more convincing that the statutes of a hundred republics.[12]

The eponymous Altowan is of mixed race, and combines the physical presence of the native with equally natural gentlemanly speech and behaviour. The issue of race weaves itself erratically throughout the book. So often men of mixed race are portrayed as combining the worst of red and white; Altowan combines the best, but this does not protect him from an identity crisis, intensified when he discovers that the young mixed-race woman he is attracted to is in fact his half-sister. Idalie's upbringing has combined 'the vicissitudes of an Indian life' of her early childhood with the relative sophistication of the Red River settlement, where after her mother's death she was adopted by the white wife of an HBC partner.[13] She is 'the beautiful daughter of the wilds' with natural grace, courage and nobility, and the assets of education: '[she] had not failed to profit by any thing that was amiable or elegant in the society she had met in the Red River establishment'.[14] Elegance was probably a rare commodity at Red River in the 1830s, but Stewart's point is clear. He is implying a future that allows – perhaps depends on – a happy union between indigenous and incoming populations.

He stresses the way frontiersmen acquire Native American habits, and take on something of their nobility. Trapper Joe Henry, Missouri-born, is an 'American of the West, whose tall and muscular form, long hair and eagle eye, would show him a free man among the free'.[15] But the arena of freedom is changing. The buffalo and the bear are disappearing and traditional aboriginal life is being eroded: 'the frequent traces of bones overgrown with grass, of huts, and pickets, and fires, gave a sad appearance of desolation and change, to what had evidently once been the scene of crowded camps and animated life'.[16] The latter part of the novel leaves the American West for England, where the increasingly convoluted plot is played out. Altowan is killed. He had a role on the frontier, but there is no place for him in England, in spite of (or perhaps because of) the fact that his father turns out to be an aristocratic Yorkshire landowner. His half-sister, on the other hand, marries into that same aristocracy. She can leave the wilderness behind; Altowan cannot. It is often implied that women of mixed race have less difficulty than men in abandoning part of their identity.

Stewart's narrative clearly owes much to Sir Walter Scott. Like Scott, he is dealing with frontiers and lost causes, with change and the erosion of tradition, and with tribal rivalries. He tracks his characters across the landscape in similar fashion and borrows tropes and phrases: 'the three might have been seen … winding their way upward along a bank of that rapid stream' could be Scott in the Highlands as readily as Stewart in the American West.[17] The narrative also owes much to Stewart's own background of family dysfunction; he was no stranger to domestic contention. But Stewart's grasp of narrative is clumsy and the effort to portray heroic nobility is overblown.

Stewart himself tried to introduce the wilderness to Murthly, bringing botanical and zoological specimens, live buffalo and several of Miller's paintings back to Scotland. In his introduction to *Altowan* Webb claimed that Stewart 'had looked upon a country fresh from the hands of the Creator – filled with magnificent lakes, lofty mountains, and boundless prairies, which spoke the nothingness of man'.[18] In fact, Stewart employs the wild environment to enhance the stature and heroism of man, including himself, and tried to recreate something of that ambience at Murthly. He surrounded himself with Native American artefacts and trophies of buffalo, bear and bighorn as reminders of his own personal engagement with the wilderness.

In 1834, the year after William Drummond Stewart made his first trip to the West, another second son of the Scottish nobility was travelling in the United

States. Charles Augustus Murray's father was the 5th earl of Dunmore, and he arrived in the United States at the age of twenty-eight, having behind him an Eton and Oxford education and two unsuccessful attempts as a parliamentary candidate. He sailed from Liverpool on the appropriately named American ship *Waverley*, and spent time in Pennsylvania, Maryland and Virginia before heading west. In his account of his travels he comments on Scottish settlement in the New World. He found Gaelic-speaking Highlanders who had left Scotland after the '45 industriously farming in Virginia. He was impressed by the emigrants' hard work and tenacity in transforming untilled land, and believed Scots to be particularly successful in making something of American opportunity: 'the Scotchmen who have settled in the United States, have earned for themselves a higher than average character for honesty, perseverance, and enterprise, than their rival settlers from any other part of the world'.[19] Murray himself had with him his kilt and plaid, and was not averse to parading his Scottish identity.

Back in Scotland Murray's father was acquiring for £60,000 a large part of the island of Harris from its proprietor Alexander Norman MacLeod. When Lord Dunmore died in 1836 Charles Augustus Murray's elder brother inherited an estate which was crowded with crofter tenants and squatters whom it could not sustain. But it did include good grazing land, coveted by a local sheep farmer, also a tenant of the estate. For the 6th earl the solution to his tenantry's drain on his resources was to turn his land over to sheep. The crofters were offered land elsewhere or free passage to Canada, but turned both options down and refused to move. Dunmore brought in troops, who quickly overcame this resistance. Although initially most of the tenants were resettled in other parts of the island, eventually 600 of them departed for Canada. Charles Murray's account of his American travels was published in 1839, the year in which the evictions took place; he may have wished to portray Scottish settlement in the New World in a good light, though he was probably deaf to the echoes of America's displacement of Indian nations, who were forcibly repopulated when they were not altogether eliminated.

Murray travelled through Ohio and Kentucky, where he acquired a German companion, Mr Verrunft, and continued on through Missouri to Fort Leavenworth, near present-day Kansas City. It was there that he met a band of Pawnee, and was intrigued enough by these 'genuine children of the wilderness' to set off with them to visit the main Pawnee encampment.[20] Although he found the Pawnee attractive and friendly, it was not an experience to be undertaken lightly. They headed into Nebraska, setting off each day at 4 am and travelling nine hours before stopping for food. When they reached the camp Murray found a community of about 5,000, which he observed with fascination and described in some detail. His familiarity with the novels of Fenimore Cooper had not prepared him for what appeared to be a thriving traditional life. He was received with courtesy and hospitality, and was impressed by Sa-ni-tsa-rish, the Pawnee chief. During his month in the camp, he was invited to feasts and to participate in buffalo hunts – he was critical of some of the native tactics, but admired their tracking abilities. There were numerous adventures, some of them life-threatening, including an attack by Cheyenne, traditional enemies of the Pawnee.

Murray is a more detached observer than Stewart, and perhaps more aware of the lurking paradoxes of frontier life. He was clearly attracted, as were many Scottish visitors to the United States, by what he calls 'a real republican equality' which he found was already being eroded in the eastern states, where equality was 'daily infringed on and modified'.[21] In cities such as Boston and Philadelphia 'distinctions of rank and station' were apparent, but in the Far West 'where society is in its infancy' the demands of settlement and exploiting the potential of natural resources had an equalising effect. With the focus on survival, physical and financial, 'men of leisure are unknown, and the arm of the law is feeble in protecting life and property'. Life was rough and ready, 'the tone of manners, conversation, and accomplishment, is necessarily much lower than in states and cities longer established'. Only in these circumstances, argued Murray, can 'true republican equality' exist.[22]

Yet Murray cannot escape his background or throw off his own class instincts, and although there was much about Pawnee life that irked and dismayed him he was not immune to noble savagery. Fascinated as he was by the wilderness and the challenge of the frontier, he travelled with a valet, and his tolerance of discomfort was limited. After his month with the Pawnee he was pleased and relieved to return to the relative comforts of Fort Leavenworth. Although he invested in 20,000 acres of Wisconsin land, he did not share Stewart's relish for the wilderness and returned to Britain where he wrote first an account of his travels and then a novel, which pre-dated Stewart's *Altowan* by two years and like it owes much to both Cooper and Scott.

The Prairie-Bird (1844) is without the florid extravagance of Stewart's *Altowan*, but is nevertheless highly flavoured and equally convoluted. With a pedestrian narrative and a cast of two-dimensional characters, its story-telling leaves much to be desired, but it does have some interest as a vehicle for an anthropological examination of Native American life east and west of the Mississippi and the impact of white settlement. He provides detailed descriptions of the dress, accoutrements and habits of the Delaware and Osage people. Like Stewart's, his native heroes are handsome, dignified and courteous. His Delaware chief War-Eagle has a 'light, free step upon the grass ... like that of a young elk on a prairie'. War-Eagle's younger brother

Wingenund is good-looking and gentlemanly, with, according to Scot Colonel Brandon, feelings and manners that 'would put to shame those of many who think themselves fine gentlemen'.[23] Brandon, a former Jacobite who lost his property after the '45, expands on the theme:

> I have seen among [Indians] so much cruelty, cunning and drunkenness, that the romantic notions which I once entertained respecting them are completely dissipated. Nevertheless, I confess that many of their worst faults have arisen from their commerce with the whites; and they still retain some virtues which are completely rare among us.

These virtues are, he says, 'patience under suffering', the ability to keep a secret, and loyalty.[24]

The colonel's son Reginald is the novel's central character, 'a powerful, athletic young man with a countenance strikingly handsome, and embrowned by exercise and exposure'. Reginald is the idealised frontier hero, dressed in deer-skin, his long hair curling under his wolf-skin cap, bear-skin moccasins on his feet, a rifle in his hand and 'an ornamented *couteau-de-chasse* hanging at his belt'.[25] He is as comfortable in his sister's boudoir as in the forest or on the plains. He saves War-Eagle's life, and his own life is in turn saved by Winegund, thus binding the three together as friends and brothers. There are other less gentlemanly characters among both Indians and whites who play an equal part in brutality; the message here is that the naturally noble, whether savage or refined, will recognise and acknowledge each other in an environment which fosters barbarity.

The action concerns Reginald's eventual recovery of a young white woman, the eponymous Prairie-Bird, who was abducted by a band of Osage as a child. Stewart is more daring in his portrayal of white and red relations, but he and Murray were clearly both exercised – and perplexed – by the impact of white expansion on indigenous life and vice versa. Perhaps taking their lead from Cooper, they grasped the dramatic potential inherent in the environment they portrayed, but did not know how to resolve the implications or, indeed, how to explore them fully. Imitative of Scott as they clearly were, they make no attempt to emulate his efforts at resolution.

Around half a century after the adventures of Stewart and Murray, Ewan Cameron from Argyll arrived in Montana to raise polo ponies intended for the British market. He had little success, but noted the potential for sport in Montana's Badlands. It was, at the end of the nineteenth century and in spite of intensive agricultural activity, still an area where 'miles may be traversed without finding sign of human being or hearing sound more civilised than the howling of a wolf'.[26] Peter Doig, who in the 1890s brought his family from Dundee to Montana's Big Belt Hills, was familiar with that wildness as in a series of jobs he helped out on scattered sheep farms. His concern, however, was not with sport but with the need to sustain his family.

The response of Stewart and Murray to the call of the wild was largely recreational. They sought adventure, Stewart especially, and were impelled by curiosity and attracted by the exotic. They did not, like Peter Doig and many other Scottish families in Montana, seek a livelihood in the wilderness and their futures did not depend on what they made of their experiences. Stewart collected material, dead and alive, to bring back to Scotland, but these were trophies rather than professional assets. The opportunity to collect, however, was irresistible to those who wished to understand and learn from the wilderness rather than exploit and dominate it.

DAVID DOUGLAS: 'I CRAWLED, FOR I COULD HARDLY WALK'

In 1823, a twenty-four-year-old Scot from Perthshire was sent by the Horticultural Society of London to collect botanical specimens in the eastern United States and British North America. Impressed by his abilities, the society sent him off again the following year, this time to the largely unexplored Pacific Northwest. The aim was to observe and collect material, especially species that might thrive on the European side of the Atlantic and thus be of commercial benefit. The young man was David Douglas, son of a stonemason from Scone near Perth (and not far from Murthly Castle), who after a few years at the local parish school had become an apprentice gardener at the earl of Mansfield's Scone Palace. In 1818, he moved on to Valleyfield near Dunfermline, an estate owned by Sir Robert Preston, where he worked under the head gardener Alex Stuart. Encouraged by Sir Robert, he attended botany lectures at the University of Glasgow, where William Hooker, the professor of botany, became his mentor. It was Hooker who recommended Douglas to the Horticultural Society.

Douglas was not the first Scottish gardener to explore and collect in North America. In 1782, John Fraser from Kiltarlity near Inverness set off for Newfoundland as a self-taught plant collector. Later he was in the Carolinas and Georgia, and later still, after a trip to Russia where he was commissioned by Catherine the Great to collect American plants, in Tennessee, Kentucky and Ohio. In Tennessee he climbed Bald Mountain, at the southern end of the Blue Ridge Mountains that divide Tennessee and North Carolina, where he found rhododendrons (*Rhododendron catawbiense*) growing in profusion. Specimens were duly collected and became the first to grow successfully in Britain. Fraser was also responsible for introducing to Britain species of azalea, laurel and magnolia. One of those to whom he sent plants was William Aiton from Lanarkshire, head gardener at Kew. The Scottish gardening network was widespread and productive. It was Aiton who recommended

Francis Masson from Aberdeen to accompany Captain Cook on his second voyage in 1772, which took him to South Africa. Masson returned to South Africa some years later and collected extensively. Then, in 1797, at the age of fifty-six he went to America, where he spent seven years investigating New York State, and areas around lakes Ontario, Michigan and Huron. It was his last chance to pursue his passion for plants and collecting; he died in Montreal in 1805.

Douglas made the journey to the mouth of the Columbia River by sea and, like the ill-fated *Tonquin*, the *William and Ann* which had brought him from Liverpool had great difficulty in entering the river to reach landfall at Astoria. For six weeks storms and high seas prevented an approach. It was a dramatic introduction to two and a half years of life in the wild. He arrived at Fort Vancouver, which was to be his base, in April 1825 and there was welcomed and supported by Dr John McLoughlin. He also met at the fort James Douglas (no relation), a HBC trader who helped to pioneer an overland route from the Fraser River to Fort Vancouver. He would later be based at Fort Vancouver, before moving on to Fort Victoria on Vancouver Island and eventually becoming governor of British Columbia.

David Douglas was eager to get down to work, and quickly adapted to travelling by canoe, on horseback and on foot through a formidable landscape. He had to carry with him the means of storing and preserving specimens, but in terms of his own comfort he travelled light. Although he sometimes had a tent, he frequently slept under an upturned canoe or with no shelter at all.

> In England people shudder at the idea of sleeping with a window open; here, each individual takes his blanket and with all the complacency of mind that can be imagined throws himself on the sand or under a bush just as if he were going to bed. I confess, at first, although I always stood it well and never felt any bad effects from it, it was looked on by me with a sort of dread. Now I am well accustomed to it, so much so that comfort seems superfluity.[27]

And comfort was, of course, relative. The search for plants and trees took him beyond the established trade routes and demanded huge effort.

> The luxury of a night's sleep on a bed of pine branches can only be appreciated by those who have experienced a route over a barren plain, scorched by the sun, or fatigued by groping their way through a thick forest, crossing gullies, dead wood, lakes, stones, etc. Indeed so much worn out was I three times by fatigue and hunger that twice I crawled, for I could hardly walk.[28]

His feet were blistered, and he had one biscuit in his knapsack.

While the fur traders who assisted Douglas were intent on the least demanding route from one post to the next, Douglas constantly diverted, usually with a native guide, to climb a peak or penetrate a forest. On one such expedition near the Columbia River he tackled a summit carrying only a blanket, 3 ounces of tea (Douglas was a firm believer in the reviving qualities of a cup of tea), 1 lb of sugar and four small biscuits. He shot and ate a white-headed eagle – 'very good eating' – to supplement this meagre diet.[29] He spent the night on the mountain top, where it was so cold that he had to keep moving about to keep warm. On the way down the mountain he killed five ducks with a single shot, which seems improbable but he was by all accounts an excellent marksman. The twenty-five-day trip was not a great success: 'I experienced more fatigue and misery, and gleaned less than in any trip I have had in the country.'[30]

By the end of that year, 1825, Douglas was suffering from an infected knee, which would cause him problems for the rest of his time in the northwest. But it did not deter him. The following March he was travelling with HBC Factor John Macleod up the Columbia and to Fort Colvile. Macleod then headed northwest making for Hudson Bay, while Douglas continued to Fort Spokane. There he found the Finlay family nearly starving. They were subsisting on lichen soaked in water, compressed into cakes and cooked. Douglas was able to help them out as on this occasion his supplies included dried buffalo meat.

There were occasions when Douglas himself had cause to be grateful for assistance. In June 1826, he was in the Blue Mountains where he was lashed by storms, so cold and wet he could hardly move. 'If I have any zeal', he recorded in his journal, 'for once and the first time it began to cool.'[31] He was at a low ebb when he met an HBC brigade, which included Archibald McDonald from Glencoe, who would become a leading figure in the company's activities. He was provided with a clean shirt and supper, but the sheer relief of 'seeing a person again' counted for more. By 'person', of course, he meant a white person. 'After travelling in the country of savages for days together … assuredly the face of a Christian although strange speaks friendship.'[32] But most important was the fact that the brigade carried letters from home, which he spent much of the night reading and re-reading: 'in fact before morning I might say I had them by heart'.[33]

Douglas was dependent on HBC support and on native guides. His comments on the Native Americans he encountered are ambivalent. He seemed to be attracted by the simplicity of aboriginal life, but at the same time saw that simplicity as a sign of indolence and resistance to learning new skills. He spent a lot of time in native company, and applied himself to learning some of the languages, but there is no sense of real relationships developing and nothing to hint at the kind of admiration expressed by Irving, Stewart and Murray. On occasion Douglas found himself facing hostility or caught up in preparations for warfare between different bands, situations which he handled with perspicacious coolness. In the autumn of 1826 Douglas finally fulfilled his aim of collecting cones from the sugar pine, only to find he had attracted the interest of suspicious natives. He spent the night lying on the grass with his gun beside him, calmly writing his journal by the light of a pine resin torch.

By the end of that year Douglas had travelled around 6,000 miles, up the Columbia and Okanogan rivers, into the Blue Mountains, along the Snake River, and into the Willamette Valley. He had experienced extreme heat and cold, hunger, exhaustion and threats to his life, most of which he describes in undramatic fashion, though he is occasionally driven to complain. In the Blue Mountains in November 1826 he records that he has travelled thirty-three miles 'drenched and bleached with rain and sleet, chilled with a piercing north wind'. He faced 'the comfortless consolation of lying down wet without supper or fire. On such occasions I am very liable to become fretful.'[34]

Three months later, David Douglas took leave of Fort Vancouver and set off to cross the Rockies on the first leg of a journey to Hudson Bay and eventually across the Atlantic. He joined an HBC brigade, and travelled at first in the company of John McLoughlin, John McLeod and Francis Ermatinger. It was February, with thick snow on the ground, and Douglas had to learn to use snowshoes. He describes making his way through soft snow, 'sinking, ascending two steps and sometimes sliding back three, the snow-shoes twisting and throwing the weary traveller down ... so feeble that lie I must among the snow, like a broken-down wagon-horse entangled in his harnessing, weltering to rescue myself'.[35] In spite of the hard going, the rough camps at night sleeping on branches, clothing which was never dry and snowshoes in need of constant repair, Douglas decided to climb one of the Rocky Mountain peaks. It took him five hours:

> The sensation I felt is beyond what I can give utterance to. Nothing as far as the eye could perceive, but mountains such as I was on, striking the mind with horror blended with a sense of the wondrous work of the Almighty. The aerial tints of the snow, the heavenly azure of the solid glaciers, the rainbow-like hues of their broken fragments, and huge mossy icicles hanging from the perpendicular rocks with snow sliding down from the steep southern rocks, with amazing velocity, producing a crash and grumbling like the shock of an earthquake, the echo of which resounding in the valley for several minutes.[36]

Douglas had by this time considerable experience of the sheer power of the natural world, but here he articulates it strikingly and we are made particularly aware of his own vulnerability.

The party, now without McLeod and McLoughlin, reached Jasper House and continued east to Fort Edmonton and across a vast tract of wilderness to Norway House at the northern end of Lake Winnipeg. On the way they encountered John Franklin and John Richardson returning from their second expedition. With them was botanist Thomas Drummond, from Forfar, Angus, on the other side of the Sidlaw Hills from Douglas's birthplace. Douglas was impressed by Drummond, a cheerful, self-reliant young man and as determined a collector as Douglas himself. He had spent much of the winter alone in the Rockies. From Norway House Douglas went south to the Red River settlement, where he stayed with Donald Mackenzie, governor of the colony, before setting off on the final leg of the journey, reversing the trek of the original settlers fourteen years earlier. He reached York Factory in eighteen days, and embarked for London.

Douglas had successfully collected and preserved hundreds of samples and specimens, which were duly delivered to the Horticultural Society. Many of them are now familiar features of the British landscape and British gardens. Lupins, clarkias, sunflowers and Californian poppies are just some of the descendants of the seeds that Douglas carefully preserved and brought back; but perhaps most conspicuous in Scotland are the Douglas fir and the Sitka spruce, the latter ubiquitous in forestry plantations. They are living links with the North American wilderness.

Douglas did not adjust readily to life in London. As a Scot of humble origins and rough manner he might always have found it difficult, but his years in the wilderness did nothing to prepare him for a situation where his achievements were recognised, but he himself was considered uncouth. He would not conform to the expectations of London society, retaining his wilderness style of dress and address. He could be short-tempered and rude. The Horticultural Society did not know what to do with him, other than to send him back to the wild, where his skills could be put to productive use. So in 1829 he was again in the United States, spending several months collecting in California and visiting Hawaii before returning to the Columbia. While in Honolulu the news that the Horticultural Society was in financial difficulties and that Joseph Sabine, his mentor there, had resigned prompted his own resignation and the decision to continue collecting on a freelance basis. He was now entirely dependent on his own efforts, a situation which perhaps heightened his awareness of vulnerability.

Back in the Pacific northwest he quickly returned to the search for specimens, in spite of an environment of growing instability. He wrote to William Hooker:

> You may judge my situation, when I say to you that my rifle is in my hand day and night; it is by my side under my blanket when I sleep, and my faithful little Scotch terrier, the companion of all my journeys, takes his place at my feet. To be obliged thus to accoutre myself is truly terrible. However, I fail not to do my best, and if unsuccessful in my operations can make my mind easy with the reflection that I used my utmost endeavours.[37]

As a freelancer, Douglas had a reputation to sustain in circumstances that were increasingly precarious. At worst, failure could cost him his life, but survival with his reputation damaged was not an attractive alternative. The difficulties he encountered did not diminish his effort, although rheumatism and deteriorating eyesight slowed him down. In spite of these difficulties he planned to make his way back to Britain overland, via Alaska and Siberia, but this extraordinarily ambitious journey on foot had to be abandoned. On the return up the Fraser River through the Fort George Canyon his canoe was seized by the rapids and whirled downriver. He was lucky to escape with his life, his instruments and Billy, the small terrier he had brought with him from Britain; his diary and over 400 species of plants were lost. It was a bitter blow, and although he comforted himself with the knowledge that no lives were lost and that such mishaps were common, he admitted in a letter to Hooker that 'this disastrous occurrence has much broken my strength and spirits'.[38]

By the end of 1833 Douglas was back in Hawaii, where he stayed for some months. The following summer, at the age of thirty-five, he went walking in the mountains. On 12 July his body was found, trampled and bloody, at the bottom of a pit dug to trap wild cattle. The exact circumstances of his death have never been determined, but it is very likely that, with his diminished eyesight and notwithstanding the vigilance of Billy, he simply fell into the pit. In the North American wilds he contemplated the possibility of death through starvation, exposure or violence, but he could hardly have anticipated such an end.

For David Douglas the call of the wild was quite specific. He was not looking for adventure or recreation, although he clearly had a need for a physically demanding existence. For him, the wilderness was a resource, not to be exploited – indeed, he was critical of the depredations of fur trapping – but to be studied, learnt from and, literally, transplanted. But it was also a means to fulfilment for a young man whose restless talents meant that he was not best suited to join the ranks of the many Scottish gardeners working throughout the United Kingdom or to become a member of the horticultural establishment. The wilderness was a gateway, as it was for many Scots whose aspirations, while often encouraged by education and early experience, were frustrated.

In the year of Douglas's death Charles Augustus Murray and William Drummond Stewart were both enjoying their travels in the American West. When in 1834 Stewart spent several months at Fort Vancouver he must have heard something of David Douglas, who owed much to the support he found there. In that year also the first organised wagon train crossed the Great Divide through the South Pass. The tentative trails through the Rockies were beginning to become established routes, with landmarks that would take on iconic identities. Routes, striking topographical features and stopping places were given names that reflected the incoming people and their experiences and perceptions. The very act of naming was a reassurance, a means of rendering an often threatening landscape less alien. (It could also be seen, as Greg Gillespie has persuasively argued, as appropriation, an assumption that the wilderness was a blank canvas awaiting description and identity.[39]) Further north, the first part of the route David Douglas took from Fort Vancouver to Hudson Bay was now established as a means by which HBC brigades transported pelts out of the mountains and down the Columbia River for onward shipment from the Fort. This movement across the land-scape in itself made little impact on its wild nature, although the trapping was shrinking the beaver population, something that concerned Douglas. But wild country continued to make a huge impact on the men who depended on it for their livelihoods.

JAMES CARNEGIE IN PURSUIT OF NOBLE BEASTS

By 1843 the thirty-year-old Red River settlement at the southern end of Lake Winnipeg had a population of around 5,000, with a few substantial buildings and reasonably thriving farms, but beyond lay a vast hinterland with a sparse indigenous population and, it seemed, little potential for development. Twelve years later the isolation of the little colony, still not much more than a village, forcefully struck a visiting American journalist: 'Deserts, almost trackless, divide it from the habitations of men. To reach it, or once there to escape, is an exploit of which one may almost boast.'[40] A man who played an important role in opening up the routes from the upper Fraser River was David Douglas's namesake James Douglas, by 1834 a Chief Trader with the Hudson's Bay Company. Douglas was the son of a Glasgow sugar merchant, with a plantation in British Guiana, and a Creole. He had had a few years education in Scotland before being apprenticed to the North West Company, soon to merge with the Hudson's Bay Company. Douglas went on to take the lead in opening up New Caledonia, as Simon Fraser had named the territory west of the Rockies and north of the Columbia. But settlement came slowly, and the prairies to the east of the Rockies remained virtually empty, without settlers and without wagon trains rolling west in search of the fertile valleys on the far side of the mountains.

The year 1843 saw the last fur-trading rendezvous further south in what would become the territory of Wyoming. Here the Rocky Mountain wilder-ness was now no longer the sole province of native and fur trapper. By the early 1840s hundreds of covered wagons were crossing the Great Plains and struggling through the mountain passes. There were forts and trading posts at strategic points where entrepreneurs clustered in the hope of profiting from the westward trekkers. But these were minute excrescences on the vast rolling prairie and the massive flanks of the mountains. Whatever respite they offered weary travellers they did not shrink the wilderness, which still began well east of the Mississippi. For a family setting out from Wisconsin, say, a journey of many months would take them from dense forest to empty prairie, across mighty rivers, into forest again, through formidable mountains. The landscape could be beautiful, but it was always potentially dangerous, and that combination of beauty and danger remained a powerful attraction for those who saw wilderness as a source of fun and rugged fulfilment. The call of the wild did not diminish.

One who responded in 1859 was James Carnegie, 9th earl of Southesk in Angus. Seeking health, solace and diversion after the death of his wife, he left Scotland and headed west to Saskatchewan and the Rockies. It was particularly the prospect of hunting big game that appealed to him. His home territory, near the foot of the Grampians, offered wild country and red deer, but it could not compete with grizzly bears, wolves and herds of buffalo. Unlike Stewart and Murray, who participated in native buffalo hunts for sustenance and the materials for survival, Carnegie's sole objective was sport. He wanted to kill beasts with fine heads which could be displayed as trophies, as evidence of skill and prowess.

Carnegie, accompanied by Duncan Robertson from Perthshire, one of his estate gamekeepers, travelled from New York to Lachine on the St Lawrence, where he was welcomed by George Simpson, who placed the resources of the Hudson's Bay Company at his disposal. (Without the fur trade, none of these adventures would have been possible.) From Lachine Carnegie made his way west to Red River via Toronto and Detroit. At Red River he was entertained in style by William Mactavish at Fort Garry, and spent time with John Rae, who assisted with the preparations for his hunting expedition. While there he attended a service at the Presbyterian church and commented on its 'extreme plainness' and its strong Scottish identity:

> It was easy to see that the Scottish race prevailed in the congregation, the tunes and the manner of singing so forcibly recalling the sober deliberate fashion of my own country, that I could scarcely believe myself thousands of miles away in the innermost heart of America.[41]

This familiarity was sustaining. Most of those who assisted Carnegie in planning and executing his trip were Scots or of Scottish descent. Apart from the connection with the homeland, it meant that he could rely on an appropriate acknowledgement of his status. By this time, a year before his death, George Simpson had received a knighthood and had a substantial estate in Montreal; he was more than happy to mix with aristocracy. If Carnegie's gamekeeper had appeared at Fort Garry asking for help to hunt buffalo he would no doubt have received a dusty answer.

On 15 June a bulky entourage of carts, horses, dogs and men set off from the Red River settlement. They were loaded with provisions, weapons, ammunition, tents, blankets, utensils and gifts for the natives. Carnegie's guide was James McKay, an impressive Métis HBC employee, 'broad-chested and muscular', weighing 18 stone but tough, agile and an excellent horse-man.[42] McKay dressed in Red River style: a blue hooded coat (*capot*) with brass buttons over a red and black flannel shirt, and moccasins on his feet. With McKay was his younger brother John, James Short, another Métis, two Scots, Morrison McBeath and Donald Matheson, and Toma, an Iroquois attendant and canoe-man loaned by Sir George. They headed west, on the look out for buffalo.

Carnegie kept a journal, which he later revised for publication in 1875. In it he describes in detail the pursuit and slaughter of buffalo.

> I stood in the stirrups and leant over [his horse's] head, held my gun forward at arm's length, took the level of the cows, and fired into the heaving mass where the best ones seemed to be. To my joy one of them instantly stopped; the others rushed madly on their course, but she crawled slowly along, her bowels protruding from a great wound in her flank torn by the bullet of my No. 12.[43]

Not satisfied with felling a cow, Carnegie went on to pursue a bull 'with very long perfect horns, and most luxuriant mane and beard' which he duly killed.[44] He pulled up his horse and looked down at the dead beast, 'feasting my eyes on his noble proportions as he lay lifeless on the crisp brown turf of that utterly deserted plain'.[45] Carnegie tempers the thrill of the chase and the triumph of the kill with his assurances that indiscriminate slaughter 'would have weighed heavy on my conscience', and he is also self-critical, acknowledging that he lacked skill in managing horse and gun.[46] But it is his enthusiasm that predominates, and his conviction that hunting is of itself a noble pursuit enhanced by wild terrain, wide open spaces and the magnifi-cence of the quarry.

Carnegie expressed some uneasiness at the slaughter involved, often indiscriminate and always wasteful, but it did not deter him. The excite-ment of the chase and the opportunity to present himself in heroic mould predominated. It was enough justification to stress that the animals were given a sporting chance of escape – a 'good run' was expressed as the possi-bility of freedom for the hunted rather than added thrills for the hunter:

> Not counting two or three bulls shot after a fine run and allowed every chance for their lives, or slain under some sudden excitement, I could safely

say that no buffalo had been killed by myself or my men except for good, or at all events definite and sufficient reasons.[47]

However, the buffalo herds, the staple of the Plains nations, were already dwindling.

From Edmonton House they continued west, following the McLeod River into the mountains and then working their way south. The landscape was both magnificent and forbidding. They had to fight their way through dense woods and deep morasses, and men and horses became exhausted. Food was scarce (Carnegie was alarmed at the greed of the men who recklessly ate their way through the stores of provisions) and there was a variety of new culinary experiences. Carnegie sampled beaver, moose, porcupine and skunk: 'soft and white, but there was a suspicion of *skunkiness* about it that prevented me from finishing the plateful'.[48] He longs for a 'good larder and an educated cook'.[49]

The mountains provided another quarry for the hunt: mountain sheep with splendid horned heads. On one occasion the party brought down twelve of the animals. Carnegie was pleased to have 'fine heads' to take back to Scotland, but was troubled at the slaughter: 'conscience rather reproached me'. He quickly justified his actions: 'a man who travels thousands of miles for such trophies may be excused for taking part in one day's rather reckless slaughter'. It did not occur to him to question the motive for such travel, although the killing of especially large animals made him uneasy:

> there is something repugnant to the feelings in carrying death and anguish on so large a scale amongst beautiful, inoffensive animals ... the butchery of the act comes more home, one sees with such vividness the wounds, and the fear, and the suffering.[50]

By the end of September the weather had deteriorated and the dwindling supply of provisions had become a serious concern. Tea and pemmican were rationed, it was bitterly cold and the first snow storms had set in. They were saved by the gift of a moose killed by natives, the hunters being paradoxically unable to provide for themselves. When they finally emerged from the mountains it was a great relief. For Carnegie it was like an escape from prison: 'There is something appalling in the gloom of the deep mountain valleys ... the very mass and vastness of the mountains depress and daunt the soul.'[51] They headed northeast to Edmonton, on to Carlton House and eventually back to Fort Garry. Although all the men survived, several of their horses collapsed from exhaustion and died, and others were so weak they had to be abandoned.

The size and number of beasts and the scale of the environment ensured that the experience of hunting in the American wilderness was beyond anything found in Scotland. In comparison deer stalking and grouse shooting on managed estates were tame and organised activities. For men such as Carnegie, privileged yet dissatisfied, hunting in the North American wilderness was liberating, a chance to throw off the constraints of Victorian Britain and indulge in bold activity that was a reminder of an heroic past. And, of course, like Stewart and Murray, he had the means to do this in the comfortable knowledge that, with a degree of skill, care and foresight, much of which was provided by others, he was likely to escape the most extreme wilderness hostility.

ISABELLA BIRD: 'A DREAM OF BEAUTY'

In 1869 the east and west coasts of the United States were finally connected by the railroad, which brought people and activity to the wild in immensely increased numbers. It also made it easier for those who sought a wilderness experience to reach their destination. Four decades after Stewart first enjoyed the challenge and exhilaration of the West, a diminutive forty-two-year-old daughter of an Anglican minister travelling alone stepped off a train at Truckee, California. Confident that even in the heaving turmoil of a makeshift mountain mining town, where the bars, brothels and gambling saloons spilled their customers into the streets and the air rang with profanity, she would be protected by the 'habit of respectful courtesy to women' she pursued her intention to explore the area around Lake Tahoe.[52] This was Isabella Bird from Edinburgh, though born in Yorkshire. She had visited the United States and Canada some nineteen years earlier, but this was her first visit to the West. In negotiating to hire a horse it was assumed she would need a mount with a side-saddle. When she insisted that she preferred to ride astride she was told that in Truckee she could do as she liked. Generally, though, when she approached a substantial settlement, she changed out of her specially devised riding outfit into a skirt and rode side-saddle. Safely away from towns it was with great relief that she returned to riding astride.

She rode alone to Tahoe and was transfixed by its beauty.

> I have found a dream of beauty at which one might look all one's life and sigh. Not lovable, like the Sandwich Islands, but beautiful in its own way! A strictly North American beauty – snow splotched mountains, huge pines, red-woods, sugar pines, silver spruce; a crystalline atmosphere, waves of the richest colour; and a pine-hung lake which mirrors all beauty on its surface.

There was a vitalising 'brilliancy of sky and atmosphere' and 'an elasticity in the air which removed all lassitude, and gives one spirit enough for anything'.[53] On the way back her horse, spooked by a bear, threw her and galloped off towards Truckee. She set off on foot resigned to a weary trudge of many miles, but found that a wagon driver had caught the horse and was preparing to set off in search of her. She mounted her still nervous steed and continued on her way.

The Tahoe trip was the prelude to a much more ambitious venture. After another train journey, in a railroad car that was 'hot, stuffy and full of chewing, spitting Yankees', she arrived at Denver, the terminus of the Kansas Pacific Railroad.[54] Her objective was Estes Park, in the Front Range of the Rockies northwest of Denver, an unsurveyed wilderness of striking beauty and teeming with wildlife. This time she hired a guide, a one-eyed disreputable looking former Indian scout called Jim Nugent or Mountain Jim. In a letter to her sister Henrietta (the letters were published in 1889 as *A Lady's Life in the Rocky Mountains*) she described him in high boots and deer-skin trousers held up by an old scarf, 'with three or four ragged unbuttoned waistcoats' worn over a leather shirt and 'an old smashed wide-awake, from under which his tawny, neglected ringlets hung'. Armed with knife, revolver and rifle he sat astride his beautiful Arab mare, 'his saddle covered with an old beaver skin, from which the paws hung down … and his axe, canteen, and other gear hanging to the horn'. He was, she wrote, 'as awful looking a ruffian as one could see'.[55]

In Estes Park she took up residence in a cabin owned by a Welshman called Griffith Evans who was running cattle in the valley. With Mountain Jim she explored the stunning wilderness on her pony Birdie, and climbed Long's Peak, a formidable undertaking. Jim had to heave and drag her up the final ascent. She lived, she said, mainly outdoors and on horseback, often sleeping 'under the stars on a bed of pine boughs'.[56] She rejoiced in the 'peerless sunrises and sunsets, its glorious afterglow, its blazing noons, its hurricanes sharp and furious, its wild auroras, its glories of mountain and forest, of canyon, lake, and river'.[57] Perhaps intensifying the experience was her relationship with Mountain Jim, dangerous, attractive and epitomising the wildness she embraced so enthusiastically. He proposed to her, to no avail, and sometime later was killed by Griff Evans, who protested self-defence: he believed he was protecting himself from attack by a drunk and angry wild man.

Isabella Bird claimed Estes Park for her own. It was, she said, 'no man's land' which was hers 'by right of love, appropriation, and appreciation'. Her 'appropriation' is personal rather than political, something to retain and carry with her rather than to conquer. She was absorbed by the wildlife, mountain lions, grizzly bears, coyotes, lynx, mink, marten and a great variety of birds: 'May their number never be less, in spite of the hunter who kills for food, and the sportsman who kills and marauds for pastime.'[58] She does not mention the presence of an indigenous population, although later she writes sympathetically of the natives' predicament and with anger of the Indian Agency's 'fraud and corruption'.[59]

Bird rode back to Denver alone, and continued on to Colorado Springs. She was overtaken by heavy snow, following a track unmarked by footprints or wagon wheels. Here was another and very threatening manifestation of wilderness:

> I cannot describe my feelings on this ride, produced by the utter loneliness, the silence and dumbness of all things, the snow falling quietly without wind, the obliterated mountains, the darkness, the intense cold, and the unusual and appalling aspect of nature. All life was in a shroud, all work and travel suspended.[60]

She chose to travel alone, but on her continuing exploration of Colorado she often felt an acute sense of isolation, and on occasion was seriously lost. Twenty miles or so from Boulder she missed the track and was overtaken by the dark. 'I felt very eerie and made up my mind to trudge on all night steering by the pole star but I feared Birdie would fall for want of water. It was gruesome.'[61] Eventually she reached her destination, and although she and Birdie often had to go without food and water no great harm came to them.

Bird returned to Estes Park, this time earning her keep, cooking and cleaning for the cattlemen. Her puddings and cakes were much appreciated, and she relished the physical labour: 'I cleaned the parlour and the kitchen, washed up, baked and then made 4 lbs of sweet biscuits and baked them after which I had to clean all my tins and pans and do my own room and haul water.'[62] Her clothes were in shreds and she was constantly mending and improvising repairs. Respectable Edinburgh would have been appalled, but Bird was dismissive of the assumption that such labour was unsuitable for a lady.

By the 1870s when Isabella Bird was travelling in the West there were clusters of crowded humanity, generally the consequence of the railroad and often springing up overnight. In Truckee, Denver and Cheyenne, all railroad towns, she encountered 'the scum of advancing civilisation' where 'murders, stabbings, shooting, and pistol affrays were at times events of almost hourly occurrence'.[63] 'Civilisation' brought its own kind of wildness. She also encountered worn-out, struggling settlers toiling to subsist on 160-acre claims. In Canyon, Colorado, she stayed for a while with the Chalmers family; Mr Chalmers, descended from Scottish Covenanters, was 'a frugal, sober, hard-working man', in spite of which all the homestead's equipment seemed to be broken and useless. 'It is hardly surprising', Bird commented, 'that nine years of persevering shiftlessness should have resulted in nothing but the ability to procure the bare necessities of life.'[64] By 'shiftlessness' she clearly did not mean that work was not done, but that it was unproductive and unsupported by aspirations towards improvement. It is an image that recurs over and over again in the story of frontier settlement. So often wilderness, far from fulfilling a promise of fecundity, demanded endless toil with dispiriting results and the erosion of morale. Bird's vignettes of pioneer life are in sharp contrast to her profound pleasure in wild country.

Bird would go on to travel extensively, particularly in the Far East. When she was not travelling she was based mainly in Edinburgh and Mull, and was involved in campaigns on behalf of slum dwellers and struggling crofters. She was never of robust health, but her experience of the American West seemed to toughen her. At the age of fifty she married Dr John Bishop, but the marriage was short-lived. Five years later Bishop died and she was soon on the move again. Restless, impatient of the demands of 'polite society', she relished freedom of movement for its own sake. Wilderness offered that, as it offered liberation from convention and the solitude she also craved. Robert Louis Stevenson, who six years later would make his own journey through the American West, would have understood.

In her delight in wilderness she has more in common with John Muir, seven years her junior, than with others who responded to the call of the wild, but unlike Muir (see Chapter 8) she did not find spirituality in the landscape, nor was she moved to campaign to preserve wild environments. And although she wrote several travel books, she does not present wild or alien terrain as the arena of heroic activity. Rather, it provides opportunities for genuine independence and ingenuity. For a woman in the second half of the nineteenth century these counted for a great deal. Isabella Bird was an exceptional woman, but in the context of the American wilderness her singularity was less on account of her gender as on the fact that she travelled independently. There was no supporting organisation or accompanying entourage. She had help along the way, but most of it came from modest, if not struggling, pioneer families who shared what they had. She travelled hundreds of miles alone with no motive other than to experience the wild. She felt herself to be in tune with the wilderness, and she left the Rocky Mountains with great regret. What she did share with some of her male counterparts was a restlessness and an inability to adapt to conventional life. She was still travelling in her sixties, in the Far East, and died in Edinburgh in 1904.

ISOBEL HUTCHISON: TAKING 'AN AWFUL CHANCE'

Some sixty years after Bird's travels in the Rockies, Isobel Hutchison, from Alloa and Edinburgh, set off at the age of fifty-three on a journey through Alaska and Arctic Canada. She was a botanist who collected plant samples for the Royal Horticultural Society and the Natural History Museum, but this was a winter journey with little opportunity for plant collecting. Her objective was the travelling itself, and filming and photographing the places and people she encountered. She was used to Arctic conditions as she had spent time in Greenland; nevertheless, the journey was a risky proposition. A boat up the Yukon River took her to Fort Selkirk and on to Dawson. From there she flew to Nome, a cosmopolitan gold town on the Bering Sea, to begin a journey round the coast which took her eventually to Aklavik on the Mackenzie delta. She travelled by boat and dog sled, and like Isabella Bird she was confident that she would be treated with respect. Gus Masik, an Estonian who had taken part in Vihljalmur Stefansson's 1918 Arctic Expedition, escorted Hutchison on part of her journey. He was less sanguine, commenting: 'You took an awful chance travelling alone in these parts! This is the most God-forsaken corner of Uncle Sam's attic.'[65]

When the ice closed in, Hutchison continued by dog sled, over rough sea ice and through blizzards, deep snow and temperatures reaching 62° below freezing. The dogs hauled her cameras and equipment as well as her baggage and at times herself, although she often walked. Benighted on the ice, Gus built a snow-house: 'I found myself in a tiny crystal chamber, its walls, floor and roof shining like diamonds in the light of a candle frozen into the floor.'[66] They reached Herschel Island, a former whaling station, presided over by Mr Sinclair from Orkney. She was told of footballers who froze to death when in the middle of a game they were overtaken by a sudden blizzard. On the way to Shingle Point Mission the rough trail and a high wind slowed their progress to a crawl, and it was nearly dark when she and her guide reached their destination. They were greeted with a 'supper table spread with a white cloth and silver cutlery' and half an hour after 'shambling through the icebergs' Hutchison was discussing the Oxford Movement with the ladies of the mission.[67] The Shingle Point community had been devastated by a flu epidemic some years before, but there was a thriving school, where Hutchison heard one of the Inuit children recite Stevenson's 'I have a little shadow'.

On the way back to Aklavik from a visit to a reindeer camp another blizzard blew up: 'We floundered through deep snow till the dogs were exhausted. We could not see the trail, only feel for it through snow by its greater hardness.' They negotiated switchbacks where she had to hang on to the sled 'like a spider with my head down and my feet in the air, while the poor dogs on the other side of the rise tried to heave me over'. On foot, she 'floundered up to my knees if I fell for a moment off the trail'.[68] The sixteen-hour journey left dogs and humans exhausted.

Everywhere Hutchison went she encountered Scots: Captain Campbell from Harris, master of the Yukon boat; Tom Gordon on Barter Island, with mixed-race children and grandchildren 'bearing well-known Highland names, and looking for all the world like dark-eyed sons of Harris or Skye'; Constable Mackenzie of the Royal Canadian Mounted Police, from Stornoway; at Aklavik Mrs Maclean of the post office, Dr Urquhart of the hospital, Mr Murray the minister, Mr Macnab of the reindeer camp.[69] She welcomed these meetings with compatriots and no doubt was sustained by them, but the tone of her published account, *North to the Rime-Ringed Sun* (1934), is always cheerful and upbeat. She describes her struggles with the extremes of terrain and climate with self-aware humour and seems comfortable wherever she finds herself. She had undertaken a journey to satisfy her own curiosity and zest for the Arctic wilderness. 'I had heard the call of the wild on star-lit nights under the Northern Lights; I had slept in a snow-hut; I had broken a new trail at the foot of the Endicotts, and my heart beat for the wilderness.'[70]

When she eventually left Aklavik it was on a tiny four-seater plane. She looked down on the Mackenzie delta with its: 'countless acres of forest and swamp … without a sign of life, human or animal'. It took three and a half days to reach the railhead at McMurray, with overnight stops (as they could not fly in darkness) as well as frequent stops to refuel. From her starting point in Manchester, England she had travelled more than 13,000 miles.

The Scotland that all these people left was increasingly industrialised and increasingly managed. The North American wilderness offered escape from constraint and the opportunity for adventure. It offered expansive territory, an exhilarating emptiness, and physical and psychological challenges. But these adventurers were all temporary sojourners. They may have contributed a little to opening up the frontier – Carnegie, entering mountain valleys that he believed were untrodden by Europeans, no doubt felt that he contributed more than a little – but they did not remain to pioneer a new life in the wilderness. Although the women did not give up travelling, the men returned to comfortable lives and the writing of books about their wilderness experiences. The books of all of them would help to fix North America, long identified as a land of promise, as an arena for heroic adventure which in Scotland seemed to be located only in the past.

NOTES

1. Andrew Hook, *Scotland and America 1750–1835* (Glasgow: Blackie, 1975), p. 205.
2. Washington Irving, *Tour in Scotland, 1817*, ed. Stanley T. Williams (New Haven, CT: Yale University Press, 1927), p. xxiii.
3. Ibid., p. 34.
4. Irving, *Astoria*, p. 1.
5. George Frederick Ruxton, *Life in the Far West*, ed. LeRoy R. Haten

(Norman, OK: University of Oklahoma Press, 1964), p. 133 (original emphasis).

6. Ibid., p. 135.
7. Ibid., p. 136.
8. Ibid., p. 10.
9. George MacDonald Fraser, *Flashman, and the Redskins* (London: HarperCollins, [1982] 2006), p. 72.
10. In Bernard DeVoto, *Across the Wide Missouri* (New York: Manner Books, [1947] 1998), p. 20.
11. J. Watson Webb (ed.), Introduction, William Drummond Stewart, *Altowan, or Incidents of Life and Adventure in the Rocky Mountains by an Amateur Traveller* (New York: Harper, 1846), p. v.
12. Stewart, *Altowan*, pp. 50–1.
13. Ibid., p. 223.
14. Ibid., p. 226.
15. Ibid., p. 64.
16. Ibid., p. 66.
17. Ibid., p. 47.
18. Webb, Introduction, Stewart, *Altowan*, p. ix.
19. Charles Augustus Murray, *Travels in North America* (London: 1854), vol. I, p. 108.
20. Ibid., p. 253.
21. Ibid., Vol. II, p. 113.
22. Ibid., p. 114.
23. Charles Augustus Murray, *The Prairie-Bird* (London: Richard Bentley, 1844), p. 213.
24. Ibid., p. 214.
25. Ibid., pp. 69–70.
26. In Jonathan Raban, *Bad Land: An American Romance* (London: Picador, 1996), p. 70.
27. John Davies (ed.), *Douglas of the Forests. The North American Journals of David Douglas* (Edinburgh: Paul Harris, 1979), p. 39.
28. Ibid., p. 42.
29. Ibid.
30. Ibid., p. 54.
31. Ibid., p. 73.
32. Ibid., p. 76.
33. Ibid., p. 77.
34. Ibid., p. 108.
35. Ibid., p. 125.
36. Ibid., p. 129.
37. In Ann Lindsay and Syd House, *The Tree Collector. The Life and Explorations of David Douglas* (London: Aurum, 2005), p. 153.
38. In ibid., p. 164.

39. See Greg Gillespie, *Hunting for Empire. Narratives of Sport in Rupert's Land, 1840–70* (Vancouver: University of British Columbia Press, 2007).

40. In MacLennan, *Scotchman's Return*, p. 177.

41. James Carnegie, Earl of Southesk, *Saskatchewan and the Rocky Mountains* (Boston, MA: Northeastern University Press, [1875] 1986), p. 33.

42. Ibid., p. 9.

43. Ibid., p. 92.

44. Ibid., p. 93.

45. Ibid., p. 94.

46. Ibid., p. 126.

47. Ibid.

48. Ibid., p. 175.

49. Ibid., p. 181.

50. Ibid., pp. 216–17.

51. Ibid., p. 254.

52. Isabella Bird, *A Lady's Life in the Rocky Mountains* (Sausalito, CA: Comstock Press, [1879] 1960), p. 15.

53. Isabella Bird, *Letters to Henrietta*, ed. Kay Chubbuck (London: John Murray, 2002), p. 9.

54. Bird, *A Lady's Life*, p. 27.

55. Ibid., p. 80.

56. Ibid., p. 95.

57. Ibid., p. 96.

58. Ibid., pp. 96–7.

59. Ibid., p. 171.

60. Ibid., pp. 131–2.

61. Bird, *Letters*, p. 170.

62. Ibid., p. 61.

63. Ibid., p. 23.

64. Bird, *A Lady's Life*, p. 43.

65. Isobel Wylie Hutchison, *North to the Rime-Ringed Sun* (Glasgow: Blackie, 1934), p. 152.

66. Ibid., p. 182.

67. Ibid., p. 197.

68. Ibid., pp. 226–7.

69. Ibid., p. 167.

70. Ibid., p. 237.

5

Future Prospects and Present Sacrifice

I am bound to recommend it as a new home to all those hearts and hands that are disposed to labour, and who for the sake of future prospects ... are willing to make a present sacrifice.

Charles Augustus Murray, *Travels in North America*

On the clearest night they saw no light but their own.

John McPhee, *Rising from the Plains*

North America was sold to the Old World as a place of freedom and fruit-fulness. There was space for everyone; religious and political space as well as productive land. For land-starved rural populations in Europe the message had huge appeal. In the Scottish Highlands families could turn their backs on lairds who demanded higher rents and a system which forced them to divide their ever-diminishing allocations of land among their sons. In the rural Lowlands, cottars could escape their thraldom to those who owned the land they worked and follow a dream of farming on their own behalf. In Central Scotland's industrial areas workers in the mills and factories, many of them exiles from a rural life that could no longer sustain them or from traditional crafts such as hand-loom weaving that were increasingly obsolete, could picture themselves in circumstances where at least there were choices.

Scottish visitors to North America were often critical, especially of the United States. Even those who were attracted by ideas of democracy and freedom from the tyranny of class at times found the realities of a society without Old World constraints hard to take. But the sheer attraction of the land was powerful. Laurence Oliphant, visiting Wisconsin and Minnesota from Scotland in the early 1850s, sums it up:

The aspect of the country generally was tempting for the settler ... Well-wooded hills, and valleys, and meadows with long rich grass, bore testimony to the richness of the soil, while lakes sparkled in the sunshine, and formed a most attractive picture; I could not but believe that this country, which looked so bright and smiling even in a state of savage nature, was only waiting for the hand of man still more to gladden and beautify it.[1]

The appeal of fertility was visceral. It promised the possibility of controlling one's own future.

Yet most emigrants left their old lives, however constrained and difficult, with the greatest reluctance. The majority of those who left Scotland in the eighteenth and nineteenth centuries had no land, no vote and very little control over their lives. Many of those who visited the Highlands were shocked not just at the poverty they encountered, but at the inertia of a population with apparently little will to work or improve their situation. Pennant found Highlanders 'indolent to a high degree', though he praised their generosity and 'natural politeness'.[2] In spite of poverty, exacerbated periodically by crop failure, potato blight and rising rents, and in spite of efforts to promote the attractions of the New World and entice sometimes whole communities to transplant themselves, the attachment to place and the traditions that were part of it was powerful. For the outsider, a blackhouse built of stone and turf on the island of Skye might be a filthy, smoke-filled hovel where a family shared its space with beasts, and where life was reduced to drudgery and semi-starvation. But for the family, that hovel represented generations of tradition and identity, where the landscape was woven into their lives and where language, song and story were inseparable from place.

Transplantation from the old life, whether voluntary or forced, was traumatic. The scenes of shiploads of wailing emigrants, described by many, were pitiful in their expression of human distress, but the depth of abandonment represented by such departures was hard for outsiders to understand. Alistair MacLeod catches it perfectly when in his novel *No Great Mischief* (1999) he describes the late eighteenth-century departure of the *clann Chalum ruaidh*. They have left their collie dog on the shore, but the dog leaps into the water and swims after the departing ship. The collie represents the loyalty of dog to human, but also the clan's loyalty to tradition. The descendants of that faithful collie continue down the generations alongside the descendants of the original Red Calum. The connection is maintained.

If Lowlanders appeared to be without such a distinctive tradition – and it was a romanticised version of the Highland tradition that came to dominate Scottish identity in North America – the focal points of their cultural survival were equally strong. Oral traditions of story and song crossed the Atlantic. Just as important was the Bible. A copy of the poetry of Burns often accompanied emigrating families: John Muir, setting off in 1867 on his long walk to Florida, had Burns's poems in his pack. John Muir's nephew John Love in his Wyoming ranch house recited Scott's *Lady of the Lake* and the ballads he had grown up with to his children. Canadian-born railway magnate J. J. Hill was imbued by his Scottish father with Burns and Scott. The Scots language and the language of the Old Testament were of resonant importance to migrating Lowlanders.

So if large numbers of Scots made landfall in North America after years of struggle with deprivation, with few material possessions and ill-equipped physically or psychologically to deal with the practical demands that most of them would face, they had resources that would come to their aid. Some of the *Hector*'s 200, though weakened by illness and disappointment, remained in Pictou and gradually built a community. They had assistance, from local First Nations and from some already established settlers, but without their own resources, including religious faith and a strong sense of identity, it would have been that much harder to keep going. It is clear from the account of James Macgregor, who joined the Pictou community as their minister, that his sense of religious and social duty sustained him in circumstances that were beyond anything he had imagined.

Organised Scottish settlement in North America had a few false starts and tentative beginnings, but began in earnest in the 1730s when a community of Highlanders was established in Georgia to hold the frontier against the Spanish. Three years later, in 1739, families from Argyll settled along the Cape Fear River in North Carolina. With the end of the French and Indian Wars in 1763, Scottish settlement accelerated when disbanded Scottish soldiers, responding to government enticements of land grants, elected to remain in the New World. Many of the soldiers were Highlanders for whom the army had been a release from a fragmenting clan system that would never recover from the Stewarts' final attempt to regain the throne, brought to a bloody demise at Culloden in 1746. For the British Government there were strategic advantages in encouraging settlement – who better to secure the frontier than battle-hardened soldiers, especially Scottish soldiers who had a reputation for toughness and endurance? They settled initially in the colony of New York, in Prince Edward Island and along the St Lawrence River.

Soldiers do not necessarily make good settlers, but Highlanders had an understanding of what was involved in scratching an existence from an un-yielding landscape. And it was a landscape which promised more and with which they had become familiar. There was no expectation of an easy life, but they knew what they had left behind and had already made the wrenching journey across the Atlantic. Catherine Parr Traill stresses the mountain-bred hardiness of Duncan Maxwell, father of the intrepid Hector and Catharine, and although it is love rather than land that moves him to settle in Canada, he is a useful representative figure. Through him Traill projects a distillation of Scottish character. Duncan is not only 'stern, steady, persevering, cautious', but has a profound regard for literacy and learning. This he imparts to his children, along with 'an intimate acquaintance with the songs and legends of [his] romantic country'.[3] This particular blend of stern perseverance and reliance on a rich transplanted tradition is manifested over and over again in depictions of Scottish character.

The fictional Duncan Maxwell marries a French Canadian and thus creates an emblem of reconciliation after war, but Highland settlers were more likely to send home for their families, and reinforce their Scottish identities with the material and oral culture that came with them. Tartan and bagpipes had been absorbed and in many ways enhanced by the British Army, but, however meagre, possessions from the old country, material and oral, strengthened the survival of identity. Communities reconstituted themselves in the new country. Increasingly, communities were persuaded, or forced, to cross the Atlantic and settle as a group with an existing coalescence, leaving those who remained with diminishing resources to resist social and cultural erosion.

TRANSITION: FIGURING IT OUT FOR THEMSELVES

The wilderness tempted not only the landless. Owners of substantial acres in Scotland were quick to identify business opportunities in the New World, and land settlement and the exploitation of the wild were early recognised as having immense potential. James Montgomery, for example, was a man of considerable standing. In 1767, when he began to acquire holdings in Prince Edward Island (PEI), he was Lord Advocate of Scotland and a Member of Parliament, with a successful legal career behind him. He was a committed proponent of agricultural improvement, principles which he put into practice on his Peeblesshire estates, latterly at Stobo which he acquired also in 1767.

He unobtrusively built up a substantial acreage in PEI and set about organising settlement. His plan was to develop flax farming to supply linen weaving in Scotland, an industry which was encouraged as part of post-1746 regeneration. He recruited around sixty men, who sailed from Greenock on the Clyde in April 1770. Their status was as indentured servants, or 'white negroes' as Montgomery himself described them, for a period of four years.[4] Land was leased to them at 1 shilling an acre, which sounded attractive until they set eyes on the wilderness they were expected to make profitable. 'They thought it cheap until they came out and saw it; but then they found it dear enough,' was a contemporary comment.[5] There was little support from Montgomery. They had to supply their own provisions, clear the land and build shelter. It took them two years. At the end of the four-year indenture period they would be entitled to uncleared land, at first rent-free, then paying gradually increasing rents. Their reward for clearing William Montgomery's land was the opportunity to clear more acres on their own behalf, though without actual ownership.

Although Montgomery appointed a representative, David Lawson, a flax farmer from Callendar, to manage the new venture (Montgomery never went to PEI himself, although Lawson's farm was called Stanhope after

Montgomery's Perthshire estate) the project did not turn out as he had hoped. He completely underestimated what was involved in establishing agriculture in the wilderness. Expenses multiplied, and it soon became clear that David Lawson was out of his depth as a manager. At the end of the indenture period many of the settlers abandoned their holdings. Lawson himself did well, clearing 100 acres, building a house and barns, and was able to feed his family and servants on the crops and livestock he raised. But the tenants struggled, and potential profits disappeared in an effort to support them.

Cultivating wilderness not only presented huge practical difficulties which often demanded more than realistic effort on the part of the settlers, but challenged notions about approach and the way business should be conducted. Montgomery was typical of Scotland's landowners in assuming that labour would always be cheaply available. Underlying this was a widespread belief that labour was of itself improving, and that those not prepared to work were morally weak. When in 1819 John Howison travelled through the predominantly Scottish Glengarry County in Upper Canada, which had been initially settled by disbanded Highland soldiers, he was unimpressed. The settlers had not responded to the opportunity to lead decent, hard-working lives:

> They are still the same untutored incorrigible beings that they probably were, when, the ruffian remnant of a disbanded regiment, or the outlawed refuse of some European nations, they sought refuge in the wilds of Upper Canada, aware that they would neither find means of subsistence, nor be countenanced by any civilised country … Their original depravity has been confirmed and increased by the circumstances in which they are now placed.[6]

In Howison's view, the 'lower classes' should not receive assistance to settle in Canada. 'They abuse and undervalue every thing they can obtain without exertion or individual merit,' he asserted. It was 'inexpedient to allow emigrants a free passage to Canada, or to give them anything but land when they arrive there'.[7] Yet he acknowledged the difficulties settlers faced, 'the peculiarities of the climate, the almost inaccessible situation of their farms, the badness of the roads, and the immense woods which encumber the soil', and was impressed by the activity in the forest: 'Axes rung in every thicket, and the ear was occasionally startled by the crashing of trees falling to the ground.'[8] But aware as he was of the sheer physical labour required by settlement, he could still interpret a failure to transform in thirty or forty years a one-room log cabin into a decent frame house as a sign of Scottish settlers lacking ambition and having 'no inclination to improve their mode of life, being dirty, ignorant, and obstinate'.[9] Ralph Connor's much later celebration of perseverance and 'brittle Highland courage' paints a very different picture.

J. K. Galbraith, who had no illusions about the Scottish community on the shore of Lake Erie where he grew up, applauds the speed and skill with which the original settlers adapted:

> The transition from the spare, wet, and treeless crofts of the Highlands and the Western Isles to the lush forests, deep soil, and strong seasons of the land by the Lake could scarcely have been more dramatic ... the soils, crops, crop rotation, the insects and plant diseases, the problems of farm architecture, machinery and drainage, even the wagon that went to town, were all different. Within a matter of a few months, men made the transition from an agricultural system in which they were guided by the experience of centuries to one where a very great deal depended on a man's capacity to figure things out for himself or imitate with discrimination those who could.[10]

Howison reflected the Enlightenment belief that with skill and application the conquest of nature could be achieved for the benefit and profit of humankind. This applied equally to the Scottish Highlands and to the North American wilderness. Threaded through this is the useful conviction that hard work is morally improving. (Galbraith's community reflected this, requiring 'everyone to like work or say that he did'.[11]) The amalgam of optimism and work ethic played a part in much of the movement to transplant 'excess population' from Scotland to North America. If the labour of the peasantry was not required in Scotland, it could only be beneficial for it to be exported to where it was needed. It would be good for them and good for their new country – and good for Scotland to be rid of them. Settlement was necessary to obtain a hold on the vast and 'empty' lands that were designated British North America. The fur trade, powerful though it was, could never be more than the vanguard of control. If out of settlement could come profit, so much the better. William Montgomery and others promised a better life for Scots who left the old country to enable him to make money from the wilderness. The failure to understand the character and complexity of the individual's relationship with wild country meant that many such schemes ended in disappointment for all concerned.

RED RIVER: ESCAPING THE SCALPING KNIFE

In the spring of 1813 a group of ninety-four emigrants gathered at Thurso in Caithness. They had been removed from the straths of Kildonan and Clyne in Sutherland as part of the Countess of Sutherland's project to make the land more commercially productive by turning large tracts of land into sheep runs. The plan was to re-settle her tenants in newly created coastal villages, where they would be expected to start a new life based on fishing. The people of Kildonan and Clyne had resisted clearance, and troops were

called in. Although the situation was defused, with promises of less precipi-
tate action, the Sutherland clearances left a bitter legacy. The countess's
factor, William Young, regarded her tenants as savages who required force-
ful treatment. Not surprisingly, when the possibility of assisted emigration
arose, there were many who responded.

The man who offered that possibility was Thomas Douglas, earl of
Selkirk, who was convinced that organised programmes of emigration were
a beneficent means of relieving Highland poverty. In 1803 he had successfully
settled 800 Hebridean emigrants on Prince Edward Island, which was
followed by a much more problematic venture on Lake St Clair between
lakes Erie and Huron. Undeterred by difficulties there – malaria-ridden
swamps, heavy rains which washed out homes and crops, several deaths and
many desertions – Selkirk continued to apply himself to enabling Scottish
settlement in Canada. Now, in 1813, the destination was the Red River,
approximately half way between the St Lawrence River and the Pacific
coast. Selkirk had been inspired by reading Alexander Mackenzie's account
of his travels, with some irony as Mackenzie and the North West Company
which employed him were convinced that settlement would undermine the
fur trade and destroy the economic value of the wilderness.

Selkirk held a substantial interest in the Hudson's Bay Company which
gave him considerable leverage, in spite of HBC resistance to the idea of a
colony. Simon McGillivray of the North West Company, which had a strong
foothold in the area, did his utmost to discourage the incursion of settlers.
The Nor'Westers were more vigorously opposed to settlement than the
HBC, which in 1811 granted Selkirk 300,000 square kilometres in the Red
River area, four times the area of his homeland. The land grant, for which
Selkirk paid a nominal fee of 10 shillings, was not without strings. He had
to undertake to bring people to settle the land, a thousand families in ten
years, and to supply the company with 200 workers each year. He also had
to make land available to retired HBC officers.

The responsibility for recruiting settlers, getting them to Red River and
providing support was Selkirk's. For the displaced tenants of Kildonan,
removed from their ancestral strath, the promise of a new start was a
powerful temptation. They may have had some understanding of what the
transatlantic passage involved, but the distance and difficulty of the overland journey that would follow were beyond the imagination of Highlanders
whose longest journey had probably been the thirty or so miles from Kildonan
to Scotland's east coast. Nor could they have imagined the conditions under
which their North American trek would be taken.

Two small groups of emigrants had already made the journey to Red
River, in 1811 and 1812, and gained a precarious foothold. The 1813 contingent was intended to consolidate the settlement. It was led by surgeon William

LaSerre and twenty-three-year-old Archibald McDonald from Glencoe. Although Selkirk had stressed that he was looking for single men to make up the Red River vanguard, there were thirteen families with children among the ninety-four. They left Thurso to cross the stormy Pentland Firth on the *Waterwitch*, which took them to Stromness in the Orkney Islands, the port at which HBC ships regularly took on men and supplies before crossing the Atlantic to Hudson Bay. The HBC men were sceptical at the notion of delivering emigrants to Hudson Bay, hardly the most welcoming of North American destinations, but landfall at York Factory rather than a Nova Scotian port would substantially diminish the overland distance the emigrants would have to cover to reach Red River.

At Stromness the party boarded the HBC's *Prince of Wales*, which with her sister ship the *Eddystone* and a naval escort (necessary because Britain and the United States were at war and American privateers were operating in Scottish waters) left Stromness on 28 June. Bad weather slowed their progress. Six weeks after departure typhus broke out on the *Prince of Wales*. Among the six who died was LaSerre, leaving young McDonald in charge. When they reached Hudson Strait progress was impeded by ice already forming, and although land was a welcome sight first impressions were not encouraging. Donald Gunn, a young man from Sutherland who had been taken on by the Hudson's Bay Company, noted:

> We beheld the low and uninteresting shore of Hudson Bay stretched out before us, presenting its narrow border of yellow sand and dark blue swamp in the front, with its dark and dismal-looking line of tamarack in the background. The scenery appeared bleak and desolate beyond the power of description.[12]

Today the strath of Kildonan has a different kind of bleakness, informed by the knowledge that it was once vibrant with human habitation. As Hugh MacLennan memorably wrote of Kintail, cleared in the 1830s, 'in a deserted Highland glen you feel that everyone who ever mattered is dead and gone … Those glens … are haunted by the lost lives and passions of a thousand years.'[13]

Selkirk's band of emigrants arrived at York Factory late in August. The short summer of sticky heat and plaguing mosquitoes was nearly over and it was too late in the year to continue their journey. They would have to spend the winter on Hudson Bay, but the Hudson's Bay Company was unable or unwilling to assist them. Turned away from York Factory, they were disembarked further north, at Fort Churchill. Archibald McDonald gathered his people, weakened by disease and the tribulations of the voyage, and set them to preparing for a winter that would be unimaginably colder, longer and harsher than anything they had experienced in the north of Scotland.

On the Churchill River about fifteen miles from the fort, they felled trees and built cabins. The fort's surgeon advised that the women, in his view particularly vulnerable, should 'wear constantly three petticoats, one of which must be of cloth or thick flannel, also thick leggings'.[14] Whether the women actually had the means to follow his advice is not clear. He further commented that the emigrants were 'like children, not capable of being trusted a moment out of sight': hardly promising pioneer material.[15]

They struggled through the winter, and prepared for the onward journey, making sledges and snowshoes. On 6 April, Archibald McDonald with fifty of the fittest set off for York Factory, 150 miles away. Robert Gunn played them on their way on his bagpipes as they walked in single file through the snow, the men tramping it down to make it easier for the women in their unaccustomed snowshoes. There were blizzards. Several were struck by cramp and snow blindness. The limited food supply was strictly rationed, and the slowest and weakest had to be left behind. On 19 April, they arrived at York Factory to find that there were no provisions to spare and that their barely adequate rations had to be cut further. They still had a long way to go.

In May when the ice broke up and the rivers became navigable they continued their journey by water, moving up the Hayes River on HBC York boats, and following the river and lake system until they finally reached Lake Winnipeg. An easy sail brought them to the mouth of the Red River and the land allocated to them a little to the south. What they saw looked promising, though the flat, fertile land stretching to the horizon was very different from the narrow mountain-flanked strath they had left. That this land was the habitat of buffalo, First Nations and Métis, as well as employees of the North West Company, may not at first have seemed significant. The Red River area was not an empty wilderness, although survival there would depend on an ability to adapt to wilderness realities. Paradoxically, one of the realities was that this stretch of territory which the fur traders wished to keep free of incursion was occupied by Métis, a people who emerged from unions between Scottish or French fur traders and mainly Cree women. They had strong links with the North West Company, whom it suited to encourage the Métis to develop a distinct identity. The Métis were dependent on the buffalo, the source of pemmican which they supplied to the Nor'Westers, and they feared that the incursions of a white population would disrupt the herds. Prominent among the Métis was a man called Cuthbert Grant, whose father came from Speyside, and who would go on to marry another Métis called Elizabeth Mackay.

Simon MacGillivray predicted disaster. 'Even if the emigrants escape the scalping knife, they will be subject to constant alarm and terror. Their habitations, their crops, their cattle will be destroyed and they will find it impossible to exist in the country.'[16] MacGillivray and the North West

Company were hoping to sabotage the settlement project. In fact, the local Salteaux helped the ill-provided newcomers through their first winter, supplying them with buffalo meat. The settlement was not served well by the HBC-appointed governor of Assiniboia Miles MacDonnell, who aggravated an already volatile situation by attempting to ban the supply of pemmican. (Frederick Niven's fictional account of the settlement, *Mine Inheritance*, 1940, contains a much more sympathetic portrait of MacDonnell.) Encouraged by the North West Company, Cuthbert Grant led the Métis in harassment of the settlers. Horses were stolen, cattle were killed, crops were trampled, shots were fired. In the summer of 1815 the settlement was abandoned.

The story might have ended there, to add to the tales of pioneer failure and the characterisation of Scots as victims manipulated by men of unrealistic vision, like Selkirk and John Galt, or of self-serving ambition, like James Montgomery and others who attempted to establish colonies as commercial enterprises. But the retreating settlers encountered another Scot, Colin Robertson from Perthshire, making his way to Red River on behalf of the Hudson's Bay Company. He persuaded them to return. Later that year a fresh contingent of Sutherland emigrants arrived, and the settlement began to look viable again. But there was to be another chapter of violence. The following June, Cuthbert Grant and his followers clashed with a party of men from Fort Douglas, constructed to protect the colony. About twenty of the Fort Douglas men were killed in what came to be known as the Battle of Seven Oaks. Once again the settlers retreated, and the Métis took possession of Fort Douglas.

This time Selkirk himself came to the rescue, with Swiss and German troops who had fought in the recent war with the United States. A third new start was made and eventually the Red River colony flourished. After 1821, when the North West Company and the Hudson's Bay Company merged, it was no longer caught up in the rivalry between the two great competitors for control of Assiniboia and the vast territory to the west. There were new arrivals, mainly from Scotland, and gradually the colony expanded into territory occupied by the Salteaux band who had helped to sustain them. The dispossessed appeared not to reflect on the fact that they had become dispossessors. There were still many difficulties to contend with, but eventually the Red River colony became a success story, and from it grew the city of Winnipeg.

Most of the key players in the Red River narrative were Scots or partly Scots. They battled against the terrain, the climate and each other. The story brings together all the elements of the Scottish experience in Canada: vision, courage, endurance, determined leadership, persistence, exploitation, rivalry, bitterness, near despair, greed. The story of the people from Kildonan whom Archibald McDonald led through blizzards on their unskilfully constructed snowshoes merges with that of the canny and courageous endeavours of the largely Scottish fur-trading companies. An iconic journey coalesces with liberation from Old World tyranny and the opportunity for a new life in a new land. Although the project's survival seems to have depended on key individuals, such as Archibald McDonald, Colin Robertson, even Piper Gunn, probably equally important were the shared traditions that bound the Kildonan people together.

Frederick Niven's novel *Mine Inheritance* is, though fiction, a careful account of the settlement as seen through the eyes of young David Baxter from Paisley. In his version, MacDonnell is a more heroic figure than other accounts suggest, and Cuthbert Grant and the Métis are depicted as being manipulated by the North West Company. The settlers themselves are caught in a situation beyond their control, but nevertheless display fortitude and tenacity. But what emerges most strongly from the novel is the sheer complexity of conflicting interests. Wilderness is not untouched emptiness, but a focus of violent contention. The violence comes not from those indigenous to a wild land, but from the intruders.

In Margaret Laurence's Manitoba-based novel *The Diviners* (1974), Christie Logan, born in Easter Ross, retells to young Morag Gunn the story of the trek to Red River. Christie's words lend it a mythic dimension:

> Who led the men and women and children on that march? Piper Gunn. Himself. He led them with his pipes blaring … he played the pipes like an angel right out of heaven and then like a devil right out of hell, and he kept the courage of the people beating like a drum, or like the wings of brave wild birds caught in a blizzard, for he had the faith of saints and the heart of a child and the gall of a thousand and the strength of conviction.
>
> I guess they must've walked through all of them frozen lands, and through the muskeg there and through the muck and mud of the melting snows, and through the hard snow itself although it was spring.[17]

In Christie's version the journey from Fort Churchill to York Factory becomes a 1,000-mile legend and the migrating Scots like 'wild birds'. The encounter with wilderness acquires a symbolic resonance, with the bagpipes confirming the essential Scottish identity of the experience. Robert Gunn takes his place beside the anonymous piper in George Simson's 'Coronach in the Backwoods', a symbol of individual and collective exile and endurance, defying a hostile land.

Thirty years after the people of Kildonan made their epic trek, young Edinburgh-born R. M. Ballantyne was at Red River as an HBC employee. He found a thriving community: 'a fine place it is, extending fifty miles or more along the river, with fine fields, and handsome houses, and churches, and missionaries and schools'.[18] In that same year, 1843, the claim was made that 'Scotch emigrants are hardy, industrious, and cheerful, and experience has fully proved that no people meet the first difficulties of settling wild lands with greater patience and fortitude.'[19] Red River encapsulates the contradictory characterisation of Scottish experience. Ousted in both their homeland and their new country, victims of forces beyond their understanding and control, they survived and planted a community whose roots took hold.

The evolution of a permanent community depended on bringing in people, the kind of people who would not only erect civic structures – churches, schools, court houses – but commit themselves to the civic values that these structures represented. Such permanence was resisted by those for whom wilderness was a way of life, for whom it represented freedom and an intimacy with landscape and the life it sustained. The Scots who came to North America as heroic pioneers and as near-destitute settlers were followed by ministers, teachers, doctors and bankers. James Macgregor at Pictou and later William Bell at Perth, both from Perthshire, illustrate the minister's role in holding together groups whose cohesion was constantly threatened by the land itself. The church and the school became focal points, and where there was no church hundreds would often travel great distances to gather in the open air and hear the words of a peripatetic preacher. Such gatherings were important moments of cohesion.

A century after R. M. Ballantyne was at Red River, Frederick Niven followed his Red River novel with a twentieth-century tale of Scottish emigration to Canada. In *The Transplanted* (1944) Robert Wallace, a Glasgow-born civil engineer, is captivated by the idea of pioneering in the wilderness. It is 1907 and he is in British Columbia working for a mining company. He is sustained by a vision of opening up the west, establishing a community, ensuring the means to reach markets that enable the community to thrive. It is a story of optimistic exile, of commitment to the new land while retaining cultural allegiance to the old. 'In public and in private life he was a Scot still.'[20] He still reaches for the work of William Dunbar, Robert Burns and Walter Scott. Niven is very aware of the contradictions of emigration, but *The Transplanted* is an upbeat tale of a Scottish contribution to the success of Canada. It is a very different image from Howison's 'dirty, ignorant and obstinate' Highlanders failing to improve the conditions of their lives.

HOMESTEADING: 'THE AXE AND THE PLOUGH'

Whatever the benefits of patience and fortitude, the skills and experience that Scottish settlers brought with them were varied, and their practical value depended on where they went and what was expected of them. The iconic pioneer clears the land, builds a home, tills virgin soil and raises crops and animals. The Highland crofter and Lowland cottar had some of the necessary skills, but many of those who were faced with creating a homestead in the wilderness had little in the way of appropriate practical experience. A Renfrewshire hand-loom weaver may have built his own loom and grown a few vegetables in a small garden plot. His wife's domestic skills may have included spinning and making clothes as well as tending to the basic needs of home and family. The mill worker from Lanarkshire probably had less to offer.

Daniel Muir, John Muir's father, was a shopkeeper from the small east coast port of Dunbar which had nothing in common with the Wisconsin backwoods. Most transplanted families and communities could between them provide some of the necessary skills, but the range of activities on which survival depended was formidable: felling trees; splitting logs; constructing shelter, furniture and utensils; ploughing, sowing and reaping; milking; making butter and cheese; hunting and foraging; skinning and butchering beasts; making soap and candles; shearing sheep and carding; spinning, dyeing and weaving the wool; tapping maple trees and processing the syrup; raising poultry; making baskets and rag rugs and preserves; brewing coffee from dandelions and tea from sassafras (Catherine Parr Traill provides recipes for both). In nineteenth-century Scotland levels of self-sufficiency were disappearing as an industrialised society provided increasing numbers of commodities. In the wilderness traditional skills had to be recovered or re-invented. A grounding in hard times and a tradition of resourcefulness were a useful foundation, but most pioneering settlers had a huge amount to learn. There was also a need for specialised trades. If basic carpentering could be quickly learned, shoeing a horse and fashioning ploughshares were not tasks for the amateur.

When in 1849 the eleven-year-old John Muir arrived in Wisconsin from Dunbar with his father and brothers, he exulted in the wilderness and all that it offered. He and his brother David were delighted by new species of trees, flowers, birds and beasts: 'Everything about us was so novel and wonderful that we could hardly believe our senses except when hungry or while father was thrashing us.'[21] The reality of the toil involved in clearing the land, in which the young boys were expected to play their part, and of a thrawn and abusive father did not diminish their pleasure or blunt their powers of observation. In his memoir *The Story of My Boyhood and Youth* (1913), Muir recalled both the relentless drudgery: 'it was dull, hard work leaning over on my knees all day, chopping out those tough oak and hickory stumps, deep down below the crowns of the big roots'; and the joy of the natural world: 'Oh, that glorious Wisconsin wilderness!.'[22]

When the Muir family arrived in Wisconsin they were entering frontier country. Wisconsin's western border was the Mississippi, a highway and a barrier. Beyond it lay the beginnings of the prairies that stretched for hundreds of miles until they rose to the formidable obstruction of the Rocky Mountains. To the north were Lake Superior and the largely unsettled vastness of what would become western Ontario. Scots had been among the first to cross the Appalachians, the first barrier to western expansion, and to trek west from Hudson Bay and eastern Canada. The Muir family, like hundreds of Scottish families in the mid-nineteenth century, continued the pattern of frontier settlement.

As the eldest boy much of the work of clearing and ploughing fell on John's shoulders: 'the axe and the plough were kept very busy'. The sheer scale of what was required bred a dogged persistence, and any resentment was mitigated by the reward of achievement as well as the compensating joys of the wild. 'I used to cut and split a hundred [fence rails] a day from our short, knotty oak timber, swinging the axe and heavy mallet, often with sore hands, from early morning to night.'[23] Eight years after first arriving on their land claim at Fountain Lake, during which they had built a frame house to replace the original cabin, cleared and fenced fields and built barns, Daniel Muir announced that they were moving on to take up a half-section of wild land a few miles away. The land at Fountain Lake was already exhausted, so the whole process started again: 'heartbreaking chopping, grubbing, stump-digging, rail-splitting, fence-building, barn-building, house building'.[24] The compulsion to move on and start again was not so evident in Canada, where a sense of collective identity was more likely to hold communities together. When individuals moved on it was usually because of intractable land, difficult times or the prospect of better employment elsewhere. But Daniel Muir moved his family from one hard-won homestead to another nearby that required equal effort to achieve the same level of success. His Calvinist ethic seemed to require hardship. It was his sons (and probably his wife and daughters, but we hear little about them) who bore the brunt of the new beginning.

Susan Moir, daughter of an Aberdeen family, was fifteen in 1860 when she arrived with her mother, stepfather and sister at the HBC community of Hope on the Fraser River, where they were welcomed by the Chief Factor Joe McKay. Hope was already 'a flourishing little town' with a church, a courthouse, a sawmill and several stores, but their first home was an improvised timber-framed shack lined with cloth and paper, with sheets for window blinds.[25] The women were ill-equipped for pioneering, having no idea how to wash clothes or bake bread or find their way through the bush, but they were willing learners. The family built a more permanent house and installed items that had arrived by sea, round the Horn and upriver.

Now they had a piano and a plough, crockery and candelabra, lamps and a clock, but their chairs were blocks of sawn wood and their rugs were deerskins.

In 1868, Susan Moir married John Fall Allison, an Englishman who was the first to settle at Princeton on the Similkameen River, where he was planning to raise cattle. Getting there meant crossing the Cascade Mountains, two strenuous days on horseback with a pack train, which Susan in her memoir remembered with some pleasure, in spite of the plague of mosquitoes. She relished the landscape, the flowers and the rugged existence, and was eager to learn from both pioneers and natives, but never relaxed her adherence to the standards of her upbringing. Her husband's partner Mr Hayes disapproved of her insistence on dressing for dinner, 'a habit I was drilled in as a child':

> As I did not object to his coming to table in shirt sleeves I did not see why he objected to my habits, but I think he half forgave me when he found I could milk cows and was not afraid to go into a corral full of cattle.[26]

They fell out again over her use of a tablecloth. In his view oilcloth was good enough. Later, coping with numerous children, she agreed.

John Allison built a solid timber house and made furniture from left-over planks and old tea boxes. A desk made of tea-box boards and rough lumber was covered with wrapping paper 'to hide the roughness' and then varnished with glue made from cow and deer feet.[27] This combination of commitment to the conventional standards of her upbringing and the ability to learn new skills and improvise was characteristic of Susan Moir. She readily befriended local Chinooks who helped her in numerous ways, particularly when her first child (of fourteen) was born two months prematurely. With her one-month-old baby packed in a birchbark basket she made a trip with her husband back across the mountains. They found themselves almost engulfed by a forest fire: 'the rocks were red hot and the water was boiling ... the heat was almost unbearable'.[28] When the fire brought down a huge cedar which blocked the trail Allison improvised a bridge so they could lead the blindfolded horses across, with the baby's basket wrapped in a blanket. Although Allison's leg was badly burned, they reached Hope exhausted but safe. Some years later their house and almost all its contents burnt to the ground. The family decamped to an old cabin where Moir fed the children with scones made from a rescued sack of flour, rolled out with a whisky bottle and baked on hot stones, Indian-style. She made tea from spruce twigs: 'We always joked over anything unpleasant so we laughed and joked over the table, at our looks, and at the dishes, chips of wood, and yeast powder can cups!'[29]

In 1873, the Allison family moved on, to the Okanagan Valley, and started again in an unfinished log house. Over the years, the family endured fire and flood, severe winters, loss of cattle, food shortages, illness, rattle-snakes in the kitchen, native unrest, and the depredations of 'the McLean boys', the sons of an HBC factor at Kamloops who terrorised the area and murdered two men. 'After a wild career of death and destruction these misguided boys were taken and hanged, the eldest twenty, the youngest fifteen.'[30] In spite of this, Moir described her life at this time, the 1870s in the Okanagan, as 'perfectly ideal'.[31] The following decade they were back at Princeton. When gold was discovered at nearby Granite Creek, Moir escorted pack trains to supply the mining camp with beef. She was described riding side-saddle at the head of a string of pack horses:

> I remember at the time thinking of the courage and endurance of a refined and educated woman like her to make her home so far out of the way from the comforts and conveniences of even the farming districts nearer the larger centres. She was riding on quite serenely and appeared to be enjoying the ride and the beautiful scenery, and at the same time keeping an eye on her pack-train [32]

Refinement and guts, taste and adaptability – these marked out Susan Allison and, of course, equipped her to write a memoir of her experiences. Unlike Susanna Moodie, she did not consider pioneering inappropriate or unduly arduous for a woman like herself. She moved easily between relative gentility, in Hope as it developed and in New Westminster, and a raw existence where, when food was short, she entertained her children with stories and games to distract them from the pangs of hunger. Her memoir is sanguine in the face of adversity, with a down-to-earth acceptance of the trials of the frontier, and an upbeat appreciation of wild country and its life, animal and human. She took a great deal of interest in native customs and traditions, and devoted her latter years to recording them, and registering her concern at the degradation of traditional life resulting from European influences, particularly access to alcohol.

OVERLANDERS: 'IN SEARCH OF A MORE GRATEFUL SOIL'

In the first decades of the nineteenth century many manuals of advice to emigrants were published, as well as accounts by travellers such as John Howison. The tone of these books varied, but however upbeat they were they stressed that the pioneering life was not for the faint-hearted. Eneas Mackenzie presented a picture of America's energy and progress: 'In her plains and forests an industrious, enterprising, and intelligent population are daily creating new and extensive communities, and exhibiting the whole mystery of the generation as well as the growth of nations.'[33] But although he encouraged his readers to see themselves as potentially playing a part in this creativity, he made it clear that he was addressing:

> the industrious labourer, the mechanic, the farmer, the man of moderate capital, and the father of a family who feels solicitous about settling his children, in short, all those who are prepared to encounter the numerous privations and inconveniences of emigration, in order to enjoy the great and acknowledged advantages which America offers to adventurers.[34]

Adventurers. The word implies challenge, perhaps danger, certainly strenuous physical demands and the need for courage, even heroic action. But Mackenzie was interestingly ambivalent about what he observed. If pioneering is a heroic movement westward and the creation of new communities in the wilderness, what follows in its wake can be less admirable. He recognised the underside of adventuring, the speculating, the exploitation, the opportunities for all kinds of shady activity. He was writing at a time when new United States territories were rapidly opening up: Michigan, Wisconsin, Minnesota, Iowa, Missouri, Arkansas. Indiana had become a state in 1816, Mississippi in 1817, Illinois in 1818. For the adventurer in both senses these were the areas of opportunity.

Mackenzie included some very specific advice to emigrants, on transport, provisioning and equipment. Those planning to go west should take passage on an American ship to Philadelphia, then cross the Allegheny Mountains to Pittsburgh. A 'poor family' might have to walk this journey, their baggage 'conveyed in the cheapest way by the regular stage-waggons'.[35] They could then proceed down the Ohio River. There was no easy way to reach the new territories, and those arriving from Scotland before the age of steam would already have spent several debilitating weeks at sea. For poorer families, the advice of such as Eneas Mackenzie was perhaps, however useful, more likely to be a deterrent than an encouragement, implying as it did considerable expense as well as the prospect of hardship. An anonymous guide of 1816 directly recommended realism, and warned against succumbing to the 'phantoms of ideal happiness emanating from democratic equality'. Intending emigrants should 'balance well between the reality of comforts which they now enjoy, and the uncertainty of remote ones they may never possess'.[36]

Thomas Hamilton was also sceptical of the much-hyped benefits of democracy and, as we have seen, found the evidence of settlement in remoter areas rather dispiriting. The primitive dwellings he saw were: 'about equal in comfort, I should imagine, to the cabin of an Irish peasant'.[37] Many homes were deserted, abandoned by those 'in search of a more grateful soil'.[38] The pioneer becomes less a heroic figure than a failure, and a serial failure at that. The cleared land and log cabin return to wilderness as the settler moves on to try again. The other side of the coin that presents a bright image of enterprise and fortitude reveals desolation and decay.

If the pioneer family is weighed down by unproductive toil, the individual frontiersman carries a different story. Alexander Carson emigrated from Dumfriesshire to Pennsylvania via Ulster. His son William moved on to North Carolina, his grandson to Kentucky and then Missouri, each move entailing carving out a new homestead. Then Christopher Carson, born in 1809, at the age of seventeen headed west again, not to establish another homestead but to become eventually the legendary frontiersman Kit Carson. In 1837, Robert Stuart, son of Scottish-born James Stuart, left Virginia for Illinois, and a year later crossed the Mississippi to Iowa where he cleared land and built a one-room log cabin. After five years the Stuart family moved on again to try farming near what is now Cedar Falls. In 1852, he and his two sons, Granville and James, headed for California, following the gold rush. The sons never returned to Iowa, and eventually, after many years on the move, became successful ranchers in Montana (see Chapter 7). Granville in particular would celebrate the rugged independence of the frontiersman.

By the 1830s intending settlers were beginning to cross the Missouri River, but there was a striking difference now in the pioneering journey. Until now pioneers had crossed rivers and mountain ranges to reach the next territory. Now they were looking to cross half the continent, to travel over the Great Plains, seen as an unproductive wilderness with a hostile population and nothing to offer, and conquer both stretches of desert and the massive barrier of the Rocky Mountains in order to reach Oregon and California which promised green and fertile valleys. Scots joined this flow, which began in earnest in the 1840s and increased after the end of the Civil War.

Individual Scottish stories can be plucked out of the tale of the overlanders, but the most conspicuous role of Scots was as guides and traders without whom these journeys would not have been possible. The three forts which were the 'chief recuperating and supply points of the inchoate Oregon Trail'[39] were all associated with Scots. William Sublette and Robert Campbell established Fort Laramie in 1834, the first resting place after the Missouri River which was often the scene of hundreds of encamped covered wagons and lean cattle regaining some strength after the long trek across the Plains. In the same year Thomas McKay, son of Alexander McKay who had died on the 1811 Astoria expedition and son-in-law of Dr John McLoughlin, Canadian-born but educated in Edinburgh, built Fort Boise on the Snake River. Also in 1834, Fort Hall was set up by American Nathaniel Wyeth further east on the Snake, but was taken over by the Hudson's Bay Company in 1836.

Scot Richard Grant became Chief Trader at Fort Hall in 1842. Although under instructions not to assist the overlanders, who were seen as a threat to the fur trade, he helped exhausted emigrants with supplies and horses. But he also discouraged them from heading for Oregon, because he believed the trail to be impossible for wagons, and instead pointed them in the direction of California. He seems to have acted in good faith, but it was in British interests to dissuade Americans from settling in Oregon, where the Hudson's Bay Company dominated until 1846 when the British gave up their claim to Oregon and Washington Territories. John McLoughlin at Fort Vancouver was another who warned against attempting to travel through the Rockies to Oregon.

The overlanders encountered wilderness in diverse manifestations. While some were leaving homesteads further east, and were familiar with the tasks of creating a farm and a living out of cleared forest, only the few who acted as guides knew what lay ahead when they crossed the Missouri and set off to follow the Platte River westward. The overlanders would make their way through knee-deep mud and waterless deserts, find dried-up river beds where they expected water and rivers in spate where they hoped for an easy crossing. Many were inexperienced in hunting to supplement their rations. They had to negotiate precipitous cliffs and hack their way through trees. And they had to get to the far side of the Rocky Mountains, with their wagons, their horses and cattle, and their often unrealistic loads of furniture and personal belongings. Much was jettisoned along the way.

Back in Scotland, there was keen interest in the moving frontier and the implications for potential emigrants. An *Edinburgh Review* of 1843 stressed the perils of the journey. For half the year the territory between the US frontier and Oregon was 'a howling wilderness of snow and tempests', for the other half a wasteland 'of hopeless sterility'. It was 'infested' with Indians 'of more than Scythian savageness and endurance, who cannot be tracked, overtaken, or conciliated'.[40] The journal was confident that Oregon would never be colonised by means of an overland route. Four years later the *Edinburgh Review* returned to the subject, again highlighting the dangers and the unsuitability for agriculture of an area stretching from 200 miles west of the Mississippi to the Rockies, though it conceded it might be suitable for raising cattle and sheep. By this time, hundreds of covered wagons had made that dangerous journey.

These migrations have, of course, become an emblem – *the* emblem – of the American pioneering spirit, sagas of grit and optimism in the face of an unrelenting landscape and often hostile natives. One of the early organised wagon trains assembled at Elm Grove, near Independence, Missouri, in the spring of 1842, led initially by Elijah White. Among its number was twenty-three-year-old Medorem Crawford (a Lanarkshire name), who kept a journal which reflects how difficult conditions affected individual behaviour and general progress. Also with the party were the two part-Chinook sons of

Thomas McKay, John and Alexander, who had been at school in the east: Scottish mountain men and fur traders often maintained a traditional respect for education.

From the start there were arguments, divisions and mishaps. The accumulated vexations inflicted by the terrain and the weather took their toll, described by David Lavender as 'wheels shrunken until the tires fell off, broken axletrees, sore-footed cattle, and the personal discomforts caused by sunburn, alkali water, and monotonous food cooked under difficult circumstances'.[41] Accounts of the wagon trains of the American West reveal in striking detail the attritional effects of travel in wild country. Underlying it all was the fear, if not the reality, of Indian attack.

After some respite at Fort Laramie the Elijah White group pushed on through Robert Stuart's South Pass to Green River and on to Fort Hall, where they received help and advice from Richard Grant. They abandoned their wagons and pressed on with pack horses. From Fort Hall they followed the Snake River, then trended northwest through Burnt Canyon. Crawford was one of the party bringing up the rear with the exhausted cattle. It was, he wrote, a place of 'frightful precipices & in many places if our animals make one mis-step it would be certain death'. Ahead lay the Blue Mountains, which 'struck us with terror … their lofty peaks seemed a resting place for the clouds'.[42] They reached the Whitman mission, near Fort Walla Walla where the Snake River meets the Columbia River, with a sense of huge relief. But there remained an equally challenging stretch. Elijah White had gone on ahead, by boat down the notoriously treacherous Columbia. Crawford's party, delayed by the slow progress of the cattle, followed the river on horseback until the narrowing gorge made progress impossible and they had to head into the formidable Cascade Mountains. Later, his horse 'gave out from hunger and fatigue'.[43]

Crawford made it through to the Willamette Valley, where he liked what he saw. The journey from the Missouri had taken over four months. He calculated the distance from Independence to be 1,746 miles. Crawford settled, married Adeline Brown who had been with the White party, and established a farm. Five years later he was elected a member of the territory's provisional legislature and went on to become a well-regarded civic figure contributing to the transition from frontier outpost to established community. In the early 1860s he helped to escort more wagon trains through to Oregon: he was, in the words of the introduction to his published journal, 'successful in shielding these emigrants from the outrages that those of preceding years had been suffering'. The introduction added: 'As a pioneer he was among the most intelligent, far-seeing, and energetic, and as a State-builder, he bore a very important part.'[44] The pioneer's evolution from frontiersman to statesman became rooted in American mythology.

Crawford's journal is brief, at times cryptic, recording basic details of camp sites, the trail and the wildlife, access to water and grass, weather conditions. It is an understated practical account rather than a descriptive commentary, though he noted features of the landscape and occasionally revealed more subjective impressions, commenting, for example, on the romantic character of the scenery as the wagon train approached the foot-hills of the Rockies rising from the plains. He recorded encounters with Native Americans with no sense of drama or danger, and it is clear that although there were times when the party felt threatened, on other occasions they were helped with provisions and guidance by the native groups they met. When Crawford lost his horse, it was found and returned by an Indian.

In 1844, a young coal miner from Pittsburgh made the same journey and also played a part in Oregon community-building. Though John Minto was born in England, his family was from the Scottish Borders. At the age of twenty-two he succumbed, as Crawford had, to the pull of the frontier, and joined a party of around eighty wagons and 300 people led by Cornelius Gilliam. Minto travelled with the Morrison family from Missouri (probably also of Scots descent), who treated him like a son. He would later marry their daughter Martha. In return for bed and board he gave practical assistance to the family – this was a common arrangement for single men joining the wagon trains. Unlike the cryptic Crawford, Minto's journal reveals enthusiasm and excitement. In spite of setbacks, quarrels, often appalling weather, illness, death and all the usual problems of the trail, he relished the scenery and the wildlife, and proved himself to be a proficient hunter and resourceful in many ways. Not long after he arrived in Oregon, he retraced his steps to assist other pioneers down the Columbia River. After a brief spell working in a saw mill he took up a land claim near Salem where he planted orchards and raised sheep. He went on to serve in the Oregon state legislature (Oregon became a state in 1859) and in the 1870s played a part in opening up two new passes through the Cascade Mountains, one of which is named for him.

Like Medorem Crawford, John Minto made the transition from adventurer to respected citizen. Both left the east in their early twenties, both married women they met on the trail, and both played a part in encouraging settlement and transforming Oregon from a tentatively occupied wilderness to an established community.

Among surviving diaries and accounts of the Oregon Trail, Scottish names frequently appear. The young Abigail Scott (the Scott family claimed descent from a Highland veteran of Culloden) kept a journal of her family's overland journey ten years after the Elijah White trek. The Scotts were part of a group of five wagons that set off from Peoria, Illinois after months of preparation. Abigail methodically recorded details of the terrain, the weather, distance travelled and daily activities. But an underlying theme throughout is sickness, including that of her mother who died. Her three-year-old brother William also died of what the doctor described as 'cholera infantum' or 'dropsy in the brain'. Scott writes that he told the family 'it is in vain to administer any medicine as he must surely die this to us is heart rending'.[45] Newly dug graves were a frequent sight. She also conveys the sheer scale of the migration west in that year: 'At one time to-day we saw upwards of sixty teams ahead of us besides two large droves of cattle; while behind us as far as we could see others were moving on.'[46]

In Oregon Abigail Scott would marry a farmer, Benjamin Duniway, and become a teacher, newspaper editor, novelist, lecturer and leader in the suffrage movement, again suggesting the scope for success associated with the frontier – in this case a particularly remarkable achievement for a woman. But most of those who survived the extraordinary experience of crossing the continent before the construction of the railroads went on to lead ordinary lives, at least in the context of settling a new territory. Whether the frontier delivered greater freedom is debatable, and for most it was the end of the road. A few headed back east, or south to California, but they could go no further west. Crawford and Minto were both clearly men of courage, resourcefulness and aspiration. They were also serious. Abigail Scott, painstakingly writing her journal sitting by the family tent or propped against a wagon wheel, shared those qualities. That particular combination may have owed something to their Scottish heritage. They were clearly all three primed to take advantage of any opportunities that came their way, and were probably all aware that in making the journey west they were following trails which had been blazed by men among whom Scots were prominent.

In the context of the United States, the epic treks to Oregon and California have a heroic resonance which is seen as quintessentially American. The resolve to go west, the endurance, the elemental engagement with a wild landscape, are essential ingredients of the American frontier experience. Equally, the planting of a settlement in 'empty' land, the building of the infrastructures and connections that make a community, are part of the heroic American endeavour. But there is a tension between the narrative of the trail-breaker and that of settlement, a tension first articulated in the fiction of James Fenimore Cooper, whose hero opens up the wilderness in the regretful knowledge that by doing so it will be destroyed. As Natty Bumppo helps to make the frontier safe he knows he will lose all that he celebrates in the wild country that is his livelihood.

In Cooper's Leatherstocking Tales wilderness is not just the location of heroic action but its source. The same is true of the last phase of frontier narrative which saw the rise of the Western, in fiction and film, as the frontier itself was appearing to close. Among the more distinguished twentieth-century frontier narratives are the novels of A. B. Guthrie, whose unequivocally Scottish name signals his Aberdeenshire roots. His classic tales *The Big Sky* (1947) and *The Way West* (1949) pick up Cooper's themes as they chronicle the period of the mountain men and fur trappers and the wagon trains of the 1840s. Although fiction, the books were carefully researched, drawing on journals and contemporary accounts to produce narratives convincing both in character and in detail.

The focus of *The Big Sky* is the experience of the mountain men, the often solitary and disaffected individuals who were the first Europeans to adapt to the wilderness of the American Far West. In the introduction to the 1980 edition, Walter van Tilburg Clark makes a case for the mountain man as quintessential American hero:

> He had [the world of the westering] all to himself in its cleanest and most spacious time, and then, as scout and guide he led the missionary, the pioneer settler and the forty-niner across it; and all the rest – the border cavalryman, the stagecoach driver, the pony-express rider, the buffalo skinner, the cowboy, the prairie sodbuster; the railroad and gandy dancer and the lumber jack – trooped after.[47]

Scots played a role in all these activities, but it is as mountain men and fur traders that they stand out. Clark argues that the mountain man should replace the cowboy as the mythic frontier hero. The mountain man 'moved in a much vaster and even more dangerous wilderness' than the frontiersman who had preceded him, and was 'much more completely separated from every manifestation of unheroic civilization'.[48] William Drummond Stewart and others had responded enthusiastically to both the danger and the complete separation from 'unheroic civilization'. Clark stresses the isolation of the mountain man, and in Guthrie's narrative isolation is inseparable from a sense of freedom.

His young hero is Boone Caudill (the name a version of the Scottish name Caldwell) who, aged seventeen, leaves his Kentucky home after a quarrel with a local boy called Napier (another Scottish name). Heading west, he falls in first with a young man called Jim Deakin, then with mountain man Dick Summers, who becomes mentor to both youngsters. For Boone, as for Dick, it is the freedom of a barely peopled wilderness that is the compelling attraction. His reaction when he encounters wagons and women west of the Missouri (the Whitman wagon train of 1836, making its way to the Columbia River to establish a mission near Fort Walla Walla) is dismay. 'White women! And wheels! They figured to spoil a country, except that the women would leave or die.'[49] The notion that the wild country he had come to love would be filled with people was inconceivable:

Ask any hunter who had fought Indians and gone empty-stomached and like to froze, and he'd say it was no place for women, or for preachers, either, or farmers. And no place for wagons or carts, except maybe to bring trade goods as far as rendezvous. The rocks would knock them to pieces, and the rivers wash them down, and the sun shrivel the wheels apart. All the same, he got a pinch of misery, thinking, just as he had sometimes in Kentucky when he'd been out in the woods, feeling good that he was alone, with everything to himself, and then he would spy someone and it would all be spoiled, as if the country wasn't his any more, or the woods or the quiet.[50]

The theme runs through both *The Big Sky* and *The Way West*. The heroic endeavours of the pioneers will bring an end to the origins of that heroism, the land itself with all its unforgiving severity. The sheer beauty of the landscape is an integral part of its harshness. Dick Summers, with Boone and Jim, battles through the dark, forbidding mountains, slammed by the wind, 'at back and front and sides, so there wasn't a way a man could turn his head to shelter his face'. He keeps going 'farther into the wild heights of rock, until finally on the other side he would see the Grand Teton, rising slim and straight like a lodgepole pine, standing purple against the blue sky'.[51] The rewards of a lonely, savage existence are an intimate connection with the natural world and freedom from the burdens of convention. 'This was the way to live', Boone reflects, 'free and easy, with time all a man's own and none to say no to him.' And he goes on:

A body got so's he felt everything was kin to him, the earth and sky and buffalo and beaver and the yellow moon at night. It was better than being walled in by a house, better than breathing in spoiled air and feeling caged like a varmint, better than running after the law or have the law running after you and looking to rules all the time until you wondered could you even take down your pants without somebody's say-so. Here a man lived natural.[52]

But it is the older Dick who recognises that this will all come to an end, or at least be deeply eroded, as people follow the trails blazed by the mountain men. In *The Way West* he has accepted the inevitable and, as many mountain men did, helps to guide a wagon train from Independence, Missouri, to Fort Vancouver, Oregon. A key family is that of Henry McBee (McBeatha and Macbeth are variants of the name), who is determined to make it to Oregon. The McBees have come from Ohio, where 'things ain't so good'. Oregon promises 'soil rich as anything'. McBee expands on his vision of Oregon: 'I heerd you don't never have to put up hay, the grass is that good, winter and all. And lambs come twice a year. Just set by and let the grass grow and the critters birth and get fat. That's my idee of farmin.'[53]

It is the early 1840s. The prospect of productive farming without the backbreaking toil demanded by what was once the frontier is the driving force.

Underlying the perseverance of the overlanders is a belief that America owes them something better than unremitting toil. Serial disappointment has never laid to rest that essential element of the American dream. Guthrie's overlanders have pioneering skills and grit and guts, and the journey will demand all the experience and courage they can muster, but they want to be somewhere where they do not need to depend so relentlessly on these qualities. But they are also aware of the resonance of the undertaking. 'A man didn't make history, staying close to home,' muses Henry McBee.[54] But he is a family man, and throughout is the underlying message that family will tame the frontier and in the process destroy its promise.

The wagon train is a closed community, in which relationships are intensified by external threats, from the terrain, the weather and hostile natives. It is a community that depends on mutual support, in which quarrels and lack of cooperation can be detrimental to all – a classic environment for drama. Guthrie plays off individual actions, often selfish and self-serving, against community well-being, while at the same time illustrating the generosity of mutual assistance and comfort. It is a trope that features strongly in the American imagination and is expressed in many forms in Western novels and movies. For Scots, particularly Highlanders, who carried memories of the Old World, the undermining of mutuality had a particular resonance. The disintegration of the clan system, and the cohesion and loyalty it represented had sent many of them across the Atlantic.

In 1910, John Love brought his new bride Ethel Waxham to his ranch in Wyoming's Wind River Basin. John had been born in Wisconsin, but on his mother's death his father had taken him and his sisters home to Scotland. He was twelve when the family returned to America. At the ranch there was nothing to be seen but distant mountains, the Wind River Range and the Bighorns. There was no human habitation visible.

> From the ranch buildings ... the Wind River Basin reached out in buffalo grass, grama grass, and edible salt sage across the cambered erosional swells of the vast dry range. When the wind dropped, this whole wide world was silent, and they could hear from a great distance the squeak of a horned lark. The nearest neighbour was thirteen miles away. On the clearest night they saw no light but their own.[55]

John Love's pioneering retained an indelible Scottish character: independent, pragmatic and prudent. He was used to sleeping out in gales and blizzards with just a bedroll and no shelter. He wore 'a long bearskin coat fastened with bone pegs in loops of rope' and carried a large black umbrella as a 'summer parasol'. Each night, after cooking his dinner over the camp fire, he settled down to read by the light of a kerosene lamp. When his son asked him why he did not use a tent, he replied, 'Laddie, you don't always have one available … You want to get used to living without it.'[56]

The Scottish contribution to the settlement of the American Far West, like that of other nationalities, is absorbed into an emblematic narrative which has always stressed the American nature of the enterprise. In Canada, where the imprint of Scottish identity is so much deeper and more extensive, it is often Scottish settlement that has become an emblem of its pioneering past. In both narratives, the pioneer's efforts to tame the wilderness are imbued with contradiction and loss. Heroic journeys culminate in the destruction of the features of the land that breeds heroism. Crops and barbed wire and cities impede free movement. The longing for security and the structures of civil society ensure that the pioneer vision is eroded. And when the struggle becomes too much and moving on is the only option, the wilderness reclaims its own.

NOTES

1. Laurence Oliphant, *Far West*, pp. 187–8.
2. Pennant, *Tour of Scotland*, pp. 193–4.
3. Traill, *Lost in the Backwoods*, p. 6.
4. Ian Adams and Meredith Somerville, *Cargoes of Despair and Hope* (Edinburgh: John Donald, 1993), p. 56.
5. George Patterson, in Adams and Somerville, *Cargoes of Despair*, p. 55.
6. Howison, *Sketches of Upper Canada*, p. 151.
7. Ibid., p. 80.
8. Ibid., p. 70.
9. Ibid., p. 187.
10. J. K. Galbraith, *The Non-potable Scotch. A Memoir on the Clansmen in Canada* (Harmondsworth: Penguin, [1964] 1967), p. 62.
11. Ibid., p. 53.
12. James Hunter, *A Dance Called America* (Edinburgh: Mainstream, 1994), p. 183.
13. MacLennan, *Scotchman's Return*, p. 7.
14. Hunter, *A Dance Called America*, p. 184.
15. J. F. Bumsted, *The Scots in Canada* (Ottawa: Canadian Historical Association, 1982), p. 211.
16. Hunter, *A Dance Called America*, p. 188.
17. Margaret Laurence, *The Diviners* (London: Virago, [1974] 1989), p. 69.
18. R. M. Ballantyne, *Away in the Wilderness* (London: Nisbet, 1879), p. 22.
19. C. W. Dunn, *Highland Settler* (Toronto: University of Toronto Press, 1953), p. 25.
20. Frederick John Niven, *The Flying Years* (London: Collins, 1974), p. 147.

21. John Muir, *The Story of My Boyhood and Youth*, ed. Frank Tindall (Edinburgh: Canongate, [1913] 1987), p. 36.
22. Ibid., p. 32.
23. Ibid., p. 112.
24. Ibid., p. 115.
25. Ormsby, *Pioneer Gentlewoman in British Columbia*, p. 8.
26. Ibid., p. 23.
27. Ibid., p. 26.
28. Ibid., p. 29.
29. Ibid., p. 62.
30. Ibid., p. 47.
31. Ibid.
32. Ibid., p. xxxix.
33. Mackenzie, *View of the United States*, p. iii.
34. Ibid., p. vi.
35. Ibid., p. 457.
36. 'Old Scene Painter', *The Emigrant's Guide, or A Picture of America* (London: 1816), p. 77
37. Hamilton, *Men and Manners*, vol. II, p. 168.
38. Ibid., p. 159.
39. David Lavender, *The Penguin Book of the American West* (Harmondsworth: Penguin, 1969), p. 260.
40. John D. Unruh, *The Plains Across: Emigrants, Wagon Trains and the American West* (London: Pimlico, 1992), p. 5.
41. Medorem Crawford, *Journal*, ed. F. G. Young, available at: www.archive.org/details/journalofmedoremcrawford, p. 18.
42. Ibid., p. 22.
43. Ibid., p. 27.
44. F. G. Young, Introduction, Crawford, *Journal*, n. 9.
45. Abigail Scott, *Journal of a Trip to Oregon*, available at: www.over-land.com/diaries, p. 77.
46. Ibid., p. 25.
47. Walter van Tilburg Clark, Introduction, A. B. Guthrie, *The Big Sky* (Chicago, IL: Time-Life Books, [1947] 1980), pp. xii–xiii.
48. Ibid., p. xiii.
49. Guthrie, *The Big Sky*, p. 174.
50. Ibid., p. 175.
51. Ibid., p. 189.
52. Ibid., p. 198.
53. A. B. Guthrie, *The Way West* (New York: Houghton Mifflin, [1949] 1976), p. 9.
54. Ibid., p. 13.
55. John McPhee, *Rising from the Plains* (New York: Farrar, Straus & Giroux, 1986), p. 73.
56. Ibid., p. 75.

6

Treasures of the Forest, the Field and the Mine

A fair land; rich in furs and fish, in treasures of the forest, the field, and the mine ...

George Grant, *Ocean to Ocean*

It has occurred to me that philanthropy is not the exclusive object of our visits to the Northern regions.

George Simpson, letter (quoted in Peter Newman, *Caesars of the Wilderness*)

For the Highlanders who disembarked from the *Hector* in September 1773, the Nova Scotian forest was a place of mystery and threat. You could not see the sun or be sure of your direction of travel, and there were dangers alien to those accustomed to the landscapes of the West Highlands. But trees were the key to survival. They were the most plentiful resource of Nova Scotia and New Brunswick. The settlers needed to deal with them, to make space for homes and crops, and they needed to use them. Settlement was not possible without exploitation. That was its purpose, to make use of untapped natural resources to subsist and, if possible, to generate profit and bring a recognisable order to an untamed wilderness.

'ONE ENORMOUS TIMBER CONCESSION'

Trees were emblematic of several strands of exploitation. They were a challenge and a burden, but they were necessary for settlement. They provided pioneers with the materials for their homes, their barns and fences, their furniture and utensils. They were also a product to be exported for the benefit of both new land and homeland. They sustained the colonial presence by making settlement possible and by being the source of a lucrative trade. They created jobs and made fortunes. Thanks to trees, by the 1780s Pictou had become the commercial centre of the Gulf of St Lawrence. And on the other side of the Atlantic, particularly on the River Clyde, they were the most visible evidence of North American resources.

Along most of the eastern seaboard of North America and in the hinterland that stretched to the Appalachians trees offered great potential. In the Cape Fear area of North Carolina, settled in the 1730s by Highlanders mainly from Argyll, the plentiful pine trees had to be cleared and the land planted. The pines were their building materials, but they were also the source of turpentine, resin, tar and charcoal, key materials for shipbuilding which were transported down the Cape Fear River to Wilmington and onwards. In 1773, a Scottish visitor to North Carolina described the Cape Fear Valley as a place of well-spaced villas and farmhouses 'which afforded a most enchanting scene of the ease and happiness which the present settlers enjoy'.[1] Subsistence farming was unlikely to supply that kind of ease. Exploitation of the pine trees ensured that the Cape Fear community thrived, and probably helped it to retain its Highland character.

In Nova Scotia by the end of the eighteenth century, timber felling for profit was on a modest scale; Scotland's needs were mainly supplied by the Baltic, as they had been for centuries. The timber trade between North America and Scotland came into its own during the Napoleonic Wars, when the Baltic ports were blockaded. Pictou became a focus of the trade, as did Halifax, and Miramichi in New Brunswick. Timber was now a lucrative commodity rather than the by-product of the necessary labour of settlement. Homesteads with sea or river frontages were readily accessible to the ships that picked up their cargo, but felling was increasing in the back country and employing large numbers. George Patterson, Pictou's first historian, wrote that the 'cutting, hewing, hauling, rafting and shipping of timber became, for some years, almost the business of the people of Pictou'.[2] Across the Northumberland Strait on Prince Edward Island the timber trade was also expanding.

The timber exporting areas flourished, attracting thousands of new settlers, many brought in by the ships which sailed east with timber and west with emigrants, mainly from the West Highlands. The never-ending forest was being perceived by many not as a locus of threat and dismay, but as an enduring source of profit. Trees were a ready-made crop. The harvesting was hard and often dangerous work, but there was no clearing and tilling of soil involved, no planting, no need to nurture infant crops.

The timber trade made a significant difference to many settler families, but the main beneficiaries were the merchants and ship-owners. Prominent among these was Edward Mortimer from Keith, Banffshire, who by the late 1780s was in Pictou as representative of the Liddell firm of merchants, based in Glasgow and Halifax. Mortimer energetically built up business on his own and the firm's behalf, putting in place an infrastructure of wharves and warehouses and developing contacts mainly with fellow Scots. He was involved in shipping and fisheries as well as timber, and later in coal, first discovered in Pictou County in 1798. He was generous in his dealings with fellow Scots, allowing them extensive credit. This put him in an influential position which helped him build a number of civic and political roles, and to contribute significantly to the growing community, although on his death it was found that his assets consisted primarily of debts.

Like many Scots in Nova Scotia, Mortimer represents a nexus of exploitation and benign development. He extracted timber and coal from the land and fish from the sea, of which there was clearly no shortage. In his entrepreneurial role he facilitated settlement and boosted the efforts of the pioneers. He contributed to the massive increase in the timber trade – in the six years after the Baltic blockade the trade quadrupled. In the continuing war with France there was a great demand for masts and spars for warships, which were readily supplied by Nova Scotia and New Brunswick. Many other Scots benefited from this demand, men such as William Forsyth, a general merchant in Halifax, who imported goods from his partners on the Clyde and exported fish and timber to the United States and the Caribbean as well as Britain. Huge amounts of timber crossed the Atlantic to Aberdeen and Leith as well as Port Glasgow, where surviving wooden stakes in the River Clyde mark where the massive log rafts were held.

A supplier of timber to Forsyth was William Davidson from Inverness, who in 1765, with John Cort from Aberdeenshire, had taken up a land grant of 100,000 acres on the banks of the Mirimachi River. Realising the potential of plentiful timber, Davidson also set up his own shipyard. The outbreak of America's revolutionary war interfered with his markets, but the hoped for improvement at the war's end did not materialise. Davidson had failed to fulfil the conditions of his land grant, which stipulated settlement; as a consequence he lost over 80 per cent of his land. Although shrewd and energetic, like many others Davidson was not able to reconcile the twin demands of populating the wilderness and creating commercial benefit.

But overall the trade picked up. Allan Gilmour was with his uncle's Glasgow-based timber-importing firm when in 1821 he was sent out to New Brunswick to work at the Miramichi end of the business. By 1823, the Gilmour firm had over a hundred vessels plying the Atlantic. Later, Andrew Gilmour was in Saint John where the firm expanded into shipbuilding. Trees seemed to be an inexhaustible resource, with Lower and Upper Canada also now sharing in the timber and timber product trade, especially in the tracts of land along the St Lawrence and Ottawa rivers, which provided a transport route to the Atlantic. Red and yellow pine predominated, with smaller quantities of oak, elm and ash. The forests had sustained small communities for hundreds of years with no impact on their ability to survive. Now they were being felled on a scale never contemplated by their first inhabitants, to enable settlements and fuel their growth: 'at times it almost seemed as if the entire Province [of New Brunswick] had become one enormous timber concession'.[3] Peter Clyde, Lumber Surveyor, wrote that Miramichi was 'bothered with so much timber and lumber of one kind and another that when we fairly embark into the business it is almost impossible to get away from it again'.[4]

'BOUNDARIES LARGELY DETERMINED BY THE FUR TRADE'

Long before there was significant settlement and the felling of thousands of trees, another natural resource of the forest was being exploited. Beaver were plentiful and their fur desirable. They also depended on trees to build their homes and survive, and like trees they became an emblem of exploitation. Europeans wanted furs, especially beaver, in huge quantities. In Rupert's Land the trade depended on cultivating relations with the First Nations and later with Métis, themselves a consequence of the fur trade, who acted as guides and interpreters as well as trapping the beaver. Initial understanding of the vast territory, its configuration and its extent, came from these activities and had a permanent effect: 'Canada emerged as a political entity with boundaries largely determined by the fur trade'.[5] Further south the trade in the early nineteenth century was more often in the hands of independent trappers who operated alone or in small groups, trapping in the mountains and delivering their furs to one of the rival companies which came into being as the century progressed. Detroit on Lake Erie, then St Louis on the junction of the Mississippi and Missouri rivers, became hubs of the US trade which, as north of the border, penetrated further and further west as the more accessible areas became trapped out. John Jacob Astor's plan for an American trading post on the Pacific coast was the most ambitious of these ventures.

By the 1820s, American trappers were a growing presence in the Rockies. Every year the trading companies' representatives would head west to meet the trappers at the annual rendezvous, and exchange supplies for furs. It was these expeditions that William Drummond Stewart joined. In the north the twin hubs of the trade were Montreal, the North West Company's base, and York Factory on Hudson Bay, the headquarters of the Hudson's Bay Company. The fur-trading brigades travelled hundreds, often thousands, of miles to bring in the year's catch

West of the Great Lakes and the Missouri and in the far north it was the fur traders who were the pioneers. They were the first white men to move along the rivers, across the plains and through the mountains, and all that happened thereafter came in their footsteps. They seemed to move with ease through adversity: 'they went about the blank spaces of the map like men going to the barn'.[6] Many of them, and in Rupert's Land and New Caledonia most of them, were Scots. They evolved a way of life that maximised their

chances of survival while they served their commercial masters. They overcame immense odds, as Washington Irving evoked: 'They had to traverse the
most dreary and desolate mountains, and barren and trackless wastes uninhabited by man, or occasionally infested by predatory and cruel savages.'[7]
Irving also identified the 'passionate excitement' of the traders, which 'at
times resembles a mania ... let a single track of a beaver meet his eye, and
he forgets all dangers and defies all difficulties'.[8] They all participated in the
calculated and highly organised exploitation of thousands of square miles
of wilderness. It was something more than greed that drove them, for
although a few fur traders became very influential and very rich, most did
not. They did not all stand the pace – Irving did not encounter, or did not
give space to, those who were left behind. A significant number of the Scots
entering the fur trade became sick, or disabled by accidents, or dispirited,
or simply gave up in the face of overwhelming odds. Although the HBC
recruiting in Orkney, for example, repeatedly stressed the need for young
able-bodied men, often the recruits arriving at Hudson Bay were older and
not up to the rigours of terrain and climate.

Simon McTavish was thirteen in 1763 when he left his home in Stratherrick,
east of Loch Ness, and travelled to the American colonies, where he found
employment with a New York merchant. By 1772 he was in Detroit and
becoming involved in the fur trade. Four years later he shifted his base to
Montreal, and that same year left for London with a cargo of pelts worth
£15,000. By 1779, when the North West Company was formed, he was a key
player in the fur trade and soon had a leading role in the new company. In
1787, he gained a controlling interest and proved himself a shrewd, ruthless
and highly ambitious manager. The fur-trading nabobs enjoyed parading
their success, and each year McTavish and other influential figures made a
journey in considerable style to Fort William on Lake Superior (initially to
Grand Portage, but the end of the War of Independence left it south of the
newly drawn border). Washington Irving described their progress 'wrapped
in rich furs, their huge canoes freighted with every convenience and luxury,
and manned by Canadian *voyageurs*, as obedient as Highland clansmen'.
Among the luxuries were 'delicacies of every kind, and an abundance of
choice wines for the banquets which attended this great convocation'.[9]

   Such ostentation was a statement of authority, but it was also a gesture of
defiance in the face of the extremes of an untamed country. At Fort William,
and even more lavishly in Montreal, banquets signalled over-indulgence on
a massive scale. The notorious Beaver Club, founded in 1785, held dinners
where the members competed in excess. Vast amounts of liquor were
consumed: 120 bottles of wine at one gathering of twelve diners, as well as
ale, porter, gin and brandy. Ultimate drunken collapse amid broken crockery

at the end of an evening of raucous song and dancing on the table was *de rigueur*. It was an endurance test, perhaps not rivalling survival in the wilderness but equally a demonstration of manliness.

McTavish was the son of a lieutenant in the Fraser Highlanders who had fought in North America in the Seven Years War, but, like most of the young men and boys who made the voyage across the Atlantic, he was expected to make his own way. And like most he would make use of any contacts, family and other, that he might have. The North West Company and the Hudson's Bay Company (and many other Scottish companies) were notoriously nepotistic and the network of family connections was extensive. But there was no easy route to success. An extravagant demonstration of not only survival but commercial achievement was, for many of the Scots prominent in the two companies, a personal issue. They were aware that the riches and influences they achieved would have been unlikely rewards if they had stayed in Scotland.

When Simon McTavish died in 1804 it was his nephew William McGillivray who took over the North West Company. William and his brother Duncan were the sons of McTavish's sister Ann, whose education Simon had funded. By 1784, at the age of twenty, William was an employee of the NWC in Montreal, a prelude to being posted as a clerk first to Red River and subsequently to Snake Lake in Alberta where he set up a trading post. He had to prove himself on the ground, but his advancement in the company was steady. Following him was his younger brother Duncan, who spent a number of years working for the company in Saskatchewan and playing a part in its expansion west.

Most of the Scots who became prominent in the fur trade had a combination of education and contacts to set them on their way, even if their background was modest. They could not avoid the test of the wilderness, but had a head start on other fur-trade employees. Few of the hundreds of Orkneymen recruited when the HBC ships paused to provision at Stromness made their way to the top. John Rae, university educated and son of the HBC's representative in Orkney, was an exception. It was Highlanders who dominated the upper echelons. The Orkneymen, who at times provided over 80 per cent of the HBC's workforce, were valued because they were considered to be tough, hard-working, abstemious and amenable. Both the abstinence and the labour were unavoidable in the roles the fur trade allocated them. They were the heavy lifters, the oarsmen, the trail-breakers, the hewers and haulers. Often they had to learn new skills, making and paddling canoes, for example, and their proficiency in these 'country skills' could be the key to promotion and reward.

The work centred on maintaining the widely scattered trading posts and journeying into the interior to deliver trade goods and gather furs destined for shipment east. These annual treks were embarked on with robust enthusiasm. Robert Ballantyne from Edinburgh, who had joined the Hudson's Bay Company at the age of sixteen when his well-to-do family faced financial ruin, gives a flavour of their activity:

> Some of the men, jumping ashore, ran briskly to and fro with enormous burdens on their backs; whilst others hauled and pulled the heavy boats slowly up the cataract, halooing and shouting all the time, as if they wished to drown the thundering noise of the water, which boiled and hissed furiously around the rocks on which we stood.[10]

Human voices to drown the noise of thundering water, or perhaps just to announce a human presence: both were part of a need to make some kind of impression on a resistant environment. Ballantyne would transform his fur-trade experience into the stuff of adventure (see Chapter 7). But it was not the lure of adventure that took Orkneymen across the Atlantic, although the challenge of the wilderness may have played a part. It was the need to escape a meagre, in some cases unsustainable, existence in their home islands. The Hudson's Bay Company offered a route to security as well as danger, although for those based at the trading posts the long winters could be tedious as well as threatening. James Hargrave from Hawick, Chief Trader at York Factory, depended on the annual arrival of the HBC supply ships which brought books and newspapers to help him through the winter months. Wilderness imposed boredom and inactivity as well as making extreme physical demands.

The figure who towers over all in the fur trade is George Simpson. He was born probably in 1786, three years before Alexander Mackenzie set off on the journey that took him, disappointingly, to the Beaufort Sea, and seven years before Mackenzie's second journey cast doubt on the feasibility of a commercial route through the Rockies to the Pacific. Simpson was the illegitimate son of an unknown mother and George Simpson from Avoch, near Dingwall, where Mackenzie had spent his last years – the Simpson and Mackenzie families were connected. He was brought up by his father's family, and it was a family connection that started him on a career that would see him push the grip and influence of the Hudson's Bay Company to its limit. At the age of fourteen or fifteen he went to work for his uncle's sugar-importing firm in London.

Whatever his ambitions were at this stage, it was clear early on that Simpson was driven by an energetic Calvinist work ethic: 'a zestful and voracious appetite for work characterised his entire life'.[11] He was also part of a network of contacts that illustrates an important facet of Scottish success in the New World. Geddes & Simpson, the firm of which his uncle

Geddes Mackenzie Simpson was a partner, amalgamated with the firm of Wedderburn & Company, which owned sugar plantations in Jamaica. Andrew Wedderburn was the son and grandson of Jacobites. His grandfather was executed after the '45, and his father exiled to the Caribbean. The family estate at Inveresk, near Edinburgh, was confiscated but was later recovered by Andrew, who in 1814 changed his name to Colvile.

Colvile became a shareholder in the Hudson's Bay Company, and in 1810 was elected to the governing committee. His sister married Lord Selkirk, who, as we have seen, was deeply involved in promoting settlement in British North America and became an influential figure in the Hudson's Bay Company. It was Colvile who identified George Simpson as a likely lad for the HBC, which Simpson joined in 1820. From an office job in London he was precipitated not only into the North American wilderness, but into an arena of bitter and at times murderous conflict between the rival fur companies. He was despatched from Montreal to Red River and the Athabasca trading posts to mediate between the NWC and the HBC. It was a journey and a task that he undertook with considerable zest: 'instead of adapting himself to inclement conditions, he defied them'.[12] Equally, he defied the often fiercely uncontrolled actions of the men he had to deal with. Young and inexperienced he may have been, but he was uncompromising, intolerant of inefficiency and slackness, yet able to calm a situation of volatile enmity in territory where law enforcement was largely improvised. He proved himself to be an astute judge of character and a cunning manipulator of personalities. His reward was appointment as governor of first the Northern Department, then in 1826 the Southern Department also.

Simpson's initiation into the fur trade came at a crucial time in its development, when it had become clear that expansion was imperative and that competition was damaging its potential. His interventions in 1820 were the prelude to the amalgamation of the two companies and the push west which opened the final chapter of the trade's expansion. 'It is of the utmost importance that New Caledonia should be established next year,' he wrote in his account of his Athabasca sojourn.[13] But expansion needed a foundation of efficient management and accounting, and Simpson was scathing in his criticism of the deficiencies he found. He accused Neil McDonald at Fort Wedderburn on Lake Athabasca of doing little but 'eating and drinking the Company's property, smoking their Tobacco, and sleeping their time away' while the business was in a state of confusion and provisions were running low.[14] (Both Ballantyne and Stef Penney in her 2006 novel, *The Tenderness of Wolves*, highlight the HBC's alcohol problem.) Simpson was equally disgusted at the drunkenness and dishonesty he found at Red River. Many of those he condemned were Scots.

Yet there was one form of licence that the wilderness allowed and the

HBC condoned and which Simpson shared in enthusiastically. Alliances with native female partners were common and often encouraged, not just as a source of comfort to men undergoing hardship and isolation, but as a means of forging ties with the First Nations on whom the fur trade depended. The women also had skills which were an asset to men who had otherwise to rely on their own resources. They made and mended clothes, strung and repaired snowshoes, could often hunt and fish, and butchered meat and prepared food. Many, possibly most, of the men involved in the fur trade had native partners. Some of these 'country marriages' were long lasting and received at some stage, if not initially, the blessing of the church. Donald Smith, who became eventually governor of the Hudson's Bay Company, formed a union in Labrador which lasted a lifetime, and which he affirmed with repeated ceremonies. Colin Robertson, who played a prominent role in the settlement of Red River, had a life-long Métis partner.

Simpson considered such permanent arrangements to be detrimental to the HBC. His pragmatic view was that native and Métis women were a convenience and a commodity, to be disposed of when no longer of use, and to be abandoned or punished if they made a fuss. They should not be allowed to interfere with the progress or the status of HBC officials. Simpson himself had no intention of tying himself into a long-term relationship that would not enhance his increasingly powerful position. Before he left England, he had fathered two children with different mothers, and on the other side of the Atlantic continued as he had begun, managing relationships of varying kinds and durations with at least five women.

In 1830, Simpson was in London seeking a wife, and duly married his eighteen-year-old cousin, Frances Ramsay Simpson, the daughter of his former employer. Simpson's friend and colleague John George McTavish, from Argyll, married in Edinburgh at the same time, and the two couples returned to Canada together. (Later, Duncan Finlayson, a close associate of Simpson, married Frances's sister Isobel, who joined him at Red River when he became governor of Assiniboia.) McTavish had had a relationship, long enough to produce six daughters, with Métis Nancy Mackenzie, who was summarily dumped to make way for his new and respectable partner. Mr and Mrs Simpson and Mr and Mrs McTavish made their way west from Montreal by canoe, an experience that was something of a shock to the young women, especially to Frances who was not robust. On the way to Lake Winnipeg they passed – but did not pause at – Fort Alexander where Margaret Taylor, also Métis, was staying with her two sons. They were both Simpson's, and the second had been born while he was in England looking for a wife. Simpson used McTavish as his aid and accomplice when it came to dealing with redundant women. An earlier liaison was terminated with a request to McTavish at York Factory: 'if you can dispose of the Lady it will be satisfactory as she is an unnecessary & expensive appendage'.[15] 'Dispose of' meant to partner her with another HBC employee. Similarly, McTavish was asked to 'keep an Eye' on the pregnant Margaret, or 'the commodity' as he described her: 'if she bring forth anything in the proper time & of the right color let them be taken care of but if anything be amiss let the whole be bundled about their business'.[16] In other words, if there was any dubiety about the paternity of the baby, Simpson wanted rid of them.

Simpson was perhaps particularly open (to his male associates) and unapologetic about his exploitation of women, but the practice was endemic and often allied with the imperatives of commerce and an unforgiving environment. Wilderness was a liberation as well as a hard master – although Simpson's earlier liaisons do not seem to have hampered him socially or professionally. His Calvinist background and possibly his irregular birth had instilled in him an iron work ethic inflamed by ambition, but it did not encourage him to regard as equals those of a different class, colour or gender. His approach to the territory and its people was relentlessly pragmatic. His purpose was to control and maximise the fur trade. Not surprisingly, there were those among his HBC associates who found him overbearing and obnoxious. The comments of John McLean, an HBC Chief Trader, reveal how some regarded Simpson, and reflect on the trade itself:

> In no colony subject to the British Crown is there to be found an authority so despotic as it is at this day exercised in the mercantile colony of Rupert's Land; an authority combining the despotism of military rule with the strict surveillance and mean parsimony of the audacious trader. From Labrador to Nootka Sound the uncharted, uncontrolled will of a single individual gives law to the land.[17]

McLean added that with such unlimited power 'it is not to be wondered at that a man who rose from a humble situation should in the end forget what he was and play the tyrant'.[18] McLean's implication that Simpson, a bastard of modest origins, should know his place rather mars the tone of his comment; nevertheless, the evidence is clear that Simpson was unflinchingly ruthless in pursuit of his goals.

Simpson established his control by ensuring that his presence was felt in every corner of the fur-trading domain. He travelled tirelessly, determined to go further and faster than others, and combining speed with considerable state. Symbols of status – food, drink, clothes – accompanied him, to impress both his own people and the First Nations. He recruited Colin Fraser from Scotland as his personal piper, to announce his arrivals and departures. Ostentation signalled power; it was also a statement of defiance in the face of inevitable adversity.

Simpson was scornful of those who could not match his stamina, and his men, used to the most rigorous of conditions and demands, were often exhausted by early morning starts after three or four hours sleep, with only brief pauses for food and rest. Eighteen hours on the move were normal. Speed and efficiency were Simpson's watchwords; Napoleon was his hero and example.

Simpson was determined on westward expansion. Alexander Mackenzie and Simon Fraser had demonstrated the difficulties of establishing commercially viable routes through the Rockies, and Fraser, who felt he was not getting the support he needed, complained that new forts in the west could not survive without more reliable provisioning from the east. It was not just a matter of supplying the traders themselves, but of ensuring that the North West Company made a positive impact in the locality. This did not come cheap, as Fraser reminded his superiors: 'there are none of you but know that exploring new countries and seeing strange Indians is expensive, was it only to procure a welcome reception' he wrote in a request for further resources. And he added that success also depended on having the right men on the ground: 'I need not inform you Gentlemen that if it is your intention to establish further on, or keep up what is already established, that proper people will be required for the purpose.'[19] Two decades, and the endeavours of George Simpson, demonstrated that these problems could be overcome.

In 1808, the year that Simon Fraser set off on his journey through the Rockies, Robert Campbell was born in Glen Lyon, the son of a sheep farmer. At the age of twenty-two he left Perthshire, fired by the accounts of his cousin who was with the Hudson's Bay Company to take up employment with them. On 1 July 1830 he sailed out of Stromness on the HBC supply ship *Prince Rupert* and six weeks later arrived at York Factory. He had ten days to prepare himself for the journey to Red River, where, under Chief Factor Donald Mackenzie, his role was to set up an experimental farm to raise stock and crops to supply the colony. It was hard work:

> Being young in years & experience, & anxious to do my duty faithfully & efficiently, I was so constantly on the move from earliest daylight till dark that it was seldom I was more than 4 hours out of the 24 in bed – a habit I was thankful for all my life after.[20]

Campbell, very different in personality from Simpson, shared the same work ethic and made similar demands on himself. Simpson spotted his potential, and in 1834 he was appointed to the Mackenzie River district: 'Now, Campbell', warned Simpson, 'don't you get married as we want you for active service.'[21] Simpson himself had married in the year of Campbell's arrival at Red River, and had discovered that marriage to a woman of, in his view, appropriate status (and therefore unused to the rigours of the wild) was problematic. Frances Simpson returned to London, and although thereafter she spent time in the splendid Simpson residence at Lachine, she did not repeat the experience of her initiating journey west. She died at Lachine at the age of forty.

Robert Campbell made his way to Fort Simpson on the Mackenzie River, where he became a willing instrument of Simpson's westward endeavours, themselves driven by Russian competition in the northwest. An expedition west took Campbell to Dease Lake, south of what is now the border between British Columbia and Yukon Territory. It was a grim and dangerous journey which left the party thrown on their own resources through 'a long dreary winter'. 'Ten men, one family, a clerk & myself' were 600 miles from the nearest HBC fort and source of provisions. They were 'shut in by barren mountains & surrounded by a host of Indians ... anything but amicably disposed towards us'.[22] They survived by eating *tripe de roche*, animal skins and parchment. A Nahanni female chief came to their rescue, not only bringing food but keeping her rebellious warriors under control, on one occasion quelling hostilities by approaching the ringleader: 'stamping her foot ... [she] repeatedly spat in his face, her eyes blazing with anger. Peace and quiet reigned as suddenly as the outbreak had blazed forth.'[23] She was, Campbell commented, 'truly a born leader'. (Campbell was also impressed by her pale complexion and tidy appearance.) The cause of the unrest was, in her words recorded by Campbell, that 'White people had made the country stink with our presence so that all the game had fled and left them to starve.'[24] Before leaving Dease Lake in the spring provisions ran short again, and their last meal before departure was a glue-like 'savoury dish' of parchment and snowshoes now surplus to requirements.[25]

With the signing in 1839 of an agreement with the Russians which allowed HBC access to Alaska (purchased by the United States in 1868), Simpson was determined to continue his empire's expansion. Campbell continued his explorations north into the Yukon, naming Frances Lake in honour of Simpson's wife, and reaching the Pelly River. He took possession of land in the HBC's name, carving the letters 'HBC' on a tree and flying the company ensign. He was rewarded by a letter of approbation from Simpson, who wrote that his exertions were 'exceedingly creditable to you'.[26] But there was no material support forthcoming. Campbell complained at 'the meagre means at my disposal' for setting up a post on the Pelly River.[27] When in 1848 a fire destroyed part of the new post and two men died of starvation he was understandably angered when supplies from Fort Simpson failed to arrive. The boats bringing them had turned back on 'some paltry excuse'.[28]

Campbell's explorations continued and in 1843 he made his way down the Pelly River to its confluence with the Yukon, where later Fort Selkirk was established and he was promoted to Chief Trader. But the area was less productive than Campbell had hoped, and his time at Fort Selkirk was problematic. Communications were hazardous and unreliable, and there were many more occasions when Campbell felt let down by the lack of vital supplies. Although, like all the most notable HBC employees, he demanded extraordinary effort of himself, he was not adept at attending to the details of everyday management, something which aggravated the fearsomely efficient Simpson as well as other employees. In 1852, Fort Selkirk was destroyed in a Chilkat attack, and Simpson refused to sanction its rebuilding. After a period of leave in the United Kingdom, Campbell had further assignments in the Mackenzie River district and Athabasca, but although promoted to Chief Factor he was regarded as something of a maverick. There was no room in the Hudson's Bay Company for someone who was not a team player, and in 1871 he was dismissed. He spent his last years ranching in Manitoba.

The attempt to exploit the Yukon was not a success for the fur trade, yet Campbell had taken the first steps towards opening up that part of the northwest, and was highly thought of by some. 'A natural leader of men,' was the verdict of David Bryce, a 'tall commanding figure' with a 'shrewd and adaptable manner'.[29] But in a sense, like Alexander Mackenzie and Simon Fraser, he had been defeated by the wilderness, or at least defeated by the imperatives of the fur trade's exploitation of the wilderness.

GOLD AND COAL: 'IT TAKES A HOLD OF YOU'

Wilderness also defeated many of the thousands who poured west and north in pursuit of gold. Of those who in 1849 headed for California's Sacramento River few would make their fortunes, and many would give up after months or years of profitless labour. Robert Stuart, son of a Scottish immigrant, made the gruelling 2,000 mile trek from Iowa to spend two years prospecting in the Sierras with little success. He returned home, and set out again with his two teenage sons, Granville and James. They found that 'On all the streams in all the gulches and high up in the Sierras to the north, clear to the Oregon line every little camp was crowded with miners and gold was being taken out in such profusion as almost to believe that there would be over-production.'[30] By 1852 the population of California had increased fifteenfold, while San Francisco, the territory's main city, was drained of men. With each new discovery of gold and silver the mining camps shifted, imposing their own anarchic versions of exploitation. The prospectors sluiced and dug and scrabbled for nuggets and gold dust, while a vast array of predatory camp-followers gathered to supply their recreational needs. Bars, gambling halls and brothels sprang up, alongside the entrepreneurs who brought supplies and equipment to sell at inflated prices. Among these motley populations Scottish names were to be found in almost every role. In George

MacDonald Fraser's *Flashman and the Redskins*, his hero is caught up in the California gold rush. He encounters 'bearded ruffians in greasy buckskins bright with beadwork, two-foot Bowies gleaming on their hips, chattering through their noses in a language which I recognised to my amazement as Scottish Gaelic'.[31]

James Thomson from Aberdeenshire was a modest success. After two years in Nevada City working in the lumber business he bought a claim for US$1,000 which yielded a reasonable living. But it was not sustainable, and he returned to his original trade as a baker. Granville and James Stuart spent some years prospecting in California, Idaho and Oregon, before deciding that they could do better supplying the mining camps with oxen and horses. Eventually they opened a store in Virginia City, Montana, which by the early 1860s was a locus of gold mania. Between 1863 and 1866, US$30 million in gold were stripped out of nearby Alder Gulch. In 1865, alongside the other mining camp amenities, the community boasted both Presbyterian and Episcopalian congregations, which suggests a significant Scottish and Ulster Scottish population.

In 1856, James Houston from Dunfermline jumped ship in Puget Sound when he heard of a gold strike on the Columbia River. After adventures which included receiving two arrows in his back during an Indian attack, he made his way north and in 1857 discovered gold near Fort Kamloops on the Fraser River. Thousands of the disappointed in California headed north by sea, while others made the overland journey from the east. It is estimated that around 30,000 prospectors flooded into New Caledonia. The story was repeated forty years later with the discovery of gold in the Yukon. In both cases attempts were made to bring some kind of order to the stampede. James Douglas, part-Scottish, Glasgow-educated and governor of New Caledonia at the time of the Fraser River strike, constructed town sites and roads and insisted that First Nations rights should be respected. When in 1862 gold was discovered in the Cariboo Mountains further north, Douglas built the Cariboo Road to facilitate communications. When the Yukon gold rush erupted it was the Canadian Government that insisted that all those entering the Yukon should carry a minimal amount of supplies, illustrated in the well-known photographs of heavily burdened prospectors toiling up the Chilkoot Pass and in the verse of Robert Service:

> We landed in wind-swept Skagway. We joined the weltering mass,
> Clamoring over their outfits, waiting to climb the Pass.
> We tightened our girths and our pack-straps; we linked on the
>   Human Chain,
> Struggling up to the summit, where every step was a pain.[32]

Service, who grew up in Kilwinning and Glasgow, left for North America in

1895 at the age of twenty-one. Nine years of wandering brought him to Whitehorse in the Yukon, where he was employed as a bank clerk. Whitehorse had sprung into existence in 1897 as a mining camp and its character, and that of Dawson City where Service lived later, inspired his Yukon poems and ballads, in which he vividly caught the frenzy of the gold rush.

> Gold! We leapt from our benches. Gold! We sprang from our stools.
> Gold! We wheeled in the furrow, fired with the faith of fools.
> Fearless, unfound, unfitted, far from the night and the cold,
> Heard we the clarion summons, followed the master-lure – Gold![33]

The gold rushes were stampedes of individuals prepared to endure extreme hardship in pursuit of riches, followed by secondary stampedes of those who sought to benefit, directly or indirectly, from their labour. Landscapes were deeply scarred and men, women and children succumbed to every level of exploitation. But although millions of dollars were dug out of mountainsides and sluiced from riverbeds, this did not compare with the large-scale mining activities that inevitably followed. In the 1870s, gold, silver and copper were beginning to be mined on an industrial scale, and this attracted manpower, money and expertise from Scotland. There was substantial Scottish investment in mines in California, Colorado, New Mexico, Arizona, Utah, Idaho, Montana and South Dakota. Historian Turrentine Jackson identified thirty-seven mining companies registered in Scotland and operating in the American West. But although the Scottish exploitation of North American mineral wealth was very considerable, the financial returns were disappointing. Scottish shareholders, mainly based in Glasgow, with little concept of the environment where their hoped-for source of wealth was located, lost significant amounts of money.

By the end of the eighteenth century coal had been discovered and with the development of steam shipping it became an important fuel. Scots had been mining coal for many centuries, in Fife and the central belt; readily available coal was transforming Scotland into one of Europe's foremost industrial nations. Scots were prominent in initiating and developing coal mining in both the United States and Canada, both as managers and as miners. Edward Mortimer was one of them, following the lead of the first man to obtain a licence to mine coal in Pictou County, John McKay. In Cape Breton's Glace Bay area coal had been mined by the French since before the end of the seventeenth century, and used to supply their base at Louisburg. In the nineteenth century, large numbers of Scots became involved in Cape Breton coal extraction, some recruited directly to work in the mines, others turning to employment as colliers when the struggle to maintain their homesteads became too much.

Sheldon Currie's novel *The Glace Bay Miners' Museum* (1995), is set in the twentieth century, but the movement it describes from homesteading to employment in the mines was a pattern set much earlier. Currie's story centres on a Scottish mining community transplanted from Mabou on Cape Breton's west coast to Glace Bay in the east. By leaving the land, which however hard to work was theirs, they lose their independence and become thirled to an existence where they perform dangerous work for meagre wages. It is much harder to maintain their Scottish traditions, including the Gaelic language, when they lose connection with the land and the aspirations that took them across the Atlantic. James MacKinnon, principal of Glace Bay High School, lamented the movement from farming to the mines:

> Oh, isn't it a shame for a healthy Gael living in this place to be a slave from Monday to Saturday under the heels of tyrants, when he could be happy on a handsome spreading farm with milk-cows, white sheep, hens, horses, and perhaps a car, and clean work on the surface of the earth, rather than in the black pit of misery.[34]

Just as in Scotland industrial development clustered around the sources of coal, the Glace Bay and Sydney area of Cape Breton became a focus of industrialisation. By the end of the nineteenth century, Sydney was a busy port with rail connections. Shipbuilding flourished, and in 1900 a steel plant was opened. The industrial exploitation of undeveloped territory brought its own kind of wilderness. In Alistair MacLeod's story 'The Vastness of the Dark' the young hero turns his back on 'this grimy Cape Breton coal-mining town whose prisoner I have been all my life'.[35] The mines are worn out, the houses blackened with smoke, and the view from his window is composed of 'slate-grey slag heaps and ruined skeletal mine tipples'.[36] His father and grandfather are both damaged and scarred from working underground, his father 'coughing and wheezing from the rock dust on his lungs'.[37]

It is 1960. James's family have been working in the mines since 1873, and now on his eighteenth birthday the only option is to work in a bootleg mine with no safety regulations, or to leave. His grandfather explains the grip of coal mining: 'Once you start, it takes a hold of you. Once you drink underground water, you will always come back to drink some more. The water gets in your blood.'[38] But rat-infested narrow seams and the foul air do not take hold of James, who is on the road with his backpack hitching a ride west, shaking off his confined Cape Breton identity as he crosses the Strait of Canso onto the mainland. The beleaguered community James abandons echoes the townships left by his Scottish antecedents. In other stories MacLeod makes quite explicit analogies between departures from the Highlands and departures from Nova Scotia.

The close connection between Scottish and Canadian coal mining is even more striking in later developments on Vancouver Island. Robert Dunsmuir was the son and grandson of Kilmarnock coal-masters who in 1851, twenty-six years old and with a wife and three children, began work at the HBC coal mine at Fort Rupert (now Port Hardy). It was a dispiriting situation, as the coal was of poor quality and production poor. The Hudson's Bay Company shifted their interest to Nanaimo, but eventually sold out to the Vancouver Coal Mining and Land Company, who employed Dunsmuir as a supervisor. In the 1860s, he began operating clandestinely, looking for coal seams which he could develop independently. He discovered a particularly rich coal measure, the Wellington Seam, which gave him his opportunity. By the late 1870s he was managing a highly successful coal mine, responding to the demand for coal by steam ships, industry and railways – he was responsible for constructing Vancouver Island's railway, which opened in 1886. He was an astute, innovative and tough operator, quick to introduce the latest technology, and also to employ Chinese labour in his mines at less than half the wages demanded by white workers. Dunsmuir built on his Scottish coal-mining legacy and his early experience to create the largest mining enterprise in British Columbia within twenty years or so of Vancouver Island being opened up for settlement. As in so many areas of wilderness, the fur trade had led the way, but its heyday was over.

Dunsmuir was one of the generation of Scottish pioneers who in the second half of the nineteenth century helped to transform Canada into a modern industrial nation, and like others he achieved this by exploiting both land and people: 'His hands were upon the mines, the forests, the railways, and the steamships of Vancouver Island.'[39] Remote terrain, problematic communications and minimal civic infrastructure ensured that there were few barriers to taking advantage of both. At the same time, communications and infrastructure were vital to industrial development and to settlement, and both required the building of a transcontinental railway. The Canadian Pacific Railway would become an icon of the conquest of the wilderness, and it was largely devised and impelled by Scots.

RAILWAYS: PATHFINDERS AND PIONEERS

In 1845, brothers David and Sandford Fleming and their cousin Henry Fleming left their home in Kirkcaldy, Fife, to set off on a memorable ten-week journey across the Atlantic and on to Peterborough near Lake Ontario. The journey, which took them through many areas of Scottish settlement, highlighted both the advances and difficulties of travel in a developing country. The paddle steamer that took them upriver from Quebec was making her maiden voyage; she was so wide the paddle boxes had to be removed to allow her through the locks. Without paddles, the steamer had to be hauled upriver to

Montreal, from where the Flemings took a river barge up the Ottawa River to Bytown (later Ottawa). The next stage of their journey took them south to Kingston, then west on a corduroy road to Peterborough. In the 1840s railways were being talked of and planned, but none had been built. The next decade would see an explosion of railway activity.

Eighteen years after arriving in Ontario, engineer and surveyor Sandford Fleming had worked on the Ontario, Simcoe and Huron Railroad, constructed to link Toronto and Georgian Bay on Lake Huron, and had become the Province of Canada's Chief Surveyor. In these years leading up to Confederation in 1867 railways were a dominant issue. It was recognised that without such connections the Dominion of Canada was politically and commercially fragmented – no longer could government or trade depend on the intrepid activities of individuals canoeing and tramping through the wilderness. But this did not deter an unleashing of contention over routes, practicality and funding.

In 1867, the newly constituted Dominion Government appointed Sandford Fleming as Engineer-in-Chief for the Intercolonial Railway, linking Toronto and the Maritimes. It was completed in 1876, by which time Fleming was working on Canada's most challenging railway project, the construction of a transcontinental track to connect the Atlantic and Pacific coasts. Much was at stake. British Columbia would join the confederation only if such a link were built, and the prairie provinces would look south to the United States if there were not good communications with the east. The first task was to complete a survey that would require traversing some of North America's most problematic territory.

There had been earlier surveys. In 1858, Irishman John Palliser led an expedition to explore possible routes through the Rockies. With him was James Hector, a young Edinburgh-born surgeon and geologist whose unfortunate accident with a horse led to the naming of the pass which eventually became the Canadian Pacific's route through the mountains. Hector was kicked by a horse and assumed dead, but just as he was about to be lowered into a newly dug grave he was found to be alive. The pass was named Kicking Horse. The survey took three years and involved negotiating formidable terrain, travelling hundreds of miles on snowshoes, and on occasion running out of food. That such hazards came as no surprise made them no less demanding. Ten years later Fleming's remit was to organise a survey of the whole route from the Ottawa valley to the Pacific coast. The challenge of the Rockies was daunting, but perhaps even greater were the difficulties posed by carving a way through the solid rock and muskeg swamps north of Lake Superior.

In 1872, Fleming and his party set off to check the progress of the survey. It was a journey of over 5,000 miles which took him through every feature of Canadian wilderness to Burrard Inlet on the west coast. With him was George Grant, the son of Banffshire parents, born in 1835 in a Pictou County community of Gaelic-speaking Highlanders. Brought up a Presbyterian, Grant studied for the ministry at the University of Glasgow. He was a brilliant student, and during his time in Glasgow was exposed to ideas that fostered in him a more liberal and less confined Calvinism than that which had dominated his childhood. His work for a mission in Glasgow's slums brought him into contact with an environment very different from that of pioneering Nova Scotia.

Grant returned to Nova Scotia in 1861, and two years later became minister at St Matthew's Church in Halifax. An extraordinarily energetic man, he was active in numerous social and educational causes, and in his sermons stressed the importance of social responsibility. Among his congregation was Sandford Fleming, by that time based in Halifax. Although wide-ranging in his interests and certainly tough in character – he had several close encounters with death – Grant was a curious choice to accompany Fleming's expedition. Yet he embraced the opportunity and wrote about the experience in his book *Ocean to Ocean* (1873), which communicated to a wide audience his enthusiastic response to the landscapes and possibilities he encountered. As a promoter of settlement in the prairies, always highlighting their advantages over the plains to the south, and of the railway as a vital tool he was an enormous asset to the Canadian Pacific Railway (CPR) project as well as to the young Canadian Government.

Fleming and Grant had never been west. Their first sight of the prairie offered a luscious prospect of green grass studded with wild flowers. John Macoun, an Irish professor of natural history who had been recruited en route, revelled in the identification of new species. Here was a brightly coloured and apparently benign wilderness which promised fertility and the successful raising of a variety of crops. The limited number who had already settled in Manitoba were doing well, Grant reported. Two recent Scottish settlers would in five years, he predicted, have ploughed and planted 300 or 400 acres. He relished the prospect of 'boundless seas of rich land' worked by steam ploughs and reaping, mowing and threshing machines.[40] The soil was potentially a great source of wealth, but 'untilled soil is valueless'. Each emigrant prepared to plough up the prairie, which could be done without the labour of felling trees, grubbing up stumps, burning and levelling, 'represented the addition of hundreds of dollars to the wealth of the country'.[41]

After a stop at the Red River residence of Donald Smith, who would become synonymous with the Canadian Pacific Railway, they proceeded with a fleet of Red River carts to Edmonton. The carts, built entirely of wood with enormous wheels up to 7-ft diameter, were ungainly and noisy vehicles – the squealing wheels could be heard for miles – but were well adapted for the terrain they had to cover, 'the right thing in the right place' in Grant's words.[42] It was a 900-mile journey to Edmonton, with little respite. They were up most mornings at 3 am and often on the move until 9 or 10 at night, when setting up camp demanded more intense activity: 'At the halting places meals have to be cooked, baggage arranged and rearranged, horses looked to, harness mended, clothes washed or dried, observations and notes taken, specimens collected, and everything kept neat and trim; rest is therefore impossible.'[43]

There was a strong sense of united purpose. At several points Grant stressed the importance of Sunday, both as a day of rest and as a reminder of the need for both mutual and divine support. The men gathered for worship, 'praying His mercy for our far away homes, and drawn to one another by the thought that we were in the wilderness, with common needs, and entirely dependent on God and each other'.[44] If pragmatism was the order of other days, with a necessary focus on the tasks in hand, the weekly pause in their travels was also a pause for reflection. Grant was, of course, a minister, but was far from being the only Scot for whom wilderness concentrated spirituality as well as fortitude and practical skill. Sunday was also a day for pudding, improvised from pemmican, flour, water, baking soda and sugar, and relished as much as spiritual refreshment.

At Edmonton the party split. Fleming and Grant headed roughly due west through the Yellowhead Pass to the North Thompson River and on to the Fraser, which they followed to the coast. The second party took a route along Pine River, a tributary of the Peace which had been an important highway for Alexander Mackenzie and Simon Fraser. The goal had moved on from the years when a river route to the Pacific was of paramount concern. What was being sought now was a means of laying track across every kind of hostile terrain which would carry large quantities of people and goods over thousands of miles.

They followed the McLeod and Athabasca rivers into the mountains to Jasper House and on to the Yellowhead Pass, which Fleming was convinced would be the railway's route through the Rockies. He was unhappy at the slow progress of the surveys and critical of Walter Moberly, the man in charge on the ground, who vehemently differed in his views on the best route. Grant says nothing about what was a bitter disagreement, but emphasises the impediments to their progress. They negotiate mountain precipices, flounder through 'foul smelling marsh mud', clamber over stumps and fallen trees.[45] Food is short and the horses exhausted, but when Moberly arrives with supplies spirits revive: 'All the hardships of the afternoon were forgotten as the aroma of coffee steamed up our nostrils.'[46] Fresh bread, crisp bacon and porridge for breakfast set them up for the onward journey, and when they reach the Yellowhead they found 'a pleasant open meadow'.[47]

In the wilderness food is hugely important and more than a necessity for life. It was possible to keep going on a frugal and unvaried diet, but most accounts of wilderness travel highlight the effect on morale of good food. Some days later, having crossed the Thompson River and surrounded by formidable mountains and 'melancholy woods', they come on a cache of supplies left for them – canned meat, peaches, jam, Bass pale ale, bottles of claret – which they fall on with delight.[48] But here, too, they meet a solitary prospector heading for the Cariboo Mountains where gold was discovered in 1862. John Glen (probably a Scot), on foot and leading his two pack horses, was a 'martyr for gold' undeterred by hardship and loneliness:

> Nothing to him was lack of company or of newspapers, short days and approach of winter; seas of mountains and grassless valleys, equally inhospitable; risk of sickness and certainty of storms; slow and exhausting travel through marsh and muskeg, across roaring mountain torrents and miles of fallen timber; lonely days and lonely nights; – if he found gold he would be repaid.

Grant's godliness does not prevent him from admiring this 'modern missionary … advance guard of the army of material progress'. 'Who will deny', he went on, 'his virtue, his faith, such as it was? His self-reliance was sublime.'[49]

The railway surveyors were also part of the advance guard. The message of the railway builders, echoed by Grant, was the need for good communications to make possible settlement and the exploitation of the land's resources. The political context of the message had changed since the days of Mackenzie and Fraser, and the fur trade was no longer the heartbeat of exploration, but the wilderness and the impulsion to conquer it remained. Fleming's party reached Kamloops and carried on down the Fraser River. At the end of the line, Grant predicted, there would be a great railway terminus where 'the products of Australia and Polynesia, as well as of China and Japan' would converge. The railway link from the St Lawrence to the Pacific 'through a succession of loyal Provinces bound up with the Empire by ever-multiplying and tightening links' would secure 'the future of the Fatherland and of the Great Empire of which she will then be only the chief part'.[50] Canada's wilderness had already served the Empire well. It would now be transformed into a vital highway of progress, and would ensure that the exploitation of that wilderness continued.

The railway's conquest of harsh terrain did not come cheap, and the entire enterprise was fraught with political controversy and prevarication. While the manoeuvring and haggling were going on, Fleming's survey made slow and painful progress. The task was colossal, and it was difficult to recruit men of sufficient skill and calibre to carry it out: 'hundreds of men were freezing, starving, sickening and sometimes dying in the unexplored crannies of the new Canada, as they tried to chart a route for the railway'.[51] A century after the great journeys of Mackenzie and Fraser, there were still vast tracts of Canada where no white man had set foot, and the routes that were useful to the fur trade were not necessarily amenable to steam locomotion. It was unremittingly hard work in often appalling conditions. Pathfinders blazed a potential route, axemen cleared it, surveyors calculated distances and altitudes which were marked at half-mile intervals. Every aspect of the terrain that would affect track and steam was taken into account.

Scots had already for several decades played leading roles in railroad construction in the United States. In both countries the railways were statements of human achievement as well as communication links without which such vast territories were impossible to govern. If the construction of the US transcontinental railroad was a challenge, the construction of the CPR was a triumph, and not just of engineering. Both ventures involved conflicting interests and labyrinthine negotiations. Both were highly political and demanded huge investment of cash and resources. But in Canada both the distances and the equivocating were greater. The Dominion's first prime minister, John Macdonald, supported the railway; his successor, Alexander Mackenzie, who came to power in 1873 when survey work was well under way, thought it madness. It stalled and struggled, until nine years after Fleming's first transcontinental journey, a syndicate of Scots came together and rescued it.

Richard Bladworth Angus, from Bathgate in West Lothian, had emigrated to Montreal in 1857 where he was employed as a clerk by the Bank of Montreal. He worked his way up to general manager. In the same year, John S. Kennedy, from Blantyre in Lanarkshire settled in the United States to embark on a highly successful career in banking and railroad construction. He worked closely with James Jerome Hill, Canadian-born of Scottish and Irish parents, whose railroad building career had started in St Paul, Minnesota and developed into a messianic commitment to the railroad as 'pathfinder and pioneer'.[52] Duncan McIntyre had left Renfrew in 1849 to join his uncle's dry goods business in Montreal. In 1864, he became president of the expanding firm. He began to invest in railways, and joined the board of the Canada Central Railway (CCR) of which he was soon president. When he joined the syndicate he brought the CCR with him. Sir Stafford Northcote was the only English member of the syndicate. He had a high-profile career in British politics, and was briefly governor of the Hudson's Bay Company. The final member of the syndicate was George Stephen, who had grown up in Craigellachie on the River Spey, which he left at the age of twenty-one to go to Montreal. Like McIntyre he began his Canadian working life in a relative's store, this time his cousin's drapery business. By the 1870s he was a highly successful businessman and banker, becoming president of the Bank of Montreal in 1876.

Backing the syndicate was Donald Smith from Forres, George Stephen's cousin, who had arrived in Canada in 1838. After many years of service with the Hudson's Bay Company, much of it spent in Labrador where he had to adapt to severe isolation as well as to severe conditions, Smith had eventually become a director of the HBC at a time when its dominance was declining. Although his background was similar to his cousin's, their routes to prominence differed. Of all the syndicate, Donald Smith was the only member who had direct experience of the wilderness, its demands and its impact. In 1869, he had to deal with an episode which highlighted the fact that western Canada remained untamed, but for which his years in Labrador and Montreal were scarcely a preparation. The Hudson's Bay Company surrendered its rights to Rupert's Land and the Northwest Territories, and transfer to Canadian jurisdiction was agreed. William McDougall, a Canadian-born lawyer and politician of Scottish descent, was appointed lieutenant-governor and on 30 October 1869 arrived at the North Dakota border intending formally to annex Rupert's Land. He was not expecting to meet resistance – he had his four young children with him as he had recently lost his wife – and was shocked to encounter Red River Métis led by Louis Riel, who prevented his entry. The Métis feared that the transfer would open the gates to white settlement and threaten their survival. McDougall failed to reassure them and was forced to retreat and look to the HBC to restore order. The task fell to Donald Smith.

Louis Riel and the Métis had taken over Fort Garry, where they held several prisoners, and now controlled Red River. Smith was dispatched west. His journey, almost as problematic at this time as it had been for the first Red River settlers, highlighted the need for good communications to pull the country together, and brought him face to face with some of the difficulties that would be encountered in achieving them. While Smith negotiated with Riel, assuring him that Métis land grants would be confirmed and promising consultation, troops were making their way to Red River to force Riel's surrender and release his prisoners. They were no match for Riel's men, who rapidly brought them to a halt and in the process took more prisoners. Smith interceded on the prisoners' behalf, but although most were freed he was not able to prevent the execution of their commanding officer. Riel retreated into exile in the United States, but it was not the end of his role in the story of the Canadian Pacific Railway.

It was a formidable group of men that created the CPR and pushed the railway through to completion in the face of towering physical, political and financial impediments. The construction of the railway encountered much more than forests, swamps, chasms, torrential rivers and mountains. There was much personal and political resistance to be overcome, resistance that was partly the result of a belief that the Canadian wilderness was just too daunting and difficult for such a project. And also too expensive. Over and over again it seemed that money would run out, and over and over again huge efforts of personal commitment and personal funds, especially on the part of Stephen and Smith, were required to keep it all going.

Also required were armies of men: Irish, English, Americans, Scandinavians, French Canadians, First Nations, Métis, Chinese, and, of course, Scots. The work of laying track was grim; the effort of controlling hundreds of men whose main recreations were consuming illegally traded alcohol and gambling was also relentless. Discipline was vital, but the task of bringing order to the inchoate camps that followed the railhead and imposed their own very human wildness on the wilderness was almost impossible. In spite of this the law prevailed enough to ensure the work marched on. The engineer in charge of constructing the stretch west of Winnipeg was James Ross, son of a Cromarty sea captain.

Meanwhile, Louis Riel had returned to Red River to lead increasingly disaffected Métis in a last effort to reclaim land they considered their own. In March 1885, Riel's rebellious Métis defeated Northwest Mounted Police near Fort Carlton. Two months later they were overcome by troops whose rapid response had been made possible by the railway's arrival at Winnipeg the previous month. For the CPR it was in the nick of time. A desperate final appeal for more government funds had been turned down; thanks to Riel there was a change of heart. It was recognised that the railway was a vital tool for the control of the prairies and the far west, and additional funds were voted through. Six months later, in Eagle Pass that cuts through the Gold Range of the Monashee Mountains, a small white-bearded, top-hatted gentleman hammered in the last spike of the Canadian Pacific Railway. The gentleman was Donald Smith and the place Craigellachie, named for the Speyside village where George Stephen had grown up. A week after the Atlantic and Pacific coasts were united, Louis Riel was convicted and hanged.

The men, dark-coated among the pines, who gathered to witness Smith's conclusive action were captured in a photograph. Sandford Fleming stands behind the hammer-wielding Donald Smith, two inexpressive white-bearded Scots as emblems of the incomparable Scottish contribution not only to the railway itself, but to the decades of endeavour that lay behind its conception. Smith's direct association with the Hudson's Bay Company was a reminder of the fur trade's extraordinary role in spearheading exploitation of Rupert's Land and New Caledonia. The railway builders had harnessed the spirit of the fur traders. The trade itself was in decline, but the railway opened new possibilities for exploiting the land, possibilities for which the people and settlement the fur trade had for so long resisted were essential.

Scottish railway-building activities did not slacken. Across the border in the

United States, J. J. Hill was determined to complete a transcontinental route through the northern states, and Kennedy, Smith and Stephen all backed the project. Hill displayed his characteristic blend of ambition and pragmatism: 'What we want is the best possible line, shortest distance, lowest grades and least curvature that we can build. We do not care enough for Rocky Mountain scenery to spend a large sum of money developing it.'[53] Impelled by competition with the Northern Pacific, which ran further south, he set bold targets. 'We must build 783 miles of track next summer in eight months from the present end of track in Montana to insure our position of advantage,' he wrote to Kennedy in October 1886.[54] There was no easy way through the Rockies, but a route was found across the Continental Divide through Marias Pass in the Lewis Range. Tunnels were blasted, bridges built, trestles constructed across chasms and embankments built up on precipitous mountainsides. Progress was beset by flash floods, blizzards and intense cold, but Hill drove the work on, unrelenting in the demands he made of himself and the men who worked for him. As the railhead progressed new communities were founded, including Glasgow on the Milk River. At Scenic, at the western entrance to a tunnel through the Cascades, the last spike was driven on 6 January 1890.

The railroad was intended to bring people and prosperity to Montana, and Hill was unflagging in his efforts to promote both the railroad and agricultural potential. He directly involved himself in improving cattle breeds and shipped beasts from Scotland, believing that hardy breeds such as Aberdeen Angus would do well in the northern states. But, in fact, the desired great leap forward never materialised. Although there were industrial developments, iron smelting at Great Falls, for example, people did not flood into Montana. Hill's claim that 'immigration and industry have transformed a wilderness in half a century into the home of plenty' proved premature.[55]

CATTLE AND GRAIN: 'AN OCEAN OF SURGING GRASS'

When George Grant was travelling through the prairies he commented frequently on their fertility and potential for farming. Further south, the perception of the plains, long regarded as unproductive wasteland, was changing. The westward movement of settlement was accelerated by the railroad, which also encouraged the growth of communities along the way. In both Canada and the United States, the railways had massive land grants which they had to populate, both to recover funds by selling on the land and to ensure commercial viability. The railway was opening up new territory, beckoning on the settler, creating new possibilities for industry. It introduced thousands to the experience of making something of untamed country.

Many brought with them their own wildness, as thousands exploited the potential of a large isolated workforce in an environment of limited law enforcement.

Emigrants from all over Europe were caught up in the contradictions implied by the need to tame the land and make it productive. The Scottish experience mingles with that of Scandinavians and Germans, Ukrainians and Poles, Irish, English and Welsh. Robert Louis Stevenson described the polyglot nature of his fellow passengers sailing from the Clyde in 1878. They were leaving from Scotland, but they came mainly from other parts of northern Europe. The Scots, however, made a distinctive impression on this phase of settlement, particularly in Canada where many farmed in the prairie provinces. Some had come directly from Scotland; others moved on from eastern Canada, particularly the Maritimes.

The cultivation of the prairies focused on wheat production. By the 1870s Manitoba was the source of more wheat than furs. In 1880, W. Fraser Rae commented on the scale of arable production. 'The arrangements', he wrote, 'are designed to assimilate the production of grain to the operations of a manufactory ... the farmer is a capitalist; the farm-labourer is called a "hand" and treated as one.'[56] On his Red River farm William Dalrymple was planting 30,000 acres of wheat and harvesting 1,000 acres a day with a fleet of seventy-five reaping and binding machines and 450 labourers. By the turn of the century the once near-empty prairie was experiencing 'headlong occupation and exploitation' as people and machines poured in to respond to an increasing world demand for grain.[57] In 1905, Saskatchewan and Alberta joined the Canadian Confederation; Manitoba had joined thirty-five years before.

Across the border from Saskatchewan and Alberta lay North Dakota and Montana, with Wyoming to the south. For decades Wyoming had been a territory of transit, penetrated first by the fur traders, then crossed by the overlanders on their way to the far side of the Rockies. It was arid, sage brush-studded grassland with intermittent supplies of water, good for buffalo but with little to offer the prospective farmer. In the 1870s Wyoming became the focus of intensive Scottish interest and involvement.

Much further south, in Texas, Scots were making a distinctive imprint on cattle ranching. Thousands of acres of seemingly empty land were being transformed into cattle ranges, as the post-Civil War demand for beef took off and the spreading railroad network made it possible for that demand to be met. The cattle were driven to the railheads and shipped to Chicago, the centre of the meat trade. Of the many Scottish-owned and Scottish-managed cattle ranches in Texas, the most prominent was the Matador Land and Cattle Company, financed by Scottish money, registered in Dundee, and managed initially by Henry Campbell. In 1891, management was taken over by Murdo Mackenzie from Tain in Ross-shire, described by one historian as 'probably the greatest of all ranch managers'.[58]

Men like Mackenzie had to contend with many levels of wildness. Although for a while there seemed to be limitless grass with minimal restriction on grazing rights – Campbell was running 60,000 head of cattle on 30,000 Texas Panhandle acres – the business of ranching was not straightforward. A dry summer could eliminate an essential water source, and a hard winter could decimate a herd. As the pressures of settlement grew, the open range was fiercely fought over. The annual round-ups and cattle drives were gruelling and sometimes dangerous: floods, stampedes, tainted water, Indian attacks could kill beasts and men. Not all Scottish attempts to overcome these difficulties were successful. Robert Cunninghame Graham, later well known as an author and a politician, in 1880 tried his hand at ranching in southern Texas but was forced to abandon the project after his ranch was attacked by Apaches and all his stock stolen.

Like the fur trade, the raising of cattle needed men who were tough and independent, who could work long hours in a hostile environment and deal resourcefully with emergencies. Scotland had a long tradition of driving cattle through rough country, and also of shepherding, and there were numerous Scots among cowboys and sheep herders. But the independence and resourcefulness could be problematic. Very often those most suited to the demanding and often lonely life a long way from home comforts were the least adaptable to discipline and regulation. Some ranches, such as the Scottish-owned Spur, made determined efforts to control the wilder behaviour – drinking, gambling and gun-toting – of the cowhands: 'the cowboy who actually handled cattle very quickly came to feel the hand of authority governing his daily routine and morals, and his only escape lay in joining forces with the renegades who lived a precarious and often very short existence'.[59] There were Scots among those who joined the renegades, and also among those who took advantage of distance and ignorance to cheat ranch owners back in Scotland. The Rocking Horse Ranch baffled Lord Aberdeen and Lord Tweedmouth, principal shareholders who visited the ranch to try to establish why it was losing hundreds of head of cattle. They failed to spot the sleight of hand by which the manager was counting the same herd several times over. This was a not uncommon means of inflating the count and fooled some Scottish buyers into thinking they were getting a good deal. It was yet another tier of exploitation.

By the late 1870s tales of free grazing in Wyoming and Montana were attracting the interest of ranchers and investors, and Scots and Scottish money began to flow in that direction. Large herds of cattle were driven north from Texas, where increasingly the range was being fenced, on a 2,000-mile journey to the open ranges of Wyoming and the richer grasslands of

Montana. Larry McMurtry's epic novel *Lonesome Dove* (1985) chronicles just such a trek north, from southern Texas to the Milk River near the Canadian border. His two heroes, Augustus McCrae with a Scottish name and Scottish-born Woodrow Call, crave more than free grass for their cows. They want unsettled country. At first Gus is dubious and reckons that Montana 'sounds like a goddam wilderness'. He is ready for a degree of civilisation: 'I don't have to have oprys and streetcars, but I do enjoy a decent bed and a roof to keep out the weather.'[60] But later he succumbs to the magnetic pull of unsettled country: 'I'd like to see one more place that ain't settled before I get decrepit and have to take up the rocking chair.'[61] It is not a compulsion to exploit the wilderness that drives Call and McCrae, but a longing for unpressured solitude, without the limits imposed by commercial enterprise as much as settlement, and represented by banks and stores as much as churches and schools. But they recognise that their journey north will result in an erosion of its purpose, just as the mountain men understood that the wagon trains signalled the end of what they valued in the wild country they considered their own. And Gus McCrae does not live to get decrepit: the wilderness, the wildness it nourishes and his own cussedness destroy him.

The potential of grass is expressed in the words of John Clay, the son of a well-to-do tenant farmer in the Scottish Borders who settled in Wyoming. He describes riding through the area around the Belle Fourche River, in South Dakota just east of Wyoming.

> My mouth waters when I think of the feed in that region. The bottom lands of the Belle Fourche had grass three feet high, although it was November. It lay in great swaths amid the giant groves of cottonwoods, cured, as well as the best hay in a stack. The divides were an ocean of surging grass, cropped only by a few cattle and a countless number of antelope.[62]

Clay was accompanying an Edinburgh lawyer, Robert Pringle, who was representing a Scottish company interested in investment. Over the nightly campfires Pringle sang the traditional songs of Scotland, while the cowboys with them sang Texas ballads which themselves owed something to the ballad traditions of Clay's native Borders.

The expansion of cattle ranching in Wyoming and Montana, in which Scots played a major role, is another illustration of the multi-stranded character of exploitation. The attitude to the land itself was summed up by Granville Stuart. 'None of this land is surveyed and the only way of holding it is by occupying it,' he said of Montana's Judith River country which in 1879 he chose for his ranch.[63] It was still possible to assume that those who were prepared to make use of the land had a right to possess it, but such assumptions could lead to bitter and violent confrontations. In Wyoming, these confrontations came to a head with the Johnson County War of 1892, when large-scale ranchers attempted to obstruct the encroachment of more modest homesteaders.

The grasslands that made possible the beef bonanza of the 1870s and early 1880s had once been the territory of Plains Nations such as Sioux, Cheyenne, Pawnee and Crow, and of the vast herds of buffalo on which they depended. By the late 1870s there were few buffalo thanks to wholesale slaughter by whites for their skins, and most of the indigenous people were confined to reservations. Unlike the fur trade, cattle ranching did not directly exploit the native population, but their expendability was part of the exploitation process. They were an impediment to the drive to make commercial use of country that had once been thought of as inert and unproductive.

Scots were prominent among the big ranchers in Wyoming, and John Clay became a key player in the ranching fraternity. Ambitious and resourceful, he came to Wyoming by way of Canada, where he had family connections, and California. He soon found a role for himself helping Scottish investors to purchase Wyoming cattle ranches, which demanded a sharp eye and a level head. His handling of a ranch sale by John Stewart, an Ulster Scot, illustrates some of the problems. Stewart's ranch was purchased by the Edinburgh-based Wyoming Cattle Ranche Company, whose directors included Thomas Nelson the publisher and Archibald Coats of the very successful Paisley thread firm J. & P. Coats. The ranch on the banks of the Sweetwater extended for 4,000 square miles. The prospectus studied by the gentlemen in Edinburgh painted a dazzling picture of ideal cattle country, 'a pasturage relieved by the shelter of hill, bluff, and canon from winter storms, an extraordinary dryness of climate, which neutralized the cold of the severest seasons, and an abundance of rich standing grain-like hay (the grass cured by the long dry summer), throughout the entire winter months'.[64] The sale included 19,000 head of 'improved cattle'; Stewart was described as 'the most painstaking Breeder now in the Far West'. When the cattle count proved to be 4,000 head short John Clay was called in to investigate. When Clay confronted Stewart he got short shrift: 'The ingenious gentleman was rather proud evidently of having made such a smart trade.'[65] Eventually, the case went to court and after many months and several court hearings the Edinburgh company got about a third of the money they were owed.

John Stewart's ranch was sold to Scots in 1882. The beef bonanza was at its height, but would not last much longer. The savage winter of 1886/7 'almost cleared the country of cattle, and from this blow the ranchmen never recovered'.[66] The assumption that cattle needed minimal care to survive the winter out on the range was shattered. With ferocious blizzards blowing in from the north and vast acres of grass under deep snow the cattle starved or froze. And not only did the cattle freeze. James Mackenzie managed a sheep ranch on the Sweetwater River, where he employed as a shepherd a Northumbrian called Joe Arthur whom Clay had known in his youth. Joe had drifted into Wyoming after a life of wandering, which included a spell failing to make a go of things in the Canadian backwoods. Clay visited a neighbouring ranch on a bright February day:

> It was a long steady pull to the Divide. After it is reached you trot merrily down the hill, passing through Crook's Gap, and as you progress the valley of the Sweetwater opens gradually to your view. It was a glorious day, clear and bright. The valley was bathed in sunshine ... Down the valley, amid a forest of sagebrush, ran the sinuous Sweetwater, a streak of silver; high up were granite crags and rock-ribbed hills, the silent peaks turned by the sun's flashing rays into jewelled pillars.[67]

This was Wyoming's wilderness at its most stunning. The next morning saw a total transformation, a roaring blizzard that kept them indoors all day. When the storm subsided news reached them that Joe Arthur was missing. A search party found him in the snow, his faithful collie guarding his frozen body. In a scene reminiscent of the pathos of Greyfriars Bobby, the dog lingered by his owner's grave in Wild Horse Canyon. After several days he made his way to a trapper's cabin, but refused food and soon died.

John Clay, astute, ambitious, pragmatic and relentless in matters of business, his own and that of those he represented, relished Wyoming's wild country while not underestimating its harshness. In his memoir *My Life on the Range* (1924) Clay, who died in 1934 at the age of eighty-three, celebrates the coming to Wyoming of the fruits of civilisation – the railroad, the telegraph, the telephone, schools and churches, the comforts of the Cheyenne Club where he and his associates spent many convivial hours – while at the same time mourning the passing of the Old West. Like George Simpson, he presented himself as a sophisticated businessman who savoured the finer things in life at the same time as demonstrating his frontier toughness and wilderness skills. He had experienced directly a hostile terrain and the threat of Indian attack. He had ridden the range in every kind of weather and had tracked down rustlers and horse thieves. He had great respect for the skill and endurance of the cowboys who led an often lonely and sometimes dangerous life and, like his Montana associate Granville Stuart who also left a memoir, contributed to the heroic frontier myth which helped to disguise the cowhands' meagre rewards. Stuart and Clay both believed that it was the 'big outfits' that had transformed wilderness into productive land:

> [They] brought millions of capital into a sparsely settled country and their herds converted the million tons of grass that had for thousands of years

gone to waste into millions of dollars worth of beef. Their heavy taxes built roads and schools and did much for the advancement of civilisation.[68]

After the huge losses during the severe winters of the 1880s many cattle-men turned to sheep, and this brought another wave of Scots to Wyoming and Montana. Scottish hill farming was at least a partially adequate training for shepherding in the hills and mountains of the West, and Scottish shepherds and their dogs were well regarded, although ranchers who continued with cattle abhorred sheep. Among the late nineteenth-century influx was Peter Doig from near Dundee, who in 1893 left his home country at the age of nineteen to join a growing if scattered community of Scots, including members of his family who had gone before, in Montana's Big Belt Mountains south of Great Falls. In Scotland he had been a tailor's assistant; in Montana he worked on sheep farms. He met and married another Scot, Annie Campbell from Perthshire, and the two filed a claim for a quarter-section homestead hoping to manage a sheep ranch of their own. But a quarter-section, the 160 acres which were the standard land grant, nearly 6,000 ft up was quite a different proposition from the quarters on good well-watered land which earlier settlers claimed. Peter Doig's grandson described the problem:

> Homesteads of 160 acres, or even several times that size, made no sense in that vast and dry and belligerent landscape of the high-mountain west. As well try to grow an orchard in a window-box as to build a working ranch from such a patch.[69]

Peter built a pine-log house and they settled down to make a go of raising sheep and cattle – and children, six sons with names that 'began to resound like the roll-call of a kilted regiment'.[70] The work was hard and endless, and at night, high up on the mountain, they could hear the howl of wolves and coyotes. Then, at the age of thirty-six, Peter Doig collapsed with a heart attack and died. The boys had to take on their father's work and later to hire themselves out as ranch hands to bring money into the home. By 1919 they were clear of debt and their prospects were looking brighter. Then came the winter against which local people 'would measure all other winters'.[71] They desperately battled through blizzards and snow drifts to feed their stock with fodder for which they had to pay astronomical prices, but 'the animals died a little every day, until the carcasses began to make dark humps on the white desert of snow'.[72] By the spring they had lost most of their stock and all of their money.

For most of these Scottish mountain settlers, survival was a hand-to-mouth existence. Back in the 1860s gold had been found in the area, and Helena to the west was for a while a thriving mining town. The miners moved on, but the homesteaders clung to their inadequate patches of land, trying to force out of them more than they could realistically offer. In a sense, it was the settlers' own tenacity and refusal to accept defeat that was being exploited.

NOTES

1. 'Scotus Americanus', *Information Concerning the Province of North Carolina* (Edinburgh: James Knox and Charles Elliot, 1773), p. 19.
2. Mackay, *Scotland Farewell*, p. 245.
3. Donald Creighton, *The Story of Canada* (London: Faber, [1959] 1971), p. 113.
4. Allan McInnes, Marjory-Ann D. Harper and Linda G. Fryer, *Scotland and the Americas, c. 1650–c. 1939* (Edinburgh: Scottish History Society, 2002), p. 83.
5. Harold A. Innis, *The Fur Trade in Canada* (Toronto: University of Toronto Press, [1930] 1970), p. 379.
6. DeVoto, *Wide Missouri*, p. 5.
7. Washington Irving, *The Adventures of Captain Bonneville* (London: Bohn, 1850), pp. 2–3.
8. Ibid., p. 7.
9. Irving, *Astoria*, p. 10.
10. Ballantyne, *Hudson's Bay*, p. 75.
11. J. K. Galbraith, *The Little Emperor* (Toronto: Macmillan, 1976), p. 16.
12. Ibid., p. 32.
13. James Raffan, *Emperor of the North: Sir George Simpson and the Remarkable Story of the Hudson's Bay Company* (Toronto: HarperCollins, 2007), p. 113.
14. Ibid., p. 123.
15. Galbraith, *The Little Emperor*, p. 69.
16. Raffan, *Emperor of the North*, p. 231.
17. John McLean, *Notes of a Twenty-Five Year Service in the Hudson's Bay Territory* (London: Richard Bentley, 1844), p. 235.
18. Ibid., p. 334.
19. Lamb, Fraser, *Journals*, p. 250.
20. Robert Campbell, *Two Journals of Robert Campbell* (Seattle, WA: The Shorey Book Store, 1967), p. 8.
21. Ibid., p. 27.
22. Ibid., p. 47.
23. Ibid., p. 49.
24. Ibid., p. 50.
25. Ibid., p. 55.

26. Ibid., p. 61.
27. Ibid., p. 79.
28. Ibid., p. 91.
29. G. Bryce, *Sketch of the Life and Discoveries of Robert Campbell*, Historical and Scientific Society of Manitoba Transaction No. 52 (Manitoba Free Press, 1898), p. 3.
30. Granville Stuart, *Forty Years on the Frontier, as seen in the Journals and Reminiscences of Granville Stuart, Gold-miner, Trader, Merchant, Rancher and Politician*, ed. Paul C. Phillips (Cleveland, OH: Arthur H. Clark, 1925), p. 67.
31. Fraser, *Flashman*, p. 66.
32. Robert Service, 'Trail of Ninety-Eight', *Collected Verse* (London: Ernest Benn, 1943), vol. I, p. 179.
33. Ibid., p. 177.
34. Dunn, *Highland Settler*, p. 132.
35. Alistair MacLeod, *Island* (London: Vintage, [2001] 2002), p. 33.
36. Ibid., p. 39.
37. Ibid., p. 34.
38. Ibid., p. 35.
39. G. Bryce, *The Scotsman in Canada* (London: Sampson, Low, Marston, 1912), p. 340.
40. George Grant, *Ocean to Ocean. Sandford Fleming's Expedition Through Canada in 1872* (London: Sampson Low, Marston, Searle & Rivington, 1877), p. 95.
41. Ibid., p. 96.
42. Ibid., p. 130.
43. Ibid., p. 123.
44. Ibid., p. 274.
45. Ibid., p. 246.
46. Ibid., p. 247.
47. Ibid., p. 249.
48. Ibid., p. 270.
49. Ibid., p. 271.
50. Ibid., p. 344.
51. Pierre Berton, *The National Dream. The Last Spike* (Toronto: McLelland & Stewart, 1974), p. 98.
52. James J. Hill, *Highways of Progress* (London: Hodder & Stoughton, 1910), p. 235.
53. Albro Martin, *James J. Hill and the Opening of the Northwest* (New York: Oxford University Press, 1976), p. 366.
54. Ibid., p. 345.
55. Hill, *Highways of Progress*, p. 142.
56. William Fraser Rae, *Newfoundland to Manitoba* (London, 1881), p. 183.
57. Creighton, *The Story of Canada*, pp. 193–4.

58. Lewis Atherton, *The Cattle Kings* (Bloomington, IN: Indiana University Press, 1962), p. 232.
59. Ibid., p. 44.
60. Larry McMurtry, *Lonesome Dove* (London: Pan, [1985] 1986), p. 80.
61. Ibid., p. 699.
62. John Clay, *My Life on the Range* (Norman, OK: University of Oklahoma Press, [1894] 1962), p. 44.
63. Stuart, *Forty Years on the Frontier*, p. 144.
64. Clay, *My Life on the Range*, p. 155.
65. Ibid., p. 159.
66. Ibid., p. 56.
67. Ibid., p. 58.
68. Stuart, *Forty Years on the Frontier*, p. 239.
69. Doig, *House of Sky*, p. 28.
70. Ibid., p. 29.
71. Ibid., p. 35.
72. Ibid., p. 36.

7

Regions of Adventure

We were in a region of adventure; breaking our way through a country hitherto untrodden by white man, except perchance by some solitary trapper.

Washington Irving, A Tour on the Prairies

'You bet,' Augustus said. 'We might all get killed this afternoon for all I know. That's the wild for you – it's got its dangers, which is part of the beauty.'

Larry McMurtry, Lonesome Dove

No writer has drawn adventure out of landscape as Walter Scott did. In his fiction and narrative poems wild terrain, of the Borders and the Highlands, are the arena of confrontation, steadfast endeavour and lost causes. His historical tales generate adventure through characters organic to the landscape he describes, and through others who intrude on it. Wilderness shapes action and provokes it, and, Scott suggests, breeds defiance, obduracy and sometimes anarchy. Wild country is dynamic as well as scenic, participant as well as backdrop.

A recurrent feature of Scott's work is the journey, actual and metaphorical. Scotland is geographically a small country fragmented by mountains, rivers and lochs, and includes hundreds of islands, skerries, wild seas, formidable cliffs, treacherous quicksands and mudflats. At the heart of Scott's narratives is the understanding that you can connect up the fragments only by making journeys, and that these journeys necessitate overcoming huge obstacles, both topographical and cultural. He repeatedly employs the trope of a journey into unknown territory to illuminate difference and to explore the possibility of connection. And he was writing at a time when the Enlightenment had planted stirring notions of human capability and achievement.

Scott was widely read on both sides of the Atlantic, and it is no surprise that his novels provided a narrative model for a new world founded on journeys and a belief in progression, outward and upward. The settlement of North America depended on journeys into unknown and untamed territory inhabited by strange peoples who had widely varying material cultures and spoke many different languages. Many of these peoples were themselves nomadic. Without journeys, there could be no America and no American narrative. In the context of Scottish experience, an American narrative was constructed first of all by Scots who described their travels in the New World, and by those with a keen eye for the economic potential and the possibilities of settlement. Given the opportunity, *Rob Roy*'s Bailie Nicol Jarvie, conscious of what Glasgow owed to New World trade and dreaming of developing Loch Lomond, could well have been one of them. Settlement, as John Galt examined in his frontier novels, is about more than survival and subsistence. It requires actively confronting wilderness and laying the foundations for progress.

It was almost inevitable that the first American novelist of westward expansion, James Fenimore Cooper, should look to Scott for guidance. Scottish writers, but Scott above all, had demonstrated that a small nation with a larger, more powerful neighbour could have a distinctive literature that spoke to the world. For a new nation determined to establish its own cultural identity Scott was an inspiration. His narratives also provided an example of how a developing country could accommodate the frontier, and absorb the frontier experience into heroic tales underpinned by both romance and loss. Like Rob Roy on his frontier mountainside, Natty Bumppo, in his final incarnation in *The Prairie* (1827), is an anachronism, an old man dressed in skins, 'a pouch and horn ... suspended from his shoulders', leaning on 'a rifle of uncommon length, but which, like its owner, exhibited the wear of long and hard service'.[1] He has one last task to perform, which facilitates exactly the progress that will make him redundant. Among his inheritors is A. B. Guthrie's Dick Summers in *The Big Sky* and *The Way West*, who similarly colludes in enabling settlement, which will destroy his role and also tame the wilderness, the source of both freedom and identity.

The movement west underpins Cooper's Leatherstocking Tales (1823–41), which begin in the 1740s with *The Deerslayer* in the colony of New York, and take the reader to *The Prairie* set in 1804, the year following the Louisiana Purchase. In 1805, when Simon Fraser journeyed up the Peace River and penetrated the Rocky Mountains, Scott's *Lay of the Last Minstrel* precipitated him to fame as chronicler of an apparently lost Scotland. He was addressing an audience whose interest in the wilderness beyond the Highland Line was already primed, by the accounts of travellers such as Thomas Pennant and the dynamic duo James Boswell and Samuel Johnson, and most of all by the Ossianic tales of James Macpherson. While in the 1770s and 1880s Highland Scotland was being 'discovered', on the other side of the Atlantic a war was being fought and expeditions of exploration mounted. Both enterprises would have profound repercussions for Scotland, for her trade and industry, for her population, and for the Scottish imagination.

The first accounts of Scottish travels in North America were being published before the end of the eighteenth century, but it was the early decades of the nineteenth century when growing numbers of travellers' tales were bringing a sense of the challenges that wilderness presented to Scottish readers. Alexander Mackenzie's *Voyages from Montreal* was published in 1801. With the help of his editor William Combe, Mackenzie constructed a narrative that recorded detailed observations of environment and climate, and the actions of men faced with huge obstacles, and presented himself as leader and adventure hero. Although neither of his expeditions achieved what he had hoped for, he was the Highland chieftain, demonstrating wilderness expertise and decisive courage, and commanding loyalty. In this new terrain, the bold Highlander had become the bold explorer.

For Mackenzie, Simon Fraser and many others prominent in the fur trade, North America, and particularly British North America, offered an arena where traditional clan attributes and values, considered regressive and obstructive in the homeland, could not only be enacted but celebrated. The army channelled the same anachronisms; the regulations and discipline imposed by the fur-trading companies, particularly the Hudson's Bay Company under George Simpson, echoed those of the military. (The, at times vicious, rivalry between the HBC and the North West Company echoed clan warfare, although clan identity was subsumed by company imperatives.)

Late eighteenth-century readers were responding with interest to travellers' experiences in the Highlands. How much more exciting were the accounts of the North American wilderness and man's endeavour to conquer massive natural hazards and bring control to 'a vast and unknown continent'. The tamer narratives of Scottish travellers 'adventuring' in the infant United States and its northern neighbour clearly had an eager readership. Many of these were designed as practical advice to the intending emigrant, and were more concerned to stress the potential for building new lives than to incite a spirit of adventure; nevertheless, departure for the New World, even with limited hopes, was inevitably touched with, if not engulfed by, a sense of enterprise and hazard. In other words, a narrative of adventure was implanted in the very act of emigration.

Washington Irving's documentation of travels on the western frontier was a reminder that a vast area of the North American continent was largely unknown to Europeans. His journey west in 1832 has parallels with Scott's Edward Waverley and Frank Osbaldistone entering the Highlands, equally unknown to southerners. Irving did not translate his experiences into fiction, but his three published accounts – and especially the first, *A Tour on the Prairies* (1835) – effervesce with his excited response to entering wild country. After many years living and travelling in Europe he was now on his own country's frontier. He revelled in his meetings with the Osage, celebrating 'the glorious independence of man in a savage state' and the native's ability to 'cast himself loose from everyone, shape his own course, and take care of his own fortunes'.[2] There was a thrill in being among people for whom tribal warfare was a way of life – although the purpose of the expedition he was accompanying was to bring it to an end. He makes no analogy with the clan warfare of the Highlands or the Scottish Borders where cattle reiving had been as endemic as horse stealing among the Plains Nations, but it was likely to come to the mind of any American reader of Scott. Part of Irving's purpose in writing his 'Western' books was to re-establish his American credentials, but he was published and read in Britain too, adding to the growing body of literature making the New World available to the Old.

At around the same time as Irving's western adventures were being published, John Galt produced his two frontier novels, very different in tone from the former's enthusiastic prose. Galt presents the troubled and contradictory hopes and emotions of Bogle Corbet in Upper Canada and Lawrie Todd in New York State's Mohawk Valley. Both feel they have no choice but to leave Scotland, but both are hopeful of success in the New World. They encounter and to a degree overcome (at considerable cost) huge odds. Like Susanna Moodie and Catherine Parr Traill, Galt shows that pioneering in the wilderness is intrinsically an adventure, full of 'perils' and 'novelties' and demanding bold actions. At the same time, it is prosaic. Success – survival – depends as much on attention to mundane detail as it does on courageous enterprise. Resourcefulness is a matter of making use of what there is to hand. In *Lost in the Backwoods*, Louis, 'a provident hoarder', fashions a fishing line and hook out of a length of string and a piece of tin from his pocket.[3] Pragmatism is the key to the success of both Bogle and Lawrie, although neither is immune to the threats contained in the wilderness nor to the attractions of wild beauty and the opportunities for peaceful solitude. Galt's heroes are persistent and hard-headed, but not instinctively adventurous. Circumstances thrust adventure upon them, and they deal with it, often in a spirit of stoic resignation rather than daring.

In a frontier context, settlement, the building of shelters and the day-to-day business of labour on the land and in the home, was always a foil to the hunter, the explorer and the range rider. The creating of permanence is seen as a very different experience from the free movement and independence that untamed country allowed. Fenimore Cooper charts this contrast as he follows the frontier's westward flow and mourns the obsolescence of the trailblazer. But as example and inspiration, the trailblazer and all that he represents had a great deal of life left in him. Just as Scott reinvigorated the Highlands as a locus and as an idea, and re-imagined the Highlander, generations of writers would return to the frontier hero and augment and enhance his mythic legacy.

Galt's fiction, published in the 1830s, not only added to the growing body of material documenting the North American experience for a Scottish readership, it leant a new dimension to Scotland's imaginative encounter with the transatlantic wilderness. Once an aspect of experience, whether individual or national, has entered fiction it becomes validated. It becomes part of a cultural territory that anyone can inhabit. The vigorous immediacy of *Lawrie Todd* in particular clearly had wide appeal. There was an appetite for North American tales, an appetite that later writers would exploit.

R. M. BALLANTYNE: 'FAR REMOVED FROM THE CIVILISED WORLD'

Washington Irving got no further west than present-day Guthrie, Oklahoma, on the Cimarron River. The following year William Drummond Stewart was in the Rockies, and the year after that Charles August Murray was in Kansas among the Pawnee, frequent targets of the Osage horse-thieving forays Irving's expedition was hoping to bring to an end. They both identified the American wilderness as territory for adventure stories and helped to link British, if not specifically Scottish, experience with a romantic version of the frontier. And they, too, were clearly influenced by Scott. Their novels were published in the 1840s, over two decades before Ned Buntline went west in 1868 and brought back east a fictionalised Buffalo Bill as herald of a new genre of fiction.

Irving, Stewart and Murray all produced enhanced versions of the 'noble savage', physically impressive, picturesquely arrayed, skilled in hunting and horsemanship, courageous in war, generous in outlook. Cooper had already introduced another 'noble savage': the frontiersman who had acquired the same rapport with the environment as the native while retaining the advantages of European origin. Though harbinger of his own demise, before the end comes he operates in an arena which offers plenty of scope for frontier intelligence and bold action. He reappears over and over again, and although the arena shrinks as the nineteenth century draws to a close, the potential for re-invention does not diminish.

The engagement with the North American wilderness coincided with a growing appetite in Britain for adventure stories, especially those enacted in wild terrain or distant and exotic locations. One of the most successful writers in this vein was Edinburgh writer R. M. Ballantyne, who began to publish in the 1850s. Ballantyne's experience with the Hudson's Bay Company provided material for several books aimed at a young readership. In his preface to *The Young Fur Traders* (1856) he made clear his intention 'to draw an exact copy of the picture which is indelibly stamped on my own memory. I have carefully avoided exaggeration in everything of importance.'[4] The first chapter 'conveys [the reader] into the heart of the wilderness of North America' in the middle of an Arctic winter.[5] The heart of wilderness is in fact the Red River settlement, which Ballantyne goes on to describe as something of an oasis 'far removed from the civilised world' in a vast territory scattered with 'the desolate, solitary establishments of the Hudson's Bay Company'.[6]

The narrative centres on fifteen-year-old Charley Kennedy, son of a Scottish fur trader, who, impatient to experience the northern wilds, joins an HBC brigade which leaves Red River in a fleet of boats. The departure is a stirring scene of cheerful exertion, as the *voyageurs*, 'picturesque athletic men … spring lightly into the long, heavy boats … [and] let the oars fall into the water with a loud splash'. They move out into the river's current: 'the men bent their sturdy backs, until the thick oars creaked and groaned on the gunwales, and flashed in the stream, more and more vigorously at each successive stroke'.[7] Ballantyne describes in some detail the daily existence of the fur-trade brigades, their travelling, their camps and their equipment. There are minor mishaps and major endeavours to overcome storms, rapids and wild animals. The characters that Charley encounters are honed by a life in the wilderness. Here is Jacques, son of a Scottish mother and a French Canadian, born in Canada but raised on the Missouri, who had 'from a mere youth, spent his life as a hunter in the wilderness':

> He was a square-shouldered, muscular man, and from the ruggedness of his general appearance, the soiled hunting shirt that was strapped round his waist with a parti-coloured worsted belt, the leather leggings, a good deal the worse for wear, together with the quiet self-possessed glance of his grey eye, the compressed lip and the sunburnt brow, it was evident that he was a hunter, and one who had seen rough work in his day. The expression of his face was pleasing, despite a look of severity which sat upon it, and a deep scar which traversed his brow from the right temple to the top of his nose. It was difficult to tell to what country he belonged.

Jacques speaks English, French and 'Indian' with equal fluency, 'but it would have been hard to say which of the three was his native tongue'.[8] This mix of ethnicity and background blurs his identity, yet at the same time makes him highly distinctive. He carries the imprint of the wild environment in which he has lived rather than of nationality. Jacques has gone native, and although Ballantyne seems to imply (like Catherine Parr Traill) that the French Canadian–Scottish blend is advantageous for a pioneering life he does not stress the Scottish contribution to this particular frontier hero.

Charley experiences an environment that is sometimes beneficent – 'all nature was joyous and brilliant, and bright and beautiful'– but often threatening.[9] He and his companions struggle across hostile terrain and face intense cold, blizzards, diminishing supplies and hostility from Indians and rivals. Throughout, Jacques is Charley's guide and mentor, but always with the reminder that, although superior to the young man in knowledge of the wilderness and survival skills, he is not quite Charley's equal. Jacques addresses the young hero as 'master'. At the tale's end Charley has returned to the relative civilisation of Red River and Jacques takes off north as a guide to a missionary determined to reach 'those Indian tribes that inhabit the regions beyond Athabasca'.[10]

> On reaching the summit of a slight eminence, where the prairies terminated and the woods began, they paused to wave a last adieu; then Jacques, putting himself at the head of the little party, plunged into the forest, and led them away towards the snowy regions of the Far North.[11]

Ballantyne sets *The Wild Man of the West* (1863) among the independent fur trappers who operated in present-day Montana and Wyoming. His sixteen-year-old hero March Marston joins a group of trappers heading into the Rockies, in the hope of setting eyes on the legendary 'Wild Man'. His companions are:

> the real sort of metal, none o' yer tearin', swearin', murderin' chaps, as thinks the more they curse the bolder they are, an' the more Injuns they kill the cleverer they are; but steady quiet fellers, as don't speak much, but does a powerful quantity.[12]

As in *The Young Fur Traders*, Ballantyne writes of their adventures with hearty exuberance. They are all decent men with a 'backwoods education' and experienced in the wild.[13] They are generous to their young acolyte, who revels in the 'romantic and captivating' journey into the unknown.[14] They encounter Theodore Bertram, a wandering artist, whose aim is to 'open up the unknown wilderness' through his sketches, undeterred by the fact that he was 'unfitted, either by nature or training' to travel in a 'savage land'.[15] Bertram rhapsodises about the freedom of the wilderness, 'a species of wild romance about it, that is more captivating than I can describe'.[16]

In both these novels there are direct echoes of Scott, who leads his young inexperienced heroes into unknown country and testing situations. Bertram's 'simple-minded enthusiasm' could describe Edward Waverley.[17] Young March is a frontier lad with some appropriate skills, but he is still enthused by the sheer magnificence of the landscape. Camping in the foothills of the Rockies, he is up to meet the dawn:

> There was a saffron hue over the eastern landscape that caused it to appear like the plains of Paradise. Lakelets in the prairies glittered in the midst of verdant foliage; ponds in the hollows lay, as yet unillumined, like blots of ink; streams and rivulets gleamed as they flowed round wooded knolls, or

sparkled silvery white as they leapt over obstructions. The noble river, on the banks of which the camp had been made, flowed with a calm sweep through the richly-varied country ... it seemed as though all Nature, animate and inanimate, were rejoicing in the beneficence of its Creator.[18]

This is reminiscent of *Rob Roy*'s Frank Osbaldistone emerging into 'the refreshing fragrance of the morning air' after his uncomfortable night at the clachan of Aberfoyle to see the sun rising over the valley of the River Forth: 'Man alone seemed to be placed in a state of inferiority, in a scene where all the ordinary features of nature were raised and exalted.'[19]

Scott had prepared the way for writers of wilderness adventure and it was almost impossible for the pioneers in this genre to avoid his influence. He provided a template for locating action in wild country, and for making wild country accessible to drawing-room readers. Ballantyne's Charley Kennedy and March Marston are journeying through the wilderness towards maturity, a maturity that will take them into a settled life. Their youthful escapades have strengthened and educated them, but their adult life, it is intimated, will reflect the end of frontier days. March marries a mixed-race girl, who demonstrates nurturing and nursing skills as well as a calm intelligence in a crisis. Like Traill, Stewart and Murray, Ballantyne suggests that such a union is a satisfactory route to absorbing the indigenous population into the trajectory of civilisation. Even the Wild Man emerges from his mountain lair and embraces married life.

In Ballantyne's stories the terrain presents, as well as topographical obstacles, creatures that are a continuous source of excitement at best, danger at worst. There are buffalo, deer and wildfowl to be hunted, and encounters with grizzly bears to be avoided if possible. But the biggest threat comes from the natives, almost always depicted as 'savages'. There are a few 'good Indians', such as Hawk'swing who is one of the band of trappers, but most are hostile and not to be trusted. They are also rather inept. The Indian attackers in *The Wild Man of the West* are always outmanoeuvred or frightened off. The only fatality is the commander of Mountain Fort, an alcoholic called Macgregor who is wrecked 'in body and mind'.[20] As he is dying of his wounds he is discovered to be March Marston's long-lost father, but by that time the Wild Man himself has become the boy's father figure. The future thus combines the domesticity and rigorous demands of female pioneering with the intrepid trailblazing of the male adventurers.

A. B. GUTHRIE: 'A MAN LIVED NATURAL'

A much later writer concerned with similar territory also echoes the trope made familiar by Scott. In A. B. Guthrie's *The Big Sky* young Boone Caudill enters unknown territory under the guidance of seasoned scout and trapper Dick Summers. For Boone wilderness means beaver and a source of wealth, but it also means independence, a life in which he is in a sense his own master, although he has to obey the strictures of survival. He is free from the oppression of civilisation and the need to conform, and contemplates with gloom the possibility of intrusion on this independence. The older Summers accepts that change is inevitable. The trapper, 'pushing up the unspoiled rivers, pleased with risk and loneliness' must give way to 'the wanters of new homes, the hunters of fortune, the would-be makers of a bigger nation'. Appreciation of the terrain did not change the fact that the mountain men had no more entitlement to unspoilt terrain than anyone else, however light his footfall:

> The fur hunter didn't have title to the mountains no matter if he did say finders' keepers. By that system the country belonged to the Indians, or maybe someone before them or someone before them. No use to stand against the stream of change and time.[21]

Unlike Summers, Boone Caudill clings to the idea of appropriation. He feels he owns a space that is not shared, or shared only by a few like-minded companions. The absence of wider human pre-emption allows an undisturbed and individual relationship with the wild, and such unmediated personal connection recurs in numerous accounts of engagement with the wilderness, in fact and fiction. In Scotland's West Highlands, Samuel Johnson pretended solitude to enhance his experience of the wild. Scott repeatedly evoked isolation. In North America, John Rae and others actively sought it. And it is at the heart of the mountain man's intimacy with landscape, which in turn takes root in later mythologising of the frontier hero. To be alone, entirely thrown on one's own resources and without the need to relate to humanity, is both to intensify the connection with the wild and to reinforce fundamental human qualities. Boone has escaped from an abusive family and the law; heading west takes him into territory where he has to learn – not without tutelage – to fend for himself. An essential part of his lesson is the honing of all his senses to interpret the environment in which he operates.

With isolation comes independence: 'time all a man's own and none to say no to him'. In the wilderness, Boone reflects, 'a man lived natural', kin to the wildlife, uncaged by walls and rules.[22] When after many years Boone returns to Kentucky he feels 'cramped by the forest'. Although this is back-woods country, the openness and freedom of the real wilderness have vanished.

> The wind was dead here; not even the leaves of the great poplars, rising high over all the rest, so much as trembled. It was a still, closed-in, broody world, and a man in it felt empty and lost inside, as if all that he had counted on

had been taken away, and he without a friend or an aim or a proper place anywhere.[23]

Boone, who found himself in the wilderness, is lost in the backwoods. But the wilderness also bred violence; in a fit of angry jealousy he has killed his best friend and soured his wilderness experience. And he realises that 'his' wilderness is under threat. On his way east he arrives at Independence on the Missouri River, and in dismay watches hundreds of wagons assembling for the trek west. It is 1843.

It is this next phase of the frontier story that Guthrie narrates in *The Way West*, which charts an overland journey from Independence to Fort Vancouver, following the mixed fortunes of several families and bringing back Dick Summers as the wagon train's guide and enabler. They cross the Great Divide by way of Robert Stuart's South Pass and make their way to the Green River, through hard country which Dick knows well. The heat and the lack of water take their toll on the mixed population in his charge, with names that echo their English, Welsh, Irish, Scottish and other European origins. They have already been through hardship, disaster and loss. They are pioneers, but without the untamed independence of the lone frontiersman, burdened by families, 'settled with their women and easy with their children, the hard edges worn smooth, the wildness in them broken to harness. They looked ahead to farms and schools and government, to an ordered round of living.'[24] Dick feels that he might become one of them 'if only he hadn't known the Popo Agie'.[25] He also believes that these aspiring homemakers and nation-builders might populate the wilderness, but could not change the essential character of the mountains. A generation later John Muir would show that the rivers and mountains were not immune to damage caused by nation-builders.

Guthrie himself grew up in Montana. In 1901, his family had moved west from Indiana to settle in Choteau, 80 miles from the Canadian border. His father became the first principal of Teton County Free High School – in other words, his family were a part of exactly that process envisaged by Dick Summers. Alfred Bertram Guthrie was one of nine children, of whom only three survived into adulthood. The others were carried off by scarlet fever, whooping cough or bronchitis. Choteau may not have been wilderness, but it was on the edge of civilisation and survival remained precarious. That sense of the vulnerability of humanity pervades Guthrie's writing. Adventure stories may require battling with blizzards and grizzly bears, and fending off attacks by Indians and bandits, but the assaults of the wild were often much more insidious: disease, malnutrition, exhaustion and demoralisation were the enemies of Guthrie's families as they were of all those who attempted to survive in the wild.

Wilderness stripped life to the essentials and in the process tested the core humanity of those exposed to it. For some – Guthrie's fictional heroes or the very real John Rae and John Muir – that shedding of the unnecessary was welcomed. Others resisted it. In the 1840s, Letitia Hargrave, Campbeltown-born wife of the Chief Factor at HBC's York Factory, was the only white woman permanently based there. She maintained standards with table linen, silverware and crystal, but she would eventually die of cholera at Sault Ste Marie. John Franklin's last and fatal expedition was famously weighed down with symbols of rank and status. But most tolerated the impositions of wilderness in the hope and expectation that they would lead to something better: stability and a degree of comfort, if not riches.

The tension between the frontier hero relishing isolation and embracing risk and the pioneer who aims to settle down and build a community is at the heart of many Westerns, and is sometimes present in a single conflicted character. The very genesis of the genre was in large part a response to this tension. Fenimore Cooper wished to imprint the frontier hero on the American imagination before it was too late. He could not have anticipated that fifty years later repeated incarnations of the Western hero would be entering the imaginations of millions, already primed by accounts of exploration and trailblazing.

Western fiction and film are well populated with Scottish names, without necessarily highlighting a Scottish identity or a specifically Scottish experience. (Irish names also appear frequently, although in their case Irish identity is more likely to be a focus, often of comedy.) The Westerns of Anthony Mann are especially striking in this respect. Among his heroes are Lin McAdam in *Winchester '73* (1950), Glyn McLyntock in *Bend of the River* (1952), Home Kemp in *The Naked Spur* (1953) and Will Lockhart in *The Man from Laramie* (1955), all names indicating a Scottish connection and all played by James Stewart. They are decent but driven men, committed to fulfilling an obligation or righting a wrong, sharing a quality of isolated determination. Will Lockhart, for example, is reticent about his past and deliberately obscures his identity as if it would deflect from his pursuit of vengeance. He finds himself operating in a territory not only of raw violence, but of tangled morality from which he emerges morally, but not physically, unscathed. He is the catalyst of justice, without being its direct instrument.

Several recurring motifs in the Western echo themes that are rooted deep in Scottish history. Range war and clashes between rival land interests mirror the feuding between Highland clans and between Border families. Many of the players in the West's most famous range wars were Scots or of Scottish descent, and appear in fictionalised versions. John Chisum was a leading figure in New Mexico's Lincoln County War (1870s). The Chisholms came originally from Strathglass, near Inverness. Another key player in this episode was lawyer Alexander MacSween, a name that originates in Argyll. In Arizona in the 1880s, the Graham family engaged in a bitter and bloody feud with the Tewkesburys. The Grahams, of course, were prominent in Scottish Border feuding. Perhaps the most notorious range war was Wyoming's Johnson County War which came to a head in 1892, and in which many of the players were Scots. Leading ranchers in Johnson County, plagued by endemic rustling which they believed was carried out by local homesteaders, brought in hired gunmen to deal with the problem. Some of the biggest ranches in the area were owned and managed by Scots, and these included John Clay who wrote his own account of the episode defending their actions. One of the alleged rustlers, killed by the hired guns, was Nick Ray: Ray or Rae is a name prevalent in Orkney. The sheriff who attempted to control the situation was a Scot called William 'Red' Angus.

These episodes provided rich material for film and fiction, although again without the Scottish connection being an issue and often lost altogether. In Michael Cimino's Johnson County War movie *Heaven's Gate* (1980) the real-life leading characters are scrambled and in the presentation of a clash between bullying big guys and immigrant homesteaders the Scottish ingredient is entirely lost. But the many narratives based on these episodes (the Graham–Tewkesbury feud, for example, produced at least four novels, by Amelia Bean, Dane Coolidge, Earle Forrest and Zane Grey) illustrate the precarious hold of the law in frontier country, and the close relationship between untamed territory and vigilante action. These are themes familiar to readers of Walter Scott and other Scottish fiction.

Fenimore Cooper's precursors of the Western were heavily influenced by Scott, and arguably the very first Westerns were written by Scots: William Drummond Stewart, Charles Augustus Murray and R. M. Ballantyne. Their novels were written not to provide a paradigm of American heroic endeavour, but to register an adventurous European encounter with the wild and the exotic. They were probably unread by those who in the early decades of the twentieth century brought Westerns into mainstream readership, although Zane Grey acknowledged the influence of R. L. Stevenson.

The wilderness featured in Westerns is man-made as well as natural. Rugged and often stunningly beautiful landscape is a feature of most Westerns, but lawlessness, vigilantism, the lack of civic structure and the tensions that these bring, result in a moral wilderness which is equally challenging to the protagonist. Many Westerns centre on an embryonic community rescued from anarchy or oppression by a single heroic individual, who is then unable or unwilling to participate in the ordered society that follows. *Shane*, story (1946) by Jack Schaeffer, and movie (1953) directed by George Stevens with screenplay by A. B. Guthrie, is the pre-eminent example. Echoing the plot of *Shane* is Lee Child's twenty-first-century thriller *Worth Dying For* (2010) in which a stranger finds himself in a bleakly remote Nebraska community terrorised by the local Duncan clan (a Scottish name, although Child does not identify the family's origin). Child's hero employs cool and calculated violence to restore some kind of sense of worth to a moral wasteland.

LARRY MCMURTRY: 'ROADS OF BONES'

A hard country invites, or even demands, savagery, and a moral vacuum unleashes the worst of human behaviour. Wilderness is not only a region of adventure, it can also be the territory of evil. In the novels of Larry McMurtry all aspects of wilderness are explored, and his two chief protagonists have overtly Scottish origins. Augustus McCrae is flamboyant, easy-going and wears his frontier skills lightly. Woodrow Call is dour, single-minded and driven. McCrae charms the ladies, while Call shuns them. There is no explicit evocation of a Calvinist influence, but it is there nevertheless, as are the echoes of David Balfour and Alan Breck Stewart in Stevenson's *Kidnapped*. They begin their career in *Dead Man's Walk* (1995) as Texas Rangers battling against the fearsome cruelty of the land itself and the native resistance to white encroachment on it. Call, who 'had never been a man who could think of much reason for acting happy' has a powerful sense of purpose 'to get done what needed to be done',[26] while the genial McCrae 'treated danger with light contempt or open scorn'.[27] In *Lonesome Dove* (1985) Call and McCrae, with a motley crew of misfits as uncertain of their origins as of their destinations, drive a herd of cattle on a 2,500-mile trek which takes them from the heat and aridity of Texas to the lush grasslands and severe winters of Montana. The rivers they cross are the territorial markers of their journey north, which is beset by mishaps, bloodshed and loss. There are natural hazards – turbulent rivers, waterless deserts, violent storms – and human threats, from Indians and the cruelly sinister Comanchero Blue Duck. Although driven by Call's dream of a Montana ranch, their journey becomes not an emblem of pioneering settlement, like the way west, but an odyssey almost for its own sake. There is a compulsion to be on the move, as if the wilderness itself were propelling them forward and denying the possibility of a static existence.

In the valley of the Canadian River, McCrae comes on a former mountain man who is collecting barrow-loads of buffalo bones scattered across the prairie. It is a surreal moment. The bones are a reminder that the traditional life of the Plains Nations, who depended on the buffalo, has passed. The buffalo have been hunted by whites to near-extinction, to create a new wilderness:

The sight of the road of bones stretching over the prairie was a shock. Maybe roads of bones were all that was left. The thought gave the very emptiness of the plains a different feel. With those millions of animals gone, and the Indians mostly gone in their wake, the great plains were truly empty, unpeopled and ungrazed.

In McCrae's eyes it is a strange and disturbing interim. The buffalo hunters, the advance guard of white settlement, had left 'true emptiness ... occupied only by remnants'.[28] The crazed collector works day and night to pile up a useless mountain of bones. The inevitable white settlement would leave no space for anachronistic mountain men or the vestiges of a previous life. By the novel's close Augustus McCrae is dead of wounds received in an Indian fight and Call has fulfilled his promise to return his body to Texas for burial. It is the end of his dream of ranching.

A third novel, *The Streets of Laredo* (1994), chronicles the last active years of the ageing Call. The frontier is, perhaps, coming to an end, but there is still a vast territory that appears to breed savagery, where predatory misfits pursue violence for its own sake, and the infliction of torture and death are expressions of power which few can challenge. One of the few who can is Woodrow Call, who is driven by a profound sense of duty; in this case to those who have employed him to track down a train robber, but also to himself. He has the skills and the endurance to do what most man cannot: 'He could keep riding longer and fighting harder than any man he had worked with ... he could keep going in situations where others had to stop.'[29] For Call, frontier values are not about family or community, but about loyalty to comrades. 'A man didn't desert his comrades, his troop, his leader. If he did, he was, in Call's book, worthless.'[30] Loyalty was about mutual survival, not abstract notions of honour.

Call's dour persistence, his conviction that 'remaining himself, remaining who he was, meant finishing the job he had undertaken', has a religious quality which echoes the tenacity of the Scottish Covenanters.[31] He is an old man, with arthritic joints which make it difficult to mount a horse and handle a gun. He is beginning to feel he is no longer able to confront the inhumanity of the wilderness, yet there are 'still deadly men in the West, and there was a vast space in which they could operate'. The emptiness is 'a magnet for killers'.[32] He finishes the job, kills the terrifying Mox Mox, but in the process loses an arm and a leg. Diminished, he finds a sedentary role for himself in a family environment in which community values are evolving. His comrade Pea Eye, once a Texas Ranger and Comanche fighter, is now a sodbuster. Pea Eye's wife Lorena, once a prostitute, is now a teacher. Call himself sharpens the agricultural implements necessary for cultivation. Unlike the mad mountain man collecting buffalo bones, and unlike Gus McCrae who, unable to face an inactive future, refuses to have both his gangrenous legs amputated, Call adjusts to his changed condition and changing circumstances.

By the end of *The Streets of Laredo*, McMurtry's hero has more in common with the tenacious Scottish settler who stolidly confronts the wilderness with axe and plough than with the dashing free spirit exemplified by his comrade Augustus or the self-reliant loner that he once thought himself to be. The wilderness has reduced him but not defeated him. He survives to benefit from the degree of stability that men like him have helped to bring about. There is a note of melancholy, as there often is in Western narratives that deal with the advance of settlement. Civilisation brings loss, loss of unfettered movement and an existence unrestricted by social norms, as well as an awareness of those who have perished in the process of taming the frontier. Significantly, Call accepts change. He does not choose death and he does not ride off into the sunset.

ROBERT LOUIS STEVENSON: 'ALL THE PAST UPROOTED'

When Robert Louis Stevenson, as a boy an enthusiastic reader of R. M. Ballantyne, travelled across the American continent in 1878, he began to plan his own frontier adventure story, to be called *A Vendetta in the West*. It was never completed, but Stevenson's first experience of the American wilderness had a profound impact. His journey by train from east to west coast took him through a vast expanse of alien territory. He observed the American forests, plains and mountains from inside a cramped and insalubrious railroad car and witnessed some of the effects of frontier country on both native and incomer. 'I do not know if I am the same man I was in Europe,' he wrote to his friend Edmund Gosse. He found himself 'over here in a new land, and all the past uprooted with one tug'. It was a dislocating experience, intensified when he arrived in Monterey, California, to find the woman he hoped to marry in a state of uncertainty and ambivalence. He headed for the Santa Lucia mountains, where he encountered an experience that left him with an acute sense of human frailty and his own vulnerability in particular. Already weakened by travelling, he fell seriously ill and only his chance discovery by a goat rancher saved him: 'according to all rule', he wrote to Gosse, 'it should have been my death'.[33]

Stevenson relished wild terrain, and was sensitive to landscape empty of humanity. He provided a useful definition of wilderness in his essay 'Memoirs of an Islet', where he describes the island of Erraid, which would feature so prominently in *Kidnapped*. There, apart from the lighthouse settlement which 'scarce encroached beyond its fences ... the ground was all virgin, the world all shut out, the face of things unchanged by any of man's doings'.[34] He would explore the implications of 'the world all shut out' in many different environments and manifestations.

His enthusiasm for the Scottish landscape was embedded in his understanding of its organic role in Scotland's past. He shared this with Scott, but unlike Scott he did not present landscape as a picturesque enhancement of historical narrative. And unlike his compatriot John Muir, in California at the same time as Stevenson although on an expedition to Alaska when Stevenson first arrived, he did not see wilderness as a source of spiritual nourishment. No doubt schooled by the experiences of his engineering family, his response to the harsh realities of Scottish rock, mountain and water was shaped by an understanding of its unforgiving character. At the same time, hills were always for him a place of contemplation, and seas always an invitation to adventure.

Stevenson was primed by childhood reading to find the 'frontier' a place of adventure, and by adult reading of Hawthorne, Whitman and others to find the United States both attractive and energising, but he was unprepared for the raw reality he encountered: a wilderness not only of landscape but of chaotic behaviour. The America of the imagination he had absorbed through the printed word did not equip him for the confusion and dissonance that marked his landfall on US soil. The city of New York was itself a kind of wilderness, where Stevenson's 'nightmare wanderings' took him through a series of baffling encounters.[35] The transcontinental journey that followed was full of disarray and misunderstanding. Although initially he relished the landscape he was travelling through, and savoured the names of states, territories, towns and rivers, the experience palled, especially after the transfer to the emigrant train at Council Bluffs and the crossing of the Missouri. The discomforts increased, and the scale of the plains and desert landscape, unchanging for days on end, offered little that was familiar or reassuring. He began to long for mountains, and was elated when the train finally reached the pine forests and rivers of the Sierra Nevada: 'I had come home again – home from unsightly deserts, to the green and habitable corners of the earth.'[36]

With his affinity for high country he perhaps saw a spell in the Santa Lucia mountains as a first step in locating himself, but what he found was an unequivocal reminder of the dangers of lone sojourn in inhospitable terrain and the limits of self-sufficiency. Some months later he was in the mountains to the north of San Francisco, restored to health, newly married and relishing the experience of staying in an abandoned mining camp at Silverado on Mount St Helena. But it was a mixed experience, involving an invigorating but damaged landscape and considerable toil in transforming the detritus of mine works into a habitable space. Everywhere there was evidence of human activity, yet it was a wild and isolated place. On their first night they settled into miners' bunks 'roughly filled with hay' and looked out into the night through the open door: 'a faint diffused starshine came into the room like mist; and when we were once in bed, we lay, awaiting sleep, in a haunted, incomplete obscurity'.[37] That haunting remained: 'We were surrounded by so many evidences of expense and toil, we lived so entirely in the wreck of that great enterprise, like mites in the ruins of a cheese, that the idea of the old din and bustle haunted our repose.' The abandoned buildings and equipment, 'all fallen away into this sunny silence and desertion', the forgotten 'bootjacks, old boots, old tavern bills', intensified the precariousness of the human foothold in the wild.[38]

Stevenson wrote about his Silverado sojourn in *The Silverado Squatters* (1883), and these wilderness experiences would have an impact on the fiction he wrote in the 1880s. Although *Kidnapped* is set in the Scottish Highlands, David Balfour's close encounters with death clearly reflect his creator's narrow escape in California. Stevenson returned to the United States in 1887 and spent an icy winter in the Adirondacks in upper New York State before heading west again to embark on his South Seas adventure. It was in 'the Adirondack wilderness and stringent cold of the Canadian border' that he began to write *The Master of Ballantrae* (1888).[39] The 'Adirondack wilderness' is the environment of the stark closing chapters of the novel, in which the rival Durie brothers play out the final scenes of their tortured rivalry. James, the elder brother, is dashing and charismatic, outlawed by his participation in the Jacobite Rising. Henry is colourless and insecure, resentful of the popularity of his unscrupulous brother. The alien and aggressive terrain and the cruel climate intensify the naked enmity of the brothers, and expose the sinister violence and the vulnerability of all involved. The division of the two has a very Scottish context, with the family split and the brothers warring over status, land and a woman, but it is a very American wilderness that imposes its resolution.

The Scottish landscape in *The Master of Ballantrae* is that of the southwest. The fictional Ballantrae is a wild place on the Solway coast where wild things have happened. The landscape is a place of division and lawlessness. Though not strictly Border country it is nevertheless a frontier, primarily between sea and land, and distant from the centre of government. The Solway Firth, with its treacherous tides and quicksands, is a source of mysterious arrivals and departures, appearances and disappearances, sights and sounds that defy explanation. Stevenson evokes a territory that is isolated and uncanny. The rivalry between the brothers erupts into a duel fought in the darkness of a freezing night, which ends in mystery and points forward to the even colder and stranger climax of the tale.

Stevenson's narrative takes us across the Atlantic and up the Hudson River to Albany, 'the hills singularly beautified by the colours of autumn'.[40]

It is an illusory prelude, as is Albany itself, a long-established community, one of the oldest in the Thirteen Colonies. Stevenson must have been aware that it was named for the Duke of Albany, who became James II and VII, grandfather of Charles Edward Stewart, and probably knew that the area had already in the 1740s attracted Scottish settlement. In this place of Scottish allusion a very Scottish rupture approaches its climax. Henry Durie nurses feverish expectation of revenge on his brother, his mind 'dwelling almost wholly in the Wilderness' where he conjures up visions of 'the Master's bones lying scattered in the wind'.[41] Albany may be the location of recognisable civic institutions and social conventions, but it lies on the edge of an untamed frontier.

Henry Durie and his servant Mackellar join Sir William Johnson's expedition into the interior. Johnson was an Ulster Scot who in the 1750s acquired considerable land holdings in the Mohawk Valley and helped to push settlement west to the Ohio River; it was to his advantage to tame the natives, and he was himself an opportunist. In Stevenson's narrative, the mission of Johnson's expedition is to 'nip in the bud' Indian disaffection and to prevent 'all the abominable tragedies of Indian war'.[42] It is in this dangerous territory that Henry pursues the destruction of his brother who, with a gang of 'desperate, bloody-minded miscreants' (including two Scots) is seeking a hidden cache of treasure.[43]

Mackellar in particular is susceptible to the land's hostility, intensified by his knowledge of Henry's purpose.

> I could never depict the blackness of my soul upon this journey. I have none of those minds that are in love with the unusual; to see the winter coming and to lie in the field so far from any house, oppressed me like a nightmare; it seemed, indeed, a kind of awful braving of God's power; and this thought, which I daresay only writes me down as a coward, was greatly exaggerated by my private knowledge of the errand we were come upon.[44]

Henry Durie and Mackellar carry savage intent with them as they enter savage country. Then they receive the news that James Durie and his party have been tracked by a sinister, unseen pursuer who silently butchers and scalps one member of the party after another. (This, incidentally, is a device used in several Westerns where a Native American is cast as a spectral, faceless killer.) Panic leads to flight, and flight leads to the survivors losing their way in the wilderness. James, nonchalant in the face of the country's hostility, appears to succumb to illness.

Stevenson suggests that the intruders have generated and imported evil, to find it reflected back by the bleakly alien territory they have entered. None of those involved are untainted by violence and greed, whether Sir William Johnson's colonialist force, the brothers, the ambivalent Mackellar, or the thuggish associates of James. As Stevenson has Mackellar remark, 'if human nature is even in the worst of men occasionally kind, it is still, above all things, greedy'.[45] At the root of colonial conquest is acquisitiveness, whatever other motives are in play, and at every stage of American history the frontier attracted the criminal and the misfit, the freebooter and the degenerate, individuals who chose or were forced to operate outwith the law.

One might read Stevenson's tale as the revenge on the intruders of a faceless population for whom wilderness was a livelihood rather than an obstacle to civilised life. The greed and hubris of the Durie brothers and all who are drawn into their double-edged venture are defeated by the land and those who understand it. Stevenson had already demonstrated in *Kidnapped* that the perception of wilderness depended on the degree of environmental kinship, and in *The Master of Ballantrae* there is a total lack of connection between land and incoming people. The intruders are exactly that, who see wilderness as a territory of licence and potential wealth. The indigenous inhabitants dematerialise in the protective landscape, and that ability is an organic feature of 'the horror'. The wilderness offers no redeeming features and no possibility of redemption. Stevenson takes us into a physical, moral and spiritual void which only intensifies the corrupted sensibilities of those who enter it.

The Master of Ballantrae, like *Kidnapped*, highlights the relationship between moral and physical weakness, and the effects of wild landscape on both. Wilderness is a source of horror. Explorers and others had understood this, although almost always with an emphasis on the will, courage and sagacity required for survival. Nevertheless, their accounts reveal how in this struggle for survival 'normal' human values can be relinquished. Stevenson recognised in both the Scottish and the North American landscape a territory beyond the control of humanity, or at least of humanity unaccustomed to its demands. This relationship was in the nineteenth century and into the twentieth an increasing source of fascination, reflected in the many accounts by explorers and adventurers as well as in fiction that was more concerned with the liberating effects of wild country.

JOHN BUCHAN: 'A WORLD MADE WITHOUT THOUGHT OF MANKIND'

In 1935, John Buchan, well established as a novelist, arrived in Canada as Governor-General. Over the next two years he travelled widely in Canada, including an epic 7,000-mile journey which took him beyond the Mackenzie delta into the far northwest. This would become the scene of his final novel, *Sick Heart River* (1941), written when he was in failing health and published after his death in 1940. Like Traill's *Lost in the Backwoods* it is a tale of elemental engagement with the wild, but its tone and dynamic are very different. *Sick Heart River* also echoes *The Master of Ballantrae*, although its hero's physical and spiritual journey through the most severe and unforgiving North American territory is in search of redemption not revenge.

Buchan's Edward Leithen, a character familiar to readers of his earlier novels, travels through a country that diminishes humanity, 'not built on a human scale, a world made without thought of mankind, a world colourless and formless, but also timeless; a kind of eternity'.[46] Like Stevenson, he sees wilderness as an environment on which humankind can make no impact without disastrous consequences. But unlike Stevenson's Durie brothers, possessed by selfish and self-destructive ends, Leithen recognises that survival in the wilderness demands total concentration; it is the sole focus of life and is only possible on nature's terms. This recognition leads Leithen to self-knowledge, spiritual peace and an acceptance of his own death. Stevenson allows his characters no such self-knowledge. Wilderness offers no sustenance, no enrichment. It strips away the disguises and subterfuges of 'civilised' life and exposes the stark realities of raw human need with little comfort offered. Perhaps Stevenson is suggesting that wilderness is not territory we can enter and leave at will, but is a primal space that inhabits us wherever we are.

In *Sick Heart River*, Leithen, a successful lawyer and politician, has come to the far north of Canada to die. He has TB, the consequence of being gassed in the First World War. When he is asked to search for a missing French Canadian, he seizes the opportunity for a final act of redemption, 'to make his soul' as he puts it.[47] He sets out for the far north with a Métis guide, the son of a Cree mother and a Scottish Highland father who was a Hudson's Bay Company factor. Like Traill's children, Johnny Frizel and his brother Lew have been brought up to survive in a harsh environment. They have the skills and the disposition, a tenacity and stoicism which they have learned from their severely Presbyterian father. Buchan makes a direct link between endurance and Presbyterianism.

Johnny discovers that his brother is with the man they are seeking, a successful US businessman called Francis Galliard driven by a compulsion to reconnect with the frontier legacy of his forebears. Lew is seeking a paradise he once glimpsed, the beautiful valley of the Sick Heart River, a place where he believes man and nature can lead a symbiotic existence. A narrative evolves of four men, each engaging with an unforgiving landscape in their own way, two of them with delusions of their place in the wilderness, one of them knowing he is going to die there and the fourth, Johnny, doggedly doing what is necessary to keep them all alive. In Buchan's words, 'There was a stubborn sagacious dutifulness in that bullet head, that kindly Scots face, and those steadfast blue eyes which was beyond argument.'[48]

Also involved are two Hare Indians, virtually anonymous, whose tracking and hunting skills are invaluable.

Buchan's powerful descriptions reveal a wilderness that is immensely diverse, and affects individuals in different ways. Galliard loses his mind: 'this man had chosen the wilderness, and now the wilderness had taken him and tossed him up like the jetsam of a flood'.[49] Lew's delusions of paradise are shattered when he discovers that the enticing valley sustains no life; it is not, as he had hoped, 'a bit of the Garden of Eden that God had kept private for them as could find it'.[50] Leithen accepts that he is 'without the strength to face up to the brutishness of Nature'.[51]

The aspirations of the four men coalesce when they encounter a band of Hare Indians demoralised by sickness and famine. Leithen has a new lease of life. His officer background comes to his aid; thrust by need out of dependency, he takes command. The predicament of the Hares reminds them all that life in the far north is on sufferance and demands constant alertness. Leithen organises hunting expeditions and ensures that shelters are built and fires lit. He rediscovers 'the man he once had been', and he enables the others, spiritually and psychologically lost, to find themselves.[52] The commitment to keeping others as well as themselves alive offers redemption. They all face up to the harsh realities of the north, without illusions, and in the process demonstrate 'the brotherhood of all men, white and red and brown, who have to fight the savagery of the North' and that 'the cold infernal North magnified instead of dwarfing humanity. What a marvel was this clot of vivified dust!'[53] The effort kills Leithen, but he has 'made his soul', found faith through a direct, unmediated engagement with the stark realities of the wild. Galliard returns to his old life a wiser and more contented man. The two brothers, who both fought in the First World War, set off to offer their services in a second world war which has broken out during their absence in the wilderness.

Sick Heart River, a complex and introspective novel, contains a message as direct as that of Traill's *Lost in the Backwoods*, although the emphasis is different. The wilderness is not only dangerous and physically challenging; it is spiritually and psychologically challenging also. Survival requires not only physical skills and an understanding of its demands, but also the right temperament, the right attitude to the natural world and humankind's place in it, and some form of spirituality, whether or not specifically Christian. It is the spirit that not only powers the will to endure, but is the ultimate goal of endurance.

STEF PENNEY: 'TOO BIG, TOO EMPTY FOR HUMANS'

Sick Heart River is a twentieth-century tale which reminds us that the wilderness is still an arena of elemental contest. A much more recent novel returns to the past to explore similar territory. Stef Penney's *The Tenderness of Wolves* (2006) is set in 1867, the year of Canadian Confederation, with the narrative beginning in a settlement called Dove River on the north shore of Lake Huron's Georgian Bay. Its central character, Mrs Ross (we never learn her given name), is a Scottish immigrant, who arrived with her Highlander husband when the settlement was 'nothing but trees'.[54] Now it is an uneasy mix of pioneering ways and attempts at refinement. The narrative opens with a brutal murder, an act which in itself and in its complex but elemental connections with a savage land brings wilderness into the heart of the community. But like *Sick Heart River*, *The Tenderness of Wolves* is about journeys into the wild, loss and self-discovery.

Immediately after the murder Mrs Ross's adopted son disappears. She sets off with prime suspect William Parker, a Métis fur trader, to follow the tracks of her son, who is himself in pursuit of the man he believes to be the murderer. Donald Moody, a Hudson's Bay Company employee from Glasgow, is also on the hunt for the murderer. These multiple journeys head into a snow-bound landscape, pitted with pools of frozen water and scoured by wind and hail. For Moody, not a hardy Highlander, the land is 'sullen, indifferent, hostile',[55] but Mrs Ross, who considers herself a failure as a pioneer woman, finds, in the company of the mysterious but skilful Parker, a sense of release: 'I never thought I could stray so far into the wilderness without fear.'[56] She recalls a nightmare that recurred in her early days at the settlement: 'I am in the middle of the forest, and turning round to look back the way I came, I find that every direction looks exactly alike. I panic, disoriented. I know that I am lost, that I will never get out.'[57] Trudging through the snow and the intense cold, deeply anxious about Francis her son, she reflects on her unconventionality in both pioneering and polite society.

Underlying these journeys is the memory of an episode that had many years earlier scarred the community, when the two daughters of another Scottish family never returned from a picnic in the woods. Another strand of the narrative concerns a woman and her two young children, who, heading south from a remote Norwegian settlement, lose their compass and travel in circles until they are eventually, and fortuitously, found.

Penney assembles many characters in her tale of journeys, loss and being lost, fear and intense cold, savage rivalry and unlikely comradeship, death and near-death. Not all these characters are Scots, but the wild environment bears a strong Scottish imprint, and she examines the effects of a severe land and isolation on a variety of Scottish personalities. Donald Moody, ill-equipped for wilderness heroics, is nevertheless meticulously determined to do his duty. He does not survive. His HBC colleague Mackinley is self-serving and vicious. At Hanover House, where several journeys converge, the cunning and cruel John Stewart presides over an outpost that no longer has a purpose as the country around has been trapped out. He attempts to maintain 'the Company's fragile hold over the wilderness, more in honour of the past than for any sound financial reason'.[58] His Assistant Factor Frank Nesbitt, 'a man of education and some breeding' not long arrived from Scotland, seeks refuge from isolation in alcohol.[59] Back in Dove River and neighbouring Caulfield, granite-faced Angus Ross, Mrs Ross's husband, appears emotionless. Magistrate Andrew Knox is scrupulous and fair-minded, and the Setons, the now deceased parents of the missing girls, were a 'respectable family', Charles a doctor, his wife recently arrived from Scotland when their daughters disappeared.[60] Respectability was a weapon against the untamed, but no insurance against loss.

Penney's narrative may seem a long way from Ballantyne's exuberant adventure stories, but it is in fact equally about the testing of manhood, and of womanhood also. The almost anonymous Mrs Ross, who appears to have no identity other than a private troubled past and an almost marginal present, is not a model pioneer as presented by Catherine Parr Traill, but has a persistent integrity. And she discovers a courage that she did not know she had. A key test of adversity is to bring out latent qualities that an unchallenged life may never disclose. Those qualities may not be positive. The wilderness and its dangers can breed brutality – Stewart kills out of greed – and incapacitating fear, and the will to survive can eliminate all concern for others.

Mrs Ross's sense of release does not endure. When she and Parker eventually reach 'the end of the forest that seemed to have no end' they emerge onto 'a white sea on which waves of snow march to the horizon to north, east and west'. It is beautiful, but panic mounts. The vast distance is 'too big, too empty for humans, and if we venture out onto that plain, we will be vulnerable as ants on a dinner plate'. Now the forest seems 'familiar, friendly' and she fights the urge to turn back.[61] Although dependent on Parker, it is her willpower that enables her to carry on.

Penney has clearly drawn on the accounts of fur traders, explorers and settlers to recreate an experience of extreme conditions and extremes of human behaviour, and there are echoes of both Stevenson and Buchan in her narrative. She exposes the stresses and the fallibility of individuals and families struggling to function outwith the framework of 'normal' Victorian society, and allows their fortitude and humanity to emerge out of the tale, and out of the wilderness itself. Her wilderness is not as uncompromising as Stevenson's; as in Buchan's *Sick Heart River*, there is redemption, although it is embedded in ambivalence. She sets her story in the year of the

Dominion's birth, a time when the heyday of the fur trade had passed and the country was on the threshold of a new identity and a new era. Railways were being constructed, cities were expanding, precarious settlements were becoming rooted communities. The new Dominion aspired to connect from coast to coast. Yet connection and all that it implied would not – could not – eliminate wilderness nor protect civic society from new forms of wasteland. The relationship between natural wilderness and man-made wasteland, high-lighted by John Galt in the 1830s, was half a century later a focus of concern. It would become a recurrent theme in the work of several Scottish North American writers.

NOTES

1. Irving, *Tour*, p. 34.
2. Ibid., p. 28.
3. Traill, *Lost in the Backwoods*, p. 37.
4. R. M. Ballantyne, *The Young Fur Traders* (Edinburgh: Nelson, 1856), p. i.
5. Ibid., p.1.
6. Ibid., p. 4.
7. Ibid., p. 95.
8. Ibid., pp. 160–1.
9. Ibid., p. 207.
10. Ibid., p. 428.
11. Ibid., p. 429.
12. R. M. Ballantyne, *The Wild Man of the West* (London: Routledge, 1863), p. 28.
13. Ibid., p. 39.
14. Ibid., p. 33.
15. Ibid., pp. 76, 81.
16. Ibid., p. 225.
17. Ibid., p. 81.
18. Ibid., p. 90.
19. Scott, *Rob Roy*, p. 338.
20. Ballantyne, *Wild Man of the West*, p. 197.
21. Guthrie, *The Way West*, p. 217.
22. Guthrie, *The Big Sky*, p. 198.
23. Ibid., p. 350.
24. Guthrie, *The Way West*, p. 52.
25. Ibid., p. 218.
26. McMurtry, *Lonesome Dove*, p. 80.
27. Ibid., p. 112.
28. Ibid., p. 428.
29. Larry McMurtry, *Streets of Laredo* (London: Orion, 1993), p. 423.

30. Ibid., p. 44.
31. Ibid., p. 537.
32. Ibid., p. 363.
33. Booth, Bradford A. and Ernest Mehew (eds), *The Letters of Robert Louis Stevenson* (New Haven, CT: Yale University Press, 1994), vol. III, p. 16.
34. Stevenson, *Memories and Portraits*, p. 91.
35. Robert Louis Stevenson, *The Amateur Emigrant*, in *From the Clyde to California*, ed. Andrew Noble (Aberdeen: Aberdeen University Press, 1985), p. 110.
36. Ibid., p. 157.
37. Stevenson, *Squatters*, in *From the Clyde to California*, p. 242.
38. Ibid., p. 261.
39. Robert Louis Stevenson, *The Master of Ballantrae* (London: Dent, [1889] 1976), p. vi.
40. Ibid., p. 158.
41. Ibid., p. 163.
42. Ibid., p. 177.
43. Ibid., p. 166.
44. Ibid., p. 164.
45. Ibid., p. 165.
46. Ibid., p. 175.
47. John Buchan, *Sick Heart River* (Oxford: Oxford University Press, [1941] 1994), p. 57.
48. Ibid., p. 94.
49. Ibid., p. 100.
50. Ibid., p. 91.
51. Ibid., pp. 122–3.
52. Ibid., p. 173.
53. Ibid., p.191.
54. Ibid., p. 193.
55. Stef Penney, *The Tenderness of Wolves* (London: Quercus, [2006] 2007), p. 9.
56. Ibid., p. 138.
57. Ibid., p. 180.
58. Ibid., p. 294.
59. Ibid., p. 353.
60. Ibid., p. 18.
61. Ibid., p. 191.

8

The Hope of the World?

In God's wilderness lies the hope of the world – the great fresh unblighted, unredeemed wilderness.

John Muir, *John of the Mountains*

And Piper Gunn, he was a great tall man, with the voice of drums and the heart of a child, and the gall of a thousand, and the strength of conviction.

Margaret Laurence, *The Diviners*

When in the summer of 1868 John Muir first set foot in California's Sierra Nevada he was thirty years old. Nearly twenty of those years had been spent in North America, much of the time, through circumstance or choice, in wild country. He had explored woods, lakes and hills, and had walked a long stretch of the United States north to south. Now he was in the mountains which became a gateway to levels of experience beyond anything he had encountered before and changed the trajectory of his life.

It was a place of uplifting beauty, but a place also where the detritus of human intrusion was increasingly evident. The imprint of centuries of Native American footfall was almost imperceptible, but the invasion of the white man told a very different story. It was hard to escape the evidence of mining, timber-felling and sheep ranching. In the case of mining the actual activity had moved on, leaving its scars. In 1878, Muir published an article in the San Francisco *Evening Bulletin* which illustrated how the landscape was being transformed:

> Throughout the length and breadth of this mountain-barred wilderness you everywhere come upon these dead mining towns, with their tall chimney-stacks, standing forlorn amid broken walls and furnaces, and machinery half buried in the sand, the very names of many of them forgotten amid the excitements of later discoveries, and now known only through tradition – tradition ten years old.[1]

The speed of transformation and abandonment contrasted with the ancient presence of the rocks and mountains, themselves in a constant process of change, but at a speed determined by natural means rather than human interference. The following year he wrote on abandoned mining towns in Nevada 'like the bones of cattle that have died of thirst ... monuments of fraud and ignorance – scars against science'.[2]

Some months after the publication of this article, Robert Louis Stevenson and his wife Fanny spent their honeymoon in an abandoned mining camp on Mount St Helena north of San Francisco. They found:

> mountain and house and the old tools of industry ... all alike rusty and down-falling. The hill was here wedged up, and there poured forth its bowels in a spout of broken mineral; man with his picks and powder, and nature with her own great blasting tools of sun and rain, labouring together at the ruin of that proud mountain. The view up the canyon was a glimpse of devastation; dry red minerals sliding together, here and there a crag, here and there a dwarf thicket clinging in the general *glissade*, and over all a broken outline trenching on the blue of heaven. The human impact on the mountain was profound, but in the end the mountain prevailed.[3]

Stevenson observed the 'human impact' with an acute curiosity, at the same time as relishing mountain vistas and sunrises, and the necessarily rudimentary and makeshift few weeks he spent at Silverado. Although so often characterised as a writer of 'romance', Stevenson's attitude to wilderness was pragmatic as well as open and appreciative. Experience in both Scotland and the United States had taught him that life, whether wild or tame, was precarious and temporary. He relished the challenge of hard country, but had no illusions about its potential to diminish and at times destroy humanity. The mountain prevailed. For John Muir, in San Francisco at the same time as Stevenson although there is no record that the two ever met (they may, however, have read each other's words), the power of the mountains was to be embraced, not struggled against or passively admired.

Muir was eleven when in 1849 he left Scotland, emigrating with his family to Wisconsin. In his memoir *The Story of My Boyhood and Youth*, he recalled his childhood in Dunbar on Scotland's east coast as a mixture of freedom and intolerance, of joyful explorations of shore, cliff and the Lammermuir Hills, and ruthless chastisement. It was a rough upbringing, and would get rougher when the family began a new life on a remote homestead near Portage. John and his brother responded irrepressibly to the call of the wild:

> Wildness was ever sounding in our ears, and Nature saw to it that besides school lessons and church lessons some of her own lessons should be learned, perhaps with a view to the time when we should be called upon to wander in wildness to our heart's content.[4]

Punishment for these wanderings was an ineffective deterrent, and when John learned that the family were departing for America he was elated with anticipation. More wilderness lay ahead: 'boundless woods full of mysterious good things ... no gamekeepers to stop us in all the wild, happy land'.[5] But his grandfather, left behind in Dunbar, warned: 'plenty hard, hard work'.[6] Both prognostications would prove to be correct.

Leaving Scotland brought an end to John Muir's formal schooling, but not to education. Landscape and wildlife were freely available resources which he continually absorbed: 'Nature streaming into us, wooingly teaching her wonderful glowing lessons, so unlike the dismal grammar ashes and cinders so long thrashed into us ... Oh, that glorious Wisconsin wilderness!'[7] He was equally shaped by his severe Presbyterian upbringing and a relentless father who believed in hard work, hard punishment and no mollycoddling. Daniel Muir was devoutly convinced that an independent spirit was ungodly and dangerous, but his eldest son resisted all efforts to eliminate the urge to explore and experiment. If anything, these efforts were counter-productive: John Muir's hardy resourcefulness was strengthened. And, perhaps unconsciously, he absorbed from his father's uncompromising Calvinism an ethic of tenacity and self-denial which became a driving force in his future life.

In August 1867, Muir set off on a journey of exploration. He had spent three years taking classes at the University of Wisconsin, where he had met people, in particular Ezra and Jeanne Carr, who had recognised his abilities and encouraged his studies. In 1864, he had slipped away into Canada, to escape the draft for the Civil War which had been introduced the previous year – organised and authorised killing appalled him. He found lodgings with the Campbell family in Bradford, Ontario and spent time botanising on the shores of lakes Huron and Ontario before getting work at a Georgian Bay sawmill. When the war was over he returned to the United States and found employment at a factory in Indianapolis which produced a range of wooden implements. It suited his practical and inventive skills, which he had developed from boyhood.

Equipped with a minimum of possessions and supplies, which included the New Testament, Milton's *Paradise Lost* and the poems of Robert Burns ('Wherever a Scotsman goes, there goes Burns', he would write some forty years later).[8] Muir headed east, walking around twenty-five miles a day. He crossed the Cumberland Mountains into Pennsylvania, and then turned south. He walked through a landscape devastated by war, and in the Appalachians he encountered the descendants of Scots and Ulster Scots who were living a frontier existence little changed from that of the first settlers. By the time he reached Savannah, Georgia, he had run out of money and was going without food. In Florida, he collapsed with malaria.

This 1,000-mile walk was a kind of test, a proof of his stamina and self-sufficiency (although he received help along the way, particularly when he was ill), as well as an adventure undertaken in a spirit of curiosity. But it was only a prelude, albeit enlightening. His real goal was California and the mountains of the Sierra Nevada. When he reached San Francisco, after two ocean voyages and the land crossing of the Panama isthmus, he headed at once for Yosemite.

Over the next few years he spent as much time as he could in the mountains. He found employment herding sheep and working in a saw mill. He took every opportunity to climb, to follow rivers and penetrate canyons, to observe and record the character and movement of glaciers, and generally to experience the Sierra in all conditions and weathers. His concern was not just to contemplate the natural world, but to live within it. And there was no going back. He realised that it was too late to adjust to the expectations and demands of conventional life. In a letter to his family in Wisconsin he wrote:

> I know that I could under ordinary circumstances accumulate wealth and obtain a fair position in society, and I am arrived at an age that requires that I should choose some definite course for life. But I am sure that the mind of no truant schoolboy is more free and disengaged from all the grave plans and purposes and pursuits of ordinary orthodox life than mine.[9]

Muir's habituation to wilderness made him unfit for 'ordinary orthodox life', just as it did the mountain men. As he grew older he found conformity easier, but he never neutralised the irresistible pull of the mountains – and never wanted to.

When Robert Louis Stevenson crossed America by train, he experienced great relief when it at last climbed into the mountains after traversing 'deserts of alkali and sand, horrible to man'.[10] He woke in the night to a chill in the air and a 'mountain atmosphere': 'I returned to roost with a grateful mountain feeling at my heart'. The following morning he looked out at:

> A huge pine-forested ravine upon my left, a foaming river, and a sky already coloured with the fires of dawn … you will scarce believe how my heart leapt at this. It was like meeting one's wife. I had come home again – home from unsightly deserts, to the green and habitable corners of the earth. Every spire of pine along the hill-top, every trouty pool along that mountain river, was more dear to me than a blood relation.

For Stevenson, the landscape was charged with familiarity. It was habitable, accessible territory that his imagination could deal with. His encounters with Scottish mountains had not necessarily been benign, but there is no sense here of threat. On the contrary, he shared his fellow passengers' response to the mountains of California that they signalled 'the good country' of their hopes.[11]

When Muir set off on his 1,000-mile walk he had little experience of mountains. The Lammermuirs of his youth were wild but not high and there are no mountains in Wisconsin. But he had an urgent need to be among them – they represented the ultimate wilderness experience. The mountains of California were formidable to climb, demanded the tenacity and self-denial in which he had been schooled and which he continued to seek, and afforded an intimate connection with the earth and its structures. Mountains were the source of spiritual and emotional intensity as well as a test of all the qualities Muir valued most. In September 1871, he wrote to Jeanne Carr:

> The grandest of these forces & their glorious results overpower me & inhabit my whole being, waking or sleeping I have no rest[.] In dreams I read blurred sheets of glacial writing or follow lines of cleavage or struggle with the difficulties of some extraordinary rock form.[12]

Over and over again Muir would stress that the natural world embraced humanity:

> Wonderful how completely everything in wild nature fits into us, as if truly part and parent of us. The sun shines not on us but in us. The river flows not past, but through us, thrilling, tingling, vibrating every fiber and all of the substance of our bodies as well as our souls, and every bird song, wind song, and tremendous storm song of the rocks in the heart of the mountains is our song, our very own, and sings our love.[13]

Submission to the wild was Muir's creed, and he regarded it as the truest relationship with God. He had no illusions about nature's potentially destructive power, but had a conviction, perhaps extraordinary, that a willing and generous surrender to all nature's manifestations was itself a kind of protection. It was something he wanted everyone to share. 'I care to live only to entice people to look at Nature's loveliness,' he wrote to Jeanne Carr.[14] But 'look at' was only the beginning. Muir himself had learnt how to immerse himself in nature.

An essential part of this immersion was its solitary character. Muir preferred to walk and climb alone, without the distraction of company or conversation. His ascent of the High Sierra peaks – Mount Ritter, Mount Whitney, Mount Shasta and many others – was the expression of a sense of kinship with the mountains themselves. People and things only got in the way of that kinship. He climbed without equipment, sometimes even without basic warm clothing, and with minimal supplies, often only tea, bread and oatmeal. Although he had several near-death experiences, his confidence in that kinship and his faith, in his own abilities and in God, meant that he could give himself wholly to high-risk experiences. He describes hanging on to a cliff edge or to a tree top in a gale in language almost of rapture. Here he is on Mount Shasta, which he set off to climb knowing that a snowstorm was imminent:

> Presently the storm broke forth into full snowy bloom, and the thronging crystals darkened the air. The wind swept past in hissing floods, grinding the snow into meal and sweeping down into the hollows in enormous drifts all the heavier particles, while the finer dust was sifted through the sky, increasing the icy gloom. But my fire glowed bravely as if in glad defiance of the drift to quench it … I was snug and warm, and the passionate uproar produced a glad excitement.[15]

The blizzard trapped Muir on the mountain slope for a week, during which time he observed the trees, the sky and the activities of a squirrel, examined snow crystals under a lens, and made notes.

In many ways Muir was in a privileged position. He was not driven into the wilderness by commercial pressures. He was beholden to no organisation or institution: his only agenda was his own. He had the opportunity as well as the desire to make his expeditions into the wild, although never as often as he would have liked. He had supportive friends who provided hospitality and advice, and recognised that out of his wilderness experiences came a message that it was important to communicate. Even after his marriage in 1880, which brought new responsibilities and drew him into a career as a fruit farmer and businessman, Muir found the space and the time to head for the mountains.

Muir's writing career began in San Francisco with essays for the magazine *Overland* and his *Evening Bulletin* articles. He wanted his readers to experience the natural world as he did, and he alerted them to the consequences of its erosion: deforestation, pollution of rivers, the destruction of habitats. He reflected that when New England pilgrims 'began to fish and build' it must have seemed impossible to imagine that the boundless resources of so vast a wilderness could ever come to an end, but 'neither our "illimitable" forests or ocean, or river fisheries are now regarded as inexhaustible'.[16] But it was another ten years before Muir was able to reach a wider audience, when, after his meeting with Robert Underwood Johnson, he began to write articles for the *Century* magazine, of which Johnson was editor.

In the summer of 1889, Johnson, in California to investigate Sierra gold mining, had accompanied Muir on a trip to Yosemite. Johnson's exposure to the degradation of the wilderness spurred him to persuade Muir to write about it for *Century*. It was the start of an organised campaign to alert the public to the need for conservation. 'All that is accessible and destructible', Muir wrote, 'is being rapidly destroyed, and by far the greater part of this destruction of the fineness of the wilderness is of a kind that can claim no right relationship with that which necessarily follows use.'[17] The consequence was the creation in 1890 of Yosemite National Park.

Johnson identified Muir as uniquely persuasive not just because he had an intimate knowledge of the mountains, rivers and forests and every facet of their delineation, the glaciers, the rock formations, the effects of wind and weather. It was his ability to communicate his oneness with the wilderness and the spiritual nature of his empathy that gave him so powerful a voice. By the early 1890s, Muir was acknowledged as a leading figure in a growing conservation movement. In 1892, the Sierra Club was founded and Muir became its first president. Although its conservation aims frequently brought the Sierra Club into conflict with authority and commercial interests, Muir was now an establishment figure with a public role.

In 1879, Muir had made his first trip to Alaska, and was there again the following year and in 1890. Alaska was powerfully attractive to him. It presented new mountains and the opportunity to pursue his fascination with glaciers. On the first trip he climbed Glenora Peak in the company of Samuel Hall Young, a Presbyterian missionary based at Fort Wrangell. (He later founded the first Presbyterian church at Fairbanks and was appointed General Missionary to Alaska.) Young fell, dislocated both shoulders, and had to be brought off the mountain by Muir, a slow and painfully demanding descent in the dark.

On his second Alaskan trip Muir had the adventure with Young's dog Stickeen which he recounts in the story of that name. From Taylor Bay, he set out to explore Brady Glacier in bad weather and with only a piece of bread in his pocket. The little terrier insisted on accompanying him. Towards the end of an exhausting day of hard going across snow and ice, frequently jumping fissures in the glacier, they found themselves wet, cold and hungry, stranded between two immensely wide and deep crevasses. The only way out was across a narrow ice bridge below them. 'Of the many perils encountered in my years of wandering on mountains and glaciers none seemed so plain and stern and merciless as this.'[18] Muir described how he cut steps in the ice to reach the 70-ft sliver of bridge, edged his away across and climbed the far side.

> At such times one's whole body is eye, and common skill and fortitude are replaced by power beyond our call or knowledge. Never before had I been so long under deadly strain. How I got up that cliff I never could tell. The thing seemed to have been done by somebody else. I never have held death in contempt, though in the course of my explorations I have oftentimes felt that to meet one's fate on a noble mountain, or in the heart of a glacier, would be blessed as compared with death from disease, or from some shabby lowland accident. But the best death, quick and crystal-pure, set so

glaringly open before us, is hard enough to face, even though we feel gratefully sure that we have already had happiness enough for a dozen lives.[19]

At first Stickeen, who had throughout the day demonstrated a willing courage and agility, would not follow him, but after much effort and persuasion on Muir's part at last the terrified dog also crossed the ice bridge. From that point on he attached himself firmly to Muir's side.

Stickeen is a memorable contribution to the dog story genre, but it also illustrates many aspects of Muir's relationship with the wild. He is undeterred by difficult terrain and adverse weather. He makes no special preparations and, indeed, relishes his minimalist approach. His passionate curiosity drives him on mile after mile, and his attitude to danger is both pragmatic and spiritual. Confidence in his own abilities is essential, but there are occasions when survival seems to depend on some power that is beyond human experience, and his acknowledgement of this is part of his respect for nature, which in turn is embedded in spiritual faith. The story also illustrates his empathy, in this case focused on the dog but throughout his writings demonstrated in the way he communicates genuinely and spontaneously with landscape and the creatures it sustains.

Muir was convinced that wilderness was essential to the well-being of humanity, but although he was so active in encouraging the recreational benefits of engaging with wild country, it was his solo encounters with the totally untamed that meant most to him. For Muir, the challenge of Alaska was an antidote to the national park concept, which depended on making wilderness accessible to a largely urban public without the skills and the knowledge to experience or appreciate it. The future of the conservation movement required public recognition of the value of wilderness. If wild terrain was difficult to reach, and uncomfortable and possibly unsafe to explore, such recognition was unlikely to be achieved. Muir recognised that conservation demanded compromise.

Increasingly, Muir also accepted that there was a place for limited and careful exploitation of wilderness resources – as a farmer, he was himself implicated in the degradation of the wild. The origins and development of the United States depended on such exploitation. The best future for the wilderness that remained was to find ways of benefiting from its usefulness, both economically and socially:

Thousands of tired, nerve-shaken, over-civilized people are beginning to find out that going to the mountains is going home; that wildness is a necessity, and that mountain parks and reservations are useful not only as fountains of timber and irrigating rivers, but as fountains of life.[20]

By the end of the century there were many conflicting views on conservation issues, from within the movement as well from those who opposed the very idea of protection. Although the younger Muir believed that humanity's engagement with the natural world should be direct and unencumbered and impose minimally on the environment, he understood the pressures of a public hungry for the restorative as well as the economic benefits of wilderness. Compromise was inevitable.

However, John Muir did not compromise over his last battle. In 1908, backed by the Sierra Club, he threw himself into combating the proposal to dam the Hetch Hetchy River in order to provide water for San Francisco. Hetch Hetchy canyon, where a reservoir was to be built, was within the confines of the national park. Muir, at the age of seventy-one, had lost none of his fighting spirit or his sermonising vigour:

> In these ravaging, money mad days, monopolizing San Francisco capitalists are now doing their best to destroy Yosemite Park ... these devotees of ravaging commercialism seem to have a perfect contempt for Nature, and instead of lifting their eyes to the God of the mountains, lift them to the almighty dollar.[21]

All objections were over-ruled. Muir died the following year.

Muir was a dynamic and contradictory figure. His relationship with the wilderness was both intensely personal and messianic. He cherished his solo experiences yet, although writing did not always come easily, he needed to communicate them. The very act of communication was in a sense a compromise, but language itself was an important part of his connection with nature. Putting his experiences into words confirmed their physical, emotional and spiritual reality. Although he appeared to reject the narrow Calvinism of his upbringing, he was clearly deeply influenced by it; not least was an apparently innate self-discipline and his absorption of a sense of responsibility and commitment. He shared this with other Scots who encountered extremes of wilderness, John Richardson and John Rae, for example, but his ability to transform near-death into a celebration of the natural world was probably unique.

Muir, like many other Scots, almost certainly needed America in order to make his mark. He needed not only the wilderness and the freedom it bestowed, but the social and cultural environment of the second half the nineteenth century. His youth replicated the Scottish tale of the 'lad o' pairts' transplanted into American virgin soil, a combination of independent endeavour, respect for education, and a recognition of talent by those with the means to offer support and encouragement. It was a tale that readily fitted the dream of American opportunity. Muir's ideas and his articulation of them were influenced by Emerson, whom he met, and by Thoreau who were both already expressing a sense of loss as materialism and the pace of progress severed the connection with the wild. But there is a self-consciousness, a knowingness, about both Emerson and Thoreau, which Muir does not share. He gained in sophistication as he gained experience of worlds other than the natural, but he never entirely lost a quality of innocent wonder. The climate was right for the craggy Scot who exemplified so much that the United States admired even as he passionately challenged many cherished aspirations. John Muir never relinquished his Scottish identity; at the same time he was the epitome of American rugged independence.

Isabella Bird visited Lake Tahoe, north of Yosemite, at the same time as John Muir was in the Sierras. She also preferred to travel alone, and she also immersed herself in the natural splendour surrounding her.

> The beauty is entrancing. The sinking sun is out of sight behind the western Sierras, and all the pine-hung promontories on this side of the water are rich indigo, just reddened with lake, deepening here and there into Tyrian purple. The peaks above, which still catch the sun, are bright rose-red, and all the mountains on the other side are pink; and pink, too, are the far-off summits on which the snow-drifts rest. Indigo, red, and orange tints stain the still water, which lies solemn and dark against the shore, under the shadow of stately pines. An hour later, and a moon nearly full – not a pale, flat disc, but a radiant sphere – has wheeled up into the flushed sky. The sunset has passed through every stage of beauty, through every glory of color, through riot and triumph, through pathos and tenderness, into a long, dreamy, painless rest, succeeded by the profound solemnity of the moonlight, and a stillness broken only by the night cries of beasts in the aromatic forests.[22]

Bird captures strikingly the sheer visual splendour of the scene, but not far away was the Donner Pass. The train which had brought her to Truckee had passed through it. It had acquired notoriety and its name nearly a quarter of a century earlier through the disaster that overtook the Donner party making their way west; the episode was much in Bird's mind as she explored the area around Truckee. Disease, starvation, death and cannibalism marked a harrowing blizzard-beaten journey. (Among those in the party of Scottish descent was Milton Elliot, whose body provided sustenance for the starving.) The railroad changed everything. It would bring tourists and hotels to Lake Tahoe. It would bring Robert Louis Stevenson to San Francisco. It would enable Muir to stay in contact with his family. And it brought extensive commercial benefits, and all their environmental consequences, to California.

Exploitation had not waited for the railroad. The inexorable process of transforming wilderness into wasteland had begun, in some cases long before, as both Muir and Stevenson identified. It is a process that is woven into the pioneering experience, apparently innocuous in its earliest stages –

how could a few felled trees and a few acres of planted crops have a lasting impact? But by the early nineteenth century it is apparent in accounts by numerous Scots who settled or travelled in North America. John Galt described a surreal landscape of tree stumps and scattered timber. John Howison in Upper Canada's Glengarry similarly commented on the 'profusion of decayed and half-burnt timber' and the forest enveloped with the smoke.[23] Others commented on the profligacy that came in the wake of seemingly unlimited resources, and the sometimes feral existence such profligacy encouraged. Although the taming of the wild so often seemed a Sisyphean task, even minimal impact, which achieved little for 'civilisation', could have lasting consequences. Ivan Doig, in his memoir *This House of Sky* and in his fiction, expresses the precarious existence of small-scale sheep ranchers in Montana. In *Bucking the Sun* (1996), Hugh and Margaret Duff arrive from Scotland in 1910 to take up residence in a decaying home-stead. It seems that the effort to make an impact on the environment has already failed, and over the next two or three decades there is little hope of improvement. Yet they hang on, and that very persistence becomes organic to the landscape itself, as the landscape shapes all aspects of their lives.

And whatever the consequences, the task itself retained an heroic quality. It was a proof of manhood, of courage and conviction, of endurance and skill, of individual tenacity and social responsibility. John Muir, committed to preserving rather than subduing wild country, displayed the same qualities as the pioneer who measured his achievement through trees felled, crops harvested and roads built to enable commerce and social interaction. For women pioneering demanded the same qualities, with the added challenge of childbearing. Survival often depended on mutual support; at the same time wilderness imposed self-sufficiency. Even when communities emigrated and settled together, however valuable their support structures they were unlikely to be adequate in circumstances so very different from the home country. For men and women, but perhaps particularly for women, the overlaying of the forces of nature with the forces of religious and civic authority were profoundly important. But nothing could be achieved with-out affecting the environment. By the late nineteenth century there was a growing regret at the loss of wilderness, and at the same time a growing nostalgia for the skills and fortitude that brought about that loss. And by that time there were new configurations of wilderness to impose on the lives of subsequent generation.

LEGACY AND CONTINUITY: 'COMING HOME ACROSS THE WILDNESS'

In the work of Scottish Canadian writers over the last century there are recurring themes of old and new wilderness. The old, natural wilderness survives, often unexpectedly and in circumstances where humanity is without the resources to handle it. And meanwhile, the new, man-made wilderness expands and threatens, both physically and psychologically. It is a wilderness created by backyards as well as by industrial sites, by kitchen gardens as well as by large-scale extraction. It is marked by the detritus of material life and a sterility that contrasts starkly with even the most extreme wilderness encountered by explorers and pioneers.

Margaret Laurence grew up in Manitoba, and incorporates into her novel *The Diviners* the story of the Scottish settlement at Red River. Her displaced Highlanders and their trek from Churchill to York Factory are at the heart of a mythic tale related by Christie Logan, who is proud of his Scottish origins and wants to ensure that the novel's heroine, Morag Gunn, shares his understanding and his pride. His Scottish settlers arrive at 'this almighty godforsaken land, dreadful with all manner of beasts and ice and rocks harsher than them we left', and disembark onto this 'terrible bad land' accompanied by the bagpipes of Piper Gunn, Morag's forebear. When spring arrives they struggle 'through all them frozen lands, and through the muskeg there and through the muck and mud of the melting snows, and through the hard snow itself although it was spring', always urged on by the bagpipes. And when after another trek they reach Red River they have a hard future in front of them:

> Och aye, it was hard. It was so hard you could barely feature it. Locusts. Hailstorms. Floods. Blizzards. Indians. Halfbreeds. Hot as the pit of hell in the summer, and the mosquitoes as big as sparrows. Winters so cold it would freeze the breath in your throat and turn your blood to red ice.[24]

It is an heroic tale of survival in the face of every kind of hostility, told and retold a century and a half later in a community filled with Scottish names: Cameron, Macleod, Duncan, McVitie, Melrose, Christie, Gunn.

Manawaka is a fictional community, based on Laurence's home town of Neepawa, one of the many prairie towns that came into being in the wake of the railroad, about 180 km northwest of Winnipeg. Laurence depicts a mixed community of Scots, Ukrainians and Métis, each with their own identity and their own perception of wilderness. Morag, a doctor's daughter, is adopted as a child by Christie and Prin Logan, and grows up on the wrong side of the tracks. The once brown paint on the wooden house has been blistered by hot summers and 'bone-chilling blizzard howling winters'. The front porch is:

> floored with splintered unsteady boards. The yard a junk heap, where a few carrots and petunias fought a losing battle against the chickweed, lamb's

quarters, creeping Charlie, dandelions, couchgrass, old car axles, a decrepit black buggy with one wheel missing, pieces of iron and battered saucepans which might come in useful someday but never did, a broken babycarriage and two ruined armchairs with the springs hanging out and the upholstery torn and mildewed.[25]

Junk becomes a motif in the novel, in which discarded or obsolete objects take on a symbolic resonance. They connect with the past, but take on new meanings as time passes and experiences change. Christie is the local garbage collector. He takes the town's rubbish to the dump, 'the Nuisance Grounds', and scavenges from the riches that accumulate there. This is the new wilderness, a fetid heap of old clothes, broken furniture, empty cans and bottles, rotting food, holed saucepans, a cracked toilet bowl, a rusted car, and all overlaid by 'a ZILLION crawling flies'.[26] From this place Christie has furnished his home. The new wilderness is also the collection of shanties and lean-tos inhabited by the Métis Tonnerre family, built from poles chinked with mud, flattened tin cans and tarpaper, with 'lots of old car parts and chicken wire and worn out car tires lying around'.[27] The Tonnerres also raid the dump. This, it seems, is what remains of the pioneering past.

The novel concerns Morag's attempt to find, or create, an identity that is meaningful in the context of contemporary Canada. She has a child with Jules Tonnerre, thus linking the First Nations, French and Scottish inheritance. She tries out city life. She falls in love with a married man from the Black Isle and goes to Scotland in search of him and of her family's origins. Dan McRaith's house is also full of mess and detritus: 'a beat-up table, a variety of chairs in various stages of collapse, two cats, a jumble of anoraks and rubber Wellington boots, books, buckets, cooking pots, rock and shell collections, fishing rods, piles of old newspapers … a cardboard box of broken toys …'[28] The context is entirely different, a village on the northeast coast of Scotland rather than a dusty landlocked prairie town, but there are clear echoes of the Logan and Tonnerre homes. Scotland also has a new wilderness.

To the north is Sutherland, where in the early nineteenth century the Gunns were displaced from their home. But Morag discovers that she no longer needs to make that pilgrimage. She is content with the myth of the heroic contest with the wilderness that Christie has handed down to her: 'the myths are my reality'.[29] Scotland is not, after all, her land: 'it's not mine, except a long way back. I always thought it was the land of my ancestors, but it is not,' she says to Dan. And when Dan asks what land is hers, she replies: 'Christie's real country. Where I was born.'[30] At Christie's funeral a piper, Scotty Grant, dressed in 'a blue open-necked workshirt and unpressed grey trousers', plays 'The Flowers of the Forest' at his graveside, and Morag hears Christie's voice retelling the epic tale: '*And Piper Gunn, he was a great tall man, with the voice of drums and the heart of a child, and the gall of a thousand, and the strength of conviction.*'[31] The honouring of the myth grows more important as the distance from its origins grows.

The novel ends with Morag living in southern Ontario in an old pioneer cabin and writing a novel based on the Scottish settlers from Sutherland whose story had filled her childhood.

> The novel follows them on the sea journey to Hudson Bay, through that winter at Churchill and then on the long walk to York Factory in the spring. Christie always said they walked about a thousand miles – it was about a hundred and fifty, in fact, but you know, he was right; it must've felt like a thousand. The man who led them on that march, and on the trip by water to Red River, was young Archie Macdonald, but in my mind the piper who played them on will always be that giant of a man, Piper Gunn, who probably never lived in so-called real life but who lives forever.[32]

Although Morag has severed her connection with Scotland, she takes on Christie's role as conduit of inheritance. Through her, this particular story of Scottish immigration is embedded in a Canadian narrative. It is as if the wilderness itself and the very fact of overcoming it is the passport to a new land, a new reality with all its contradictions. The piper at Christie's grave-side plays a traditional Scottish tune, but he is wearing the clothes of a Canadian working man. Morag has grown up in a twentieth-century waste-land, and now inhabits a pioneer cabin.

Laurence's contemporary Hugh MacLennan was also concerned with issues of identity, of Canada and Canadians. He describes a successful, staunchly Presbyterian Scottish Canadian elite, worthy citizens benefiting from the pioneering efforts of earlier generations, distanced from the sources of their wealth. Huntly McQueen in *Two Solitudes* (1945) is narrow-minded but not of narrow vision. His ambition is to 'organise Canada' by controlling a great range of production: mines, lumber mills, factories, construction companies, engineering works.[33] This is not the bold adventuring of George Simpson but, like Simpson, it is control McQueen wants and he believes there are empty spaces his business ambitions can fill. In the same novel, MacLennan offers different perspectives, in rural Quebec where the traditional French Canadian community is suspicious of 'English' in-comers, and in the glimpse he gives us of Nova Scotia seen through the eyes of soldiers returning from Europe after the First World War, travelling by train from Halifax to Montreal:

> They saw, as if for the first time, how empty the country looked, how silent it was. They noticed the towns like collections of grey and brown wooden

boxes scattered as if by a hand's gesture in the clearings, dirt streets running through them and perhaps a short stretch of asphalt near the brick or sandstone post-office. They saw the red brick or board railway stations, nearly every one the same … They saw the little Nova Scotia trout streams, each one shallow and freshly splashing over amber-coloured stones. They saw the Miramichi, wide and steel-grey, curving flat calm out of the spruce forests.[34]

The human imprint on the land seems tentative and dispirited, disconnected from both its pioneering past and the city of factories and wealth creation which is their destination. When they arrive at Montreal they parade through the city with the pipe band playing 'The Blue Bonnets' and 'A Hundred Pipers'.

In *The Diviners* Margaret Laurence explores the discovery of a Canadian identity, and in the process reflecting back aspects of Scotland's history which have an important place in Scotland's cultural environment as well as Canada's. Alistair MacLeod's fiction absorbs Scotland into his narratives to an even greater extent. His novel *No Great Mischief* (1999) and his stories written over thirty years and collected most recently in a volume entitled *Island* (2002) are rooted in the experience of Highland settlement in Cape Breton Island and the struggle to establish a foothold in an unrelenting environment. In 'The Road to Rankin's Point' he describes a rugged Cape Breton landscape with the Atlantic Ocean pounding at the foot of the cliffs. Once inhabited by a community of Highlanders, it could almost be Scotland. There are thistles and bluebells, birch trees and wild roses, sheep and collie dogs, all signifiers of a Highland settlement. There are patches of still-cleared land 'indicating where houses had once stood. The grey granite stones of their foundations are still visible …'[35]

This could be an abandoned Highland croft, rather than a Canadian homestead occupied by a woman in her nineties, living alone. She is the only person still remaining at Rankin's Point. If she goes the sheep, cattle, horses and dogs will go too and a continuum, damaged but not broken by crossing the Atlantic, will end. The grandmother is the only surviving link with the pioneering past. Her husband died, drunk, in the snow. Three brothers died young, 'perished in the accidental ways that grew out of their lives':

One as a young man in the summer sun when the brown-dappled horses bolted and he fell into the teeth of a mowing machine. A second in a storm at sea when the vessel sank while plying its way across the straits to Newfoundland. A third frozen upon the lunar ice fields of early March when the sealing ship became separated from its men in a sudden obliterating blizzard.[36]

The next generation have all moved on, but when they get together in the Cape Breton homestead they reconnect with their inheritance, bringing out the fiddles and harmonicas and guitars to play 'complicated jigs and reels' – Celtic music played on a mix of instruments which root it in the New World as well as in Scotland.[37] They evoke the two layers of their past, the generations of Hebridean life of minimal material comfort but with a rich cultural environment, and their more recent history as contenders in the wilderness.

More recent history is signified also by the remains of a car wreck at the foot of the cliff, as if the cliff itself had defeated the twentieth century:

> Here the twisted chassis and there the detached body and yards away the steering wheel and the trunk lid and a crumpled twisted door. The cormorants and the gulls walk carefully amidst the twisted wreckage as if hoping that each day may bring them something that they had previously missed. They peck with curiosity at the gleaming silver knobs and the selector buttons of the once-expensive radio.[38]

Again, as in Laurence, the decaying remnants of the symbol of twentieth-century mobility suggest the impermanence of the impact of progress. It is a third layer of the pioneering narrative. Abandoned mouldering cars are also found in Scottish Highland and Island landscapes.

By the end of the story Grandma is dead, choosing to remain in the place where her husband died and in the home where she raised her children alone. Her grandson Calum has cancer and himself has not long to live. His knowledge of this drives him to reach for the past, 'hoping to have more and more past as I have less and less future'.[39] He is trying to recover the half remembered. How can the legacy of language and music, of traditional beliefs and intuitions, of survival in hard lands, be maintained? Most of MacLeod's stories explore ways in which that legacy fades and transmutes and yet, after a fashion, hangs on.

No Great Mischief is a family chronicle, telling the story of '*clann Calum ruaidh*', who departed from Moidart in 1779 to settle in Cape Breton. It is a powerful story of endeavour and loss, adaptation and inevitable dispersal. The phantom-like patriarchal figure of '*Calum ruadh*', 'Red Calum', presides over each generation of the narrative. There is a reversal of expectations, as we begin to understand that the contemporary hero is not the respectable, middle-class professional man who tells the story and represents success, but his alcoholic elder brother. We meet him at the start of the novel in a seedy room in Toronto drunkenly singing a Gaelic lament, not about leaving Scotland, but about leaving Cape Breton. He is haunted by his forebears' pioneering experience and maintains an organic connection with the past, with the Cape Breton environment and with his Gaelic inheritance. He has led a wandering, but not rootless, existence which has brought him nothing of conventional stability or fulfilment. Yet it is through him that a kind of collective survival for '*clann Calum ruaidh*' is possible, which maintains faith with family and history in the old and the new country.

The narrative evolves through a series of carefully modulated flashbacks as the two brothers, and sometimes other siblings, exchange memories of the past. Memory is the pivot. It reaches back to a time before they were born, to the departure from Scotland which they have absorbed in their upbringing, and to the experiences of pioneering. It absorbs the losses inflicted by a harsh climate and difficult terrain: death at sea before even arriving, death under the ice, death in the uranium mines at the edge of the Canadian Shield, death through violence bred of rivalry in a hard country. The Gaelic language, beginning to fade, is a crucial link. Individual and collective memory, the remembered past and the remembered narratives of the past, are at the heart of MacLeod's stories, and their rhythmic echoes of an oral tradition are no accident. Like Christie Logan remembering Piper Gunn, the grandfather evokes the MacDonalds after the Battle of Killiecrankie in 1689:

> I see them sometimes coming home across the wildness of Rannoch Moor in the splendours of the autumn sun. I imagine them coming with their horses and their banners and their plaids tossed arrogantly over their shoulders. Coming with their broadswords and their claymores and their bull-hide targes decorated with designs of brass.[40]

For both, a heroic past, whether in wild Scotland or wild Canada, still lives.

There is a continuity between Cape Breton and the Scottish Highlands. It is more than the landscape and the collie dogs who make frequent appearances in MacLeod's fiction. It is more than the language and the music. It is there in the mind sets and attitudes, in, for example, the two grandfathers in *No Great Mischief*, the one stern, self-disciplined, solitary, the other easy-going and extrovert, echoing, like McMurtry's Woodrow Call and Gus McCrae, Stevenson's David Balfour and Alan Breck. It is there also in the drive of continuing migration. What these stories suggest is that leaving Cape Breton is a repetition of leaving Scotland, that the migration goes on, that it is a part of Scottish and Scottish Canadian experience that cannot be escaped, and that each new place is a potential wilderness, full of hazards and trials.

Cape Breton Island, MacLeod's territory, though connected to the mainland by a man-made causeway, has an ambience of island separateness. When at the end of *No Great Mischief* the brothers drive across the flooded causeway, Cape Breton is almost an island again. They are going home, to a place deeply imprinted by families and communities of Scottish Highland descent, communities who brought with them their own sense of separateness from

Lowland Scotland and the rest of Britain, a separateness underpinned by the designation of the Scottish Highlands as wild country. The suggestion is that the loss of culture is the direct result of the loss of a way of life that demanded self-sufficiency, a suggestion that, of course, has considerable resonance in Scotland as well as in Canada.

In Alice Munro's story 'The Wilds of Morris Township' Andrew Laidlaw and his two cousins, all from the Scottish Borders, walk with axes on their shoulders 'to try our fortunes in the wilds of Morris Township' in the Huron Tract.[41] It is November 1851. They are not anticipating an easy time: 'we expected to have some hardships to endure and we made the best of them we could'.[42] The hardships included felling huge trees in deep snow, learning to cope with isolation, and leading a spare and monastic existence 'without any visitations of grace or moments of transcendence'.[43] Life was work.

The stories in Munro's collection *The View from Castle Rock* (2006) are based on the experience of her own family and her memories of growing up in Ontario. Their starting point is a visit to Edinburgh and a climb to the castle's ramparts, where the ten-year-old Andrew looks out across a stretch of water and sees 'a pale green and greyish-blue land, part in sunlight and part in shadow, a land as light in mist, sucked into the sky' which his father tells him is America. 'There,' says his father, 'is where every man is sitting in the midst of his own properties, and even the beggars is riding around in carriages.'[44]

When in the title story Andrew Laidlaw, Munro's grandfather, reaches the real North America, rather than Fife beyond the Firth of Forth, he finds a vast and thinly peopled land 'uncultivated and covered with wood'.[45] To make something of the wilderness requires not just stamina and hard work, but discipline and denial. In 'Working for a Living' Munro remembers her grandfather as a staunch Presbyterian born 'to live by hard routines and refusals', who 'maintained his air of discipline and privacy'.[46] The link with the homeland is not relinquished. He and an elderly cousin speak 'the dialect of their childhood – discarded as they became men – which none of their descendants could understand'.[47] Their identity as Scots is organic to their pioneering life, but inevitably this identity dissipates with succeeding generations, as the pioneering experience itself dissipates. Most of the stories in *The View from Castle Rock*, and many of Munro's earlier stories, are about the legacy of emigration, for the people and for the land.

As a young boy, Munro's father trapped the wild animals whose habitat was on the family's doorstep: muskrats, mink, marten, otters and foxes. As an adult in 1925 he began to farm silver foxes for their pelts, the final chapter in the story of North American fur trapping. His skill with animals is wedded, literally, to the very different talent of his wife: 'She looked at the foxes and she did not see any romantic connection to the wilderness; she saw a new industry, the possibility of riches.'[48] But after some years the fox-farming enterprise failed. Hard work, ambition, expertise and flair do not lead to a comfortable existence, let alone to a prospect of beggars in carriages.

Munro's stories are about life on the edge, not generally on the edge of danger or thrills or passion, but on the margin of fulfilment and enrichment. The wilderness is still there, but has acquired a duality enforced by civilisation. The story 'Hired Girl' highlights the forest as a playground, which 'had eliminated all lavishness and confusion and seasonal change' but for those seeking recreation was more 'authentic': 'It seemed to me that this real forest belonged to rich people … and to Indians, who served the rich people as guides and exotic dependants, living out of sight and out of mind.'[49] In contrast, there is the bush, the forest as experienced by 'ordinary' people, which stretched along the creek that ran at the back of the Laidlaw farm, 'so that it was possible to follow it and be hardly aware of the farms, the cleared land, the straight-laid roads and fences – it was possible to imagine that you were out in the forest as it was a hundred years ago'.[50] The rich, eagerly heading north in their search for the wild, would drive past unaware of the wilderness they were missing. Here was an environment where it was not necessary to look for the heightened responses of excitement and fear that recreational adventure sought. In the world of Munro's childhood there was plenty to be afraid of: in 'Lying Under the Apple Tree' she lists 'snakes, thunderstorms, deep water, heights, the dark, the bull, the lonely road through the swamp'.[51] These were everyday fears, understood by all who shared that life. They were not ingredients of an enhanced alternative to normality.

Often in Munro's stories the inheritance of the wild is another wilderness. 'What Do You Want to Know for?' tells how decades later, she returns to the old family farm and finds it has become the site of a car-wrecking business:

> The front yard and the side yard and the vegetable garden and the flower borders, the hayfield, the mock-orange bush, the lilac trees, the chestnut stump, the pasture and the ground once covered by the fox pens, are all swept under a tide of car parts, gutted car bodies, smashed headlights, grilles, and fenders, overturned car seats with rotten bloated stuffing – heaps of painted, rusted, blackened, glittering whole or twisted, defiant and surviving metal.[52]

As in Laurence's *The Diviners*, an accumulation of redundant objects makes an ironic comment on what was once unsullied land. The childhood home is lost, taken over by a very modern dereliction. All around, the houses and barns of the pioneers have been pulled down: 'The land the buildings stood on can be identified perhaps by a slight rise in the ground, or by a clump of lilacs – otherwise it has become just a patch of field.'[53] The determined efforts of the original settlers have been overlaid by a scale of cultivation and stock-raising that they could never have imagined. The detail of past lives has disappeared, the buildings themselves, the fences and hedges, the gardens, all the small signs of human occupation and activity. 'As if you could see more then', Munro writes, 'though now you can see farther.'[54] It is losing that dominates, rather than being lost.

That sense of loss, or of missed opportunities and accumulating disappointments, permeates much of Munro's writing. Unlike MacLeod's Highlanders, her people do not sustain a Scottish identity. Their language and their origins have been subsumed by the land itself and the successive demands made by its changing face. In *The Tenderness of Wolves*, Stef Penney writes of the wilderness swallowing up emigrants pouring in from Scotland and elsewhere. Munro writes of communities that vanish a second or third time, and of buildings that are not reclaimed by the wilderness, as Macleod's abandoned Cape Breton dwellings are, but disappear under new layers of human activity. Laurence's Morag Gunn nurtures her Scottish inheritance, but chooses to free herself from its hold. Macleod writes about people who cannot or do not wish to sever the Highland connection that has influenced their lives. Munro's *The View from Castle Rock* stories are a conscious effort to remind herself and her readers of not only her Scottish Borders origins, but also the narrative of hope and disappointment that sustains that link.

Laurence, MacLeod and Munro are all twentieth-century writers, though it is hoped that there will be more from the pens of the latter two (Margaret Laurence died in 1987). A Scottish identity is still highly visible in North America, particularly in Canada, but the sense of loss and fading connection so present in MacLeod and Munro is likely to become less meaningful and more susceptible to replacement by refurbished myth. Laurence, writing of the mid-twentieth century, is able through Morag Gunn to sustain a mythic past at the same time as loosening its hold on her identity. For a younger generation writing in the twenty-first century this is probably not an option.

Yet there are echoes. They are found in D. R. MacDonald's *Cape Breton Road*, and also in Alexander MacLeod's collection of stories, *Light Lifting* (2010). The latter have no overt references to Scottish identities, apart from Scottish names, but in several stories there is an undertow of the pioneering past. Young men and women test themselves physically and mentally, seek out danger, take risks. In 'Miracle Mile' his runners (Michael Campbell and James Burns) race trains through a tunnel; in 'Adult Beginner I' young men and women dive from the roof of a hotel into the Detroit River, a busy shipping lane, in the middle of a summer night. One of the divers, Stace, has never done it before:

> There are reasons not to, of course, obvious ones, but they seem flimsy and unconvincing right now and in the end every risk has to be measured relative to doing nothing at all. She feels it coming, though. The advance presence of a killer threat. Real danger waiting off to the side. It swirls around them like faint smoke drifting in from an approaching forest fire, but nobody cares.[55]

The divers are, in a sense, pioneers, creating their own physical challenges in an urban environment, and they support each other as pioneering communities had to do. They participate in a community of risk that is also a community of care.[56] MacLeod sets his stories in Windsor, Ontario, divided from Detroit in the United States by the river connecting Lake Erie and Lake St Clair. It is border country, and his stories reflect this, often involving traversing terrain which seems to have no particular distinctiveness, and entering alien territory. In 'The Loop' a young delivery boy enters the homes of people who are potentially threatening. MacLeod's stories are full of real dangers, not all of them 'off to the side'. But they are also about survival, and the humanity and mutuality that survival requires.

LOST AND FOUND: COMPASS BEYOND MEASURE

The novelist Margaret Elphinstone was born in England, but has spent most of her life in Scotland. Her novel *Voyageurs* (2003) takes us back to the early nineteenth century. It is 1812, and British North America and the United States are about to go to war. The focus of her narrative is border country, in and around Lake Michigan and no great distance (in North American terms) from MacLeod's Windsor. Elphinstone's protagonist is an English Quaker from Cumberland who crosses the Atlantic in search of his sister. Rachel Greenhow went to Upper Canada as a missionary, but was diverted from her calling when she met and married a Scottish employee of the North West Company. She accompanied him on a fur-trading trip into Michigan Territory, and disappeared in the wilderness. *Voyageurs* is her brother Mark's account of how he searched for and eventually found his vanished sister. It is also an account of a principled and determined young man's encounter with the wild and how it changed him.

Mark Greenhow walks north from York (the embryonic Toronto) to the Quaker community of Yonge Street, following a swampy track through the forest. He has explored the Cumbrian hills and lakes since childhood, but the forest of Upper Canada is unlike anything he has experienced: 'A dense unbroken wilderness, whose compass is beyond measure, and whose depths are unfathomable. As the dark thickened the trees became a wall of whispering shadows.'[57] His journeying will take him a great distance from the supportive comfort of a Quaker community into bewildering territory which tests his convictions. In the company of his brother-in-law Alan Mackenzie, he is caught up in the commerce of the fur trade and the confusion of war. He learns to paddle a canoe, to dress animal skins and fish through ice holes. He abandons his boots and sober Quaker coat for moccasins and buckskin. He has a brief liaison with a fourteen-year-old Ottawa girl.

Mark Greenhow is a straight talker in a world he cannot understand, although he learns first French to communicate with the *voyageurs* and then the Ottawa language. He also begins to learn something of the language of the wilderness, but never quite comes to terms with its dense mysteries. The 'wall of whispering shadows' communicates little to him. It is a wall not just of uncontrolled terrain, but of the human circumstances in which he finds himself. He is surrounded by secrets and half-told truths, in a territory that is in contention, not just by armies but by values and ways of living. The outposts of commerce impinge on traditional native ways of life. Demarcations are blurred, literally when snow or mist blankets distinguishing features of landscape, but also metaphorically. Mark, seeking his lost sister, is often himself lost, emotionally and morally, as he attempts to hang on to principles of simplicity, honesty and pacifism. Crossing the border under cover of darkness he reflects: 'How any man could steer a course, with the light so uncertain and the waters so unruly, was beyond me, but the brigade held together, and pressed onwards.'[58]

The heart of the lesson Mark learns is that the wilderness is not what it seems: 'the Indian lands were no trackless wilderness; on the contrary, we could follow a pattern woven by generations of the people whose land this was'. Everywhere there are paths, although they are not obvious to the uninitiated. He begins to understand how easy it is to misconceive both landscape and people. He reflects: 'I'm niggled when the Lakers call my own country a wilderness. I learned on our journey that I'd had just the same misconception about the Indian lands of the north-west.'[59] The dynamics of Indian family life are rooted in familiar needs, for shelter and food, for care and warmth. Mark crosses a frontier of understanding – a theme that underpins the entire narrative.

Alan Mackenzie has also crossed frontiers, first, when he left his native Lochalsh for Edinburgh and found himself in alien territory populated by alien people. In the Lowlands, he recalls, telling his story to Mark, 'I was not only a stranger, but about as welcome among them as a stray dog.'[60] And to Mark the Highland world described by Alan seems 'far more remote … than the lands of the Ottawa in which we dwelt'.[61] When Alan arrived in Montreal and at the age of seventeen joined the North West Company, he felt more at home because he was with his own people, the Highland NWC employees: 'I wasn't a frightened lad; I was a man among my own folk.'[62]

When Mark finally tracks down his sister, only possible because the native people she is with allow her to be found, he has to confront the reality of her experience. She has been living with a native band for two years and has a mixed-race child. It is impossible for her to return to her old life – the Quaker community has disowned her and she has no wish to accompany her brother back to England. Her reunion with her husband is not easy, and we learn that she later dies in childbirth. The contrast between brother and sister is significant. Rachel was an independent and sometimes wilful child and became an intrepid and outspoken woman. Mark has courage and persistence, but is more stolid than his sister and more literal both in his observation and in his interpretation of Quaker principles. The fact that the story is told through his eyes is important, for that very literalness means that we accept him as a reliable narrator. It also means that we accept his detailed recording of landscape and wildlife as well as of his experiences as entirely authentic. His is an honest tale, although within it he is often lost and bemused.

Catherine Parr Traill's lost children return to their families none the worse for their experiences and well equipped to engage with a settled and progressive life. Mark Greenhow returns to Cumberland, and marries the Quaker woman he has met in Upper Canada, not the young Indian girl he briefly and intensely loves. He takes up his expected role as a Lakeland farmer. Rachel and Alan, the English Quaker and the Scottish Episcopalian, have a stillborn child before her disappearance, and after her return Alan loses both his wife and a second child. It is as if Rachel's natural place is with the indigenous people of the wilderness. Her legacy is a mixed-race child who is brought up by a Scottish Highlander who is not her father. Elphinstone has turned on its head a familiar trope of the fur-trading era. There were plenty of mixed-race children in fur-trading communities, but these were the offspring of French and Scottish fathers and their 'country wives'.

Rachel Greenhow in a sense remains lost. Part of her story is never recovered – she does not reveal exactly how she was taken or what life was like with the Indian band or what feelings she had for the father of her child. Perhaps she did not wish to be found. Alan Mackenzie is lost to the Scottish Highlands, where the way of life that sustained his family for generations is vanishing. The native people who are pivotal in Elphinstone's narrative will lose their way of life also. The reader knows that their confident assertion that Michigan Territory will never be settled is misplaced. The backwoods will soon be lost.

Like many other narratives, *Voyageurs* draws the North American wilderness within the compass of the British imagination. It demonstrates, as does Stef Penney's *The Tenderness of Wolves*, that the wild terrain of nineteenth-century North America is still a region of adventure, an arena of heroic activity and resonant emblems of endurance. The image of the hardy Scottish pioneer is embedded in the Scottish and British imperial legacy. It is re-presented and reinterpreted, absorbed into widely different contexts and narratives, but is extraordinarily robust. Its tenacity is exemplified in Scotland's renewed interest in the commanding figures of men such as John Rae and John Muir, and in the way the storyteller's imagination continues to return to the territory of wilderness.

At a time when Scotland's wild country seemed to be diminishing as a source of sustainable life except for a small number whose main concern was profit, the attraction of vast and available territory was powerful. The emphasis on individual endeavour if anything increased the attraction. Industrialisation suppressed the potential for individuals to control their own lives. Scotland saw massive and rapid industrialisation in the late eighteenth and the nineteenth centuries, and unprecedented pressure on rural life in both Highlands and Lowlands. Wilderness signalled new possibilities. For most it was the potential for social and economic benefit that mattered most, often linked with religious and political freedom, but for some the appeal lay in the wilderness itself. Learning to live in and with untamed country was seen as valuable, a source of scientific understanding, of spiritual fulfilment, even of redemption or at least of some kind of recompense for the closing in of modernity. As John Muir so vividly identified, wilderness was an unparalleled source of refreshment and regeneration.

A new world which promised much but delivered little without hard work, self-denial and self-belief was well suited to a people whose individual and collective experience so often demonstrated that achievement was not and should not be easily won. A universal lesson perhaps, but one that is arguably written on Scottish hearts and minds with particular vividness. The legacy of Scottish encounters with the North American wilderness feeds back to Scotland today, and although the experience of the hardy Scot is dissipated, diluted and reinterpreted, the undaunted figure in the forest, axe in hand, remains fixed in the imagination. Fortitude, resolve and resourcefulness, and the very facts of displacement and survival, become sources of moral authority which the inheritors of Scotland's past in both Scotland and North American are understandably reluctant to relinquish.

NOTES

1. In Frederick Turner, *John Muir. From Scotland to the Sierra* (Edinburgh: Canongate, 1997), pp. 247–8.

2. In Donald Worster, *A Passion for Nature. The Life of John Muir* (Oxford: Oxford University Press, 2008), p. 244.
3. Stevenson, 'The Silverado Squatters', in *Clyde to California*, p. 231.
4. Muir, *The Story of My Boyhood*, p. 25.
5. Ibid., p. 27.
6. Ibid.
7. Ibid., p. 32.
8. In Worster, *The Life of John Muir*, p. 31.
9. In Turner, *From Scotland to the Sierra*, p. 175.
10. Stevenson, 'Across the Plains', in *Clyde to California*, p. 155.
11. Ibid., p. 156.
12. Ibid., p. 157.
13. In Worster, *The Life of John Muir*, p. 180.
14. Linnie Marsh Wolfe (ed.), *John of the Mountains. The Unpublished Journals of John Muir* (Madison, WI: University of Wisconsin Press, 1979), p. 92.
15. In Worster, *The Life of John Muir*, p. 181.
16. Graham White (ed.), *Sacred Summits. John Muir's Greatest Climbs* (Edinburgh: Canongate, 1999), pp. 99–100.
17. In Worster, *The Life of John Muir*, p. 233.
18. In ibid., p. 315.
19. John Muir, *Stickeen. The Story of a Dog* (Boston, MA: Houghton, Mifflin, 1909), p. 18.
20. In Michael Cohen, *The Pathless Way: John Muir and American Wilderness* (Madison, WI: University of Wisconsin Press, 1984), p. 304.
21. White, Introduction, in Muir, *Sacred Summits*, p. xxvii.
22. Bird, *A Lady's Life*, p. 12.
23. Howison, *Sketches of Upper Canada*, p. 22.
24. Laurence, *The Diviners*, p. 69.
25. Ibid., p. 24.
26. Ibid., p. 58.
27. Ibid., p. 59.
28. Ibid., p. 314.
29. Ibid., p. 319.
30. Ibid.
31. Ibid., p. 329.
32. Ibid., p. 341.
33. Hugh MacLennan, *Two Solitudes* (Toronto: Stoddart, [1945] 1998), p. 118.
34. Ibid., p. 203.
35. MacLeod, *Island*, p. 151.
36. Ibid., p. 160.
37. Ibid., p. 170.
38. Ibid., p. 148.
39. Ibid., p. 176.

40. Alistair MacLeod, *No Great Mischief* (London: Vintage, 2001), pp. 83–4.
41. Alice Munro, *The View from Castle Rock* (London: Chatto & Windus, 2006), p. 111.
42. Ibid., p. 112.
43. Ibid., p. 118.
44. Ibid., p. 30.
45. Ibid., p. 79.
46. Ibid., pp. 134–5.
47. Ibid., p. 170.
48. Ibid., p. 139.
49. Ibid., p. 232.
50. Ibid., p. 131.
51. Ibid., p. 224.
52. Ibid., p. 322.
53. Ibid., p. 343.
54. Ibid., p. 344.
55. Alexander MacLeod, *Light Lifting* (London: Faber & Faber, 2012), p. 91.
56. At an event in Edinburgh on 15 May 2012, I suggested to Alexander MacLeod that his stories were exploring 'communities of risk'. He replied that he viewed them rather as 'communities of care'.
57. Margaret Elphinstone, *Voyageurs* (Edinburgh: Canongate, 2004), p. 78.
58. Ibid., p. 197.
59. Ibid., p. 302.
60. Ibid., p. 373.
61. Ibid., p. 375.
62. Ibid., p. 380.

Bibliography

Adams, Ian and Somerville, Meredith, *Cargoes of Despair and Hope* (Edinburgh: John Donald, 1993).

Andrews, E. W. with Charles McLean Andrews (eds), *Journal of a Lady of Quality* (New Haven: Yale University Press, 1934–43).

Aspinwall, Bernard, *Portable Utopia: Glasgow and the United States 1820–1920* (Aberdeen: Aberdeen University Press, 1984).

Atherton, Lewis, *The Cattle Kings* (Bloomington, IN: Indiana University Press, 1962).

Atwood, Margaret, *Survival: A Thematic Guide to Canadian Literature* (Toronto: House of Aransi Press, 1972).

Atwood, Margaret, *Surfacing* (London: Virago, 1979).

Bailyn, Bernard and Dewolfe, Barbara, *Voyagers to the West. Emigration from Britain to America on the Eve of Revolution* (London: Tauris, 1986).

Ballantyne, R. M., *The Young Fur Traders* (Edinburgh: Nelson, 1856).

Ballantyne, R. M., *Hudson's Bay or Every-day Life in the Wilds of North America* (London: Nisbet, 1876).

Ballantyne, R. M., *Away in the Wilderness* (London: Nisbet, 1879).

Ballantyne, R. M., *The Wild Man of the West* (London: Routledge, 1863).

Barcott, Bruce (ed.), *Northwest Passages. A Literary Anthology of the Pacific Northwest from Coyote Tales to Roadside Attractions* (Seattle, WA: Sasquatch Books, 1994).

Barr, Pat, *A Curious Life for a Lady. The Story of Isabella Bird* (London: Secker & Warburg, 1970).

Beebe, Lucius and Clegg, Charles, *The Age of Steam* (New York: Promontory Press, 1994).

Bell, William, *Hints to Emigrants in a Series of Letters from Upper Canada* (Edinburgh: Waugh & Innes, 1824).

Bennett, Margaret, *Oatmeal and the Catechism: Scottish Settlers in Quebec* (Edinburgh, Montreal, Kingston: John Donald and McGill-Queen's University Press, 1998).

Berton, Pierre, *The National Dream. The Last Spike* (Toronto: McLelland & Stewart, 1974).

Bird, Isabella, *A Lady's Life in the Rocky Mountains* (Sausalito, CA: Comstock Press, [1879] 1960).

Bird, Isabella, *Letters to Henrietta*, ed. Kay Chubbuck (London: John Murray, 2002).

Blaustein, Richard, *The Thistle and the River: Historical Links and Cultural Parallels Between Scotland and Appalachia*, Contributions to Southern Appalachian Studies, No. 7 (Jefferson, NC: McFarland & Co., 2003).

Booth, Bradford A. and Mehew, Ernest, *The Letters of Robert Louis Stevenson* (New Haven, CT: Yale University Press, 1994), vol. III.

Bray, Elizabeth, *The Discovery of the Highlands* (Glasgow: Collins, 1986).

Brock, William, *Scotus Americanus: A Survey of the Sources for Links Between Scotland and America in the 18th Century* (Edinburgh: Edinburgh University Press 1982).

Bronson, Edgar, *Reminiscences of a Ranchman* (Lincoln, NE: University of Nebraska Press, 1962).

Brown, Dee, *The American West* (London: Pocket Books, 2004).

Brown, Dee, *Bury My Heart at Wounded Knee* (London: Picador, 1975).

Brown, Jennifer, *Strangers in Blood: Fur Trade Company Families in Indian Territory* (Vancouver: University of British Columbia Press, 1980).

Brown, P. Hume, *Early Travellers in Scotland* (Edinburgh: David Douglas, 1891).

Bryce, G., *Sketch of the Life and Discoveries of Robert Campbell*, Historical and Scientific Society of Manitoba, Transaction No. 52 (Manitoba Free Press, 1898).

Bryce, G., *The Scotsman in Canada* (London: Sampson, Low, Marston, 1912).

Buchan, John, *The Thirty-Nine Steps* (London: Penguin, [1915] 2004).

Buchan, John, *Memory Hold-the-door* (London: Hodder & Stoughton, [1940] 1948).

Buchan, John, *Sick Heart River* (Oxford: Oxford University Press, [1941] 1994).

Bumsted, J. F., *The Scots in Canada* (Ottawa: Canadian Historical Association, 1982).

Bunyan, Ian, Calder, Jenni, Idiens, Dale and Wilson, Bryce, *No Ordinary Journey. John Rae, Arctic Explorer 1813–1893* (Edinburgh and Montreal: National Museums of Scotland and McGill-Queen's University Press, 1993).

Burroughs, John Rolfe, *Guardian of the Grasslands. First 100 Years of the Wyoming Stock Growers Association* (Cheyenne, WY: Pioneer Printing and Stationery Co., 1991).

Calder, Jenni, *There Must Be a Lone Ranger: The Myth and Reality of the American West* (London: Secker & Warburg, 1974).

Calder, Jenni (ed.), *The Enterprising Scot* (Edinburgh: National Museums of Scotland, 1986).

Calder, Jenni, 'Rae in the Arctic', in Bunyan *et al.*, *No Ordinary Journey. John Rae, Arctic Explorer 1813–1893* (Edinburgh and Montreal: National Museums of Scotland and McGill-Queen's University Press, 1993).

Calder, Jenni, *Scots in Canada* (Edinburgh: Luath Press, 2003).

Calder, Jenni, *Scots in the USA* (Edinburgh: Luath Press, 2005).

Calder, Jenni, *Frontier Scots. The Scots Who Won the West* (Edinburgh: Luath Press, 2010).

Calder, Jenni, 'Stevenson in the Wilderness: California, *Kidnapped* and *The Master of Ballantrae*', *Journal of Stevenson Studies*, 8 (2011): 166.

Campbell, D. and MacLean, P. A., *Beyond the Atlantic Roar: A Study of the Nova Scotia Scots* (Toronto: McLelland & Stewart, 1975).

Campbell, John Lorne, *Songs Remembered in Exile* (Edinburgh: Birlinn, [1990] 1999).

Campbell, Randolph B., *Gone to Texas* (Oxford: Oxford University Press, 2003).

Campbell, Robert, *Two Journals of Robert Campbell* (Seattle, WA: The Shorey Book Store, 1967).

Campey, Lucille, *'A Very Fine Class of Immigrants'. Prince Edward Island's Scottish Pioneers 1770–1850* (Toronto: Natural Heritage Books, 2001).

Campey, Lucille, *After the Hector. The Scottish Pioneers of Nova Scotia and Cape Breton 1773–1852* (Toronto: Natural Heritage Books, 2004).

Campey, Lucille, *The Scottish Pioneers of Upper Canada* (Toronto: Natural Heritage Books, 2005).

Canton, Frank, *Frontier Trails: The Autobiography of Frank M. Canton*, ed. Edward Everett Dale (Norman, OK: University of Oklahoma Press, 1966).

Carnegie, James, Earl of Southesk, *Saskatchewan and the Rocky Mountains* (Boston, MA: Northeastern University Press, [1875] 1986).

Chambers, W., *The Emigrant's Manual. British America and the USA* (Edinburgh: Chambers, 1851).

Chambers, W., *Things as They Are in America* (Edinburgh: Chambers, 1857).

Chambers, W., *The Emigrants' Guide to the United States and the Dominion of Canada* (Edinburgh: Chambers, 1872).

Child, Lee, *Worth Dying For* (London: Transworld, [2010] 2011).

Clark, D., *Selections from Scottish Canadian Poets* (Toronto: Caledonian Society of Toronto, 1909).

Clay, John, *My Life on the Range* (Norman, OK: University of Oklahoma Press, [1894] 1962).

Cockburn, Henry, *Circuit Journeys* (Hawick: Byway Books, [1888] 1983).

Cohen, Michael, *The Pathless Way: John Muir and American Wilderness* (Madison, WI: University of Wisconsin Press, 1984).

Connor, Ralph, *Glengarry School Days* (Toronto: Westminster Co., 1902).

Cooper, James Fenimore, *The Deerslayer* (New York: New American Library, [1841] 1963).

Cooper, James Fenimore, *The Prairie* (New York: New American Library, [1827] 1964).

Cracknell, Linda (ed.), *A Wilder Vein* (Ullapool: Two Ravens Press, 2009).

Crawford, Medorem, *Journal*, ed. F. G. Young, available at: www.archive.org/details/journalofmedoremcrawford.

Creighton, Donald, *The Story of Canada* (London: Faber & Faber, [1959] 1971).

Currie, Sheldon, *The Glace Bay Miners' Museum* (Wreck Cove: Breton Books, 1995).

Daniells, Roy, *Alexander Mackenzie and the North West* (London: Faber & Faber, 1969).

Davies, John (ed.), *Douglas of the Forests. The North American Journals of David Douglas* (Edinburgh: Paul Harris, 1979).

Devine, T. M. (ed.), *Scottish Emigration and Scottish Society* (Edinburgh: John Donald, 1992).

Devine, T. M., *Scotland's Empire 1600–1815* (London: Penguin Books, 2004).

Devine, T. M., *To the Ends of the Earth. Scotland's Global Diaspora* (London: Allen Lane, 2011).

DeVoto, Bernard, *Across the Wide Missouri* (New York: Manner Books, [1947] 1998).

Doig, Ivan, *This House of Sky. Landscapes of the Western Mind* (London: Harcourt, [1978] 1992).

Doig, Ivan, *English Creek* (London: Penguin, 1985).

Doig, Ivan, *Bucking the Sun* (New York: Simon & Schuster, 1996).

Duff, David (ed.), *Queen Victoria's Highland Journals* (Exeter and London: Webb & Bower and Michael Joseph, 1983).

Dunlay, Tom, *Kit Carson and the Indians* (Lincoln, NE: University of Nebraska Press, 2000).

Dunn, C. W., *Highland Settler* (Toronto: University of Toronto Press, 1953).

Elphinstone, Margaret, *Voyageurs* (Edinburgh: Canongate, 2004).

Erickson, Charlotte, *Invisible Immigrants: The Adaption of English and Scottish Immigrants in 19th Century America* (Ithaca, NY: Cornell University Press, 1972).

Fergusson, Adam, *Practical Notes Made During a Tour in Canada* (Edinburgh: Blackwood, 1839).

Fischer, David Hackett, *Albion's Seed: Four British Folkways in America* (New York: Oxford University Press, 1989).

Fitzpatrick, Rory, *God's Frontiersmen: The Scots–Irish Epic* (London: Weidenfeld & Nicolson, 1989).

Fraser, George MacDonald, *Flashman and the Redskins* (London: HarperCollins, [1982] 2006).

Fraser, Simon, *The Letters and Journals of Simon Fraser*, ed. W. Kaye Lamb (Toronto: Dundum Press, 1960).

Fry, Michael, *The Scottish Empire* (Edinburgh: Birlinn, 2002).

Fry, Michael, *Bold, Independent, Unconquer'd and Free: How the Scots Made America Safe for Liberty, Democracy and Capitalism* (Ayr: Fort Publishing, 2003).

Galbraith, J. K., *The Non-potable Scotch. A Memoir on the Clansmen in Canada* (Harmondsworth: Penguin, [1964] 1967).

Galbraith, J. K., *The Little Emperor* (Toronto: Macmillan, 1976).

Galt, John, *Lawrie Todd, or Settlers in the Woods* (London: Richard Bentley, 1830).

Galt, John, *Bogle Corbet* (London: Colburn & Bentley, 1831).

Galt, John, *Autobiography of John Galt* (London: Cochrane & McCrone, 1833).

Gard, Wayne, *Frontier Justice* (Norman, OK: University of Oklahoma Press, 1949).

Gibson, Rob, *Plaids and Bandanas: From Highland Drover to Wild West Cowboy* (Edinburgh: Luath Press, 2003).

Gillespie, Greg, *Hunting for Empire. Narratives of Sport in Rupert's Land, 1840–70* (Vancouver: University of British Columbia Press, 2007).

Graham, Ian Charles Cargill, *Colonists from Scotland: Emigration to North America, 1707–1783* (Ithaca, NY: Cornell University Press, 1956).

Graham, R. B. Cunninghame, *The North American Sketches*, ed. John Walker (Edinburgh: Scottish Academic Press, 1986).

Grahame, Fred B., *The Diary of William Richard Grahame in the United States and Canada 1831–1833* (Dundas: Magra Publishing, 1989).

Grant, Elizabeth, *Memoirs of a Highland Lady* (Edinburgh: Canongate, [1898] 1988).

Grant, George, *Ocean to Ocean. Sandford Fleming's Expedition Through Canada in 1872* (London: Sampson Low, Marston, Searle & Rivington, 1877).

Guthrie, A. B., *The Big Sky* (Chicago, IL: Time-Life Books, [1947] 1980).

Guthrie, A. B., *The Way West* (New York: Houghton Mifflin, [1949] 1976).

Guthrie, A. B., *These Thousand Hills* (New York: Houghton Mifflin, 1956).

Hamilton, Thomas, *Men and Manners in America* (Edinburgh: Blackwood, 1833).

Hargrave, James, *Letters from Rupert's Land, 1826–1840*, ed. Helen Ross (Montreal: McGill-Queen's University Press, 2009).

Harper, Marjory, *Adventurers and Exiles: The Great Scottish Exodus* (London: Profile Books, 2003).

Harper, M. and Vance, M. (eds), *Myth, Migration and the Making of Memory, Scotia and Nova Scotia c. 1700–1990* (Edinburgh and Halifax: John Donald and Fernwood Publishing, 1999).

Haws, Charles H., *Scots in the Old Dominion 1685–1800* (Edinburgh: John Dunlop, 1980).

Hewitson, Jim, *Tam Blake & Co.: The Story of the Scots in America* (Edinburgh: Canongate, 1993).

Hill, D., *Great Migrations, vol. I: The Scots to Canada* (London: Gentry Books, 1972).

Hill, James J., *Highways of Progress* (London: Hodder & Stoughton, 1910).

Hook, Andrew, *Scotland and America 1750–1835* (Glasgow: Blackie, 1975).

Hook, Andrew, *From Goosecreek to Gandercleuch: Studies in Scottish-American Literary and Cultural History* (East Linton: John Donald, 1999).

Houston, C. Stuart, *Arctic Ordeal: The Journal of John Richardson* (Montreal and Gloucester: McGill-Queen's University Press and Alan Sutton, 1984).

Howison, John, *Sketches of Upper Canada* (Edinburgh: Oliver & Boyd, 1825).

Humble, B. H., *Wayfaring Around Scotland* (London: Herbert Jenkins, 1936).

Hunter, James, *A Dance Called America* (Edinburgh: Mainstream, 1994).

Hunter, James, *On the Other Side of Sorrow* (Edinburgh: Mainstream, 1995).

Hunter, James, *Glencoe and the Indians* (Edinburgh: Mainstream, 1996).

Hutchison, Isobel Wylie, *North to the Rime-Ringed Sun* (Glasgow: Blackie, 1934).

Innis, Harold A., *The Fur Trade in Canada* (Toronto: University of Toronto Press, [1939] 1970).

Irving, Pierre, *The Life and Letters of Washington Irving* (New York: Putnam, 1862).

Irving, Washington, *Tour in Scotland, 1817*, ed. Stanley T. Williams (New Haven, CT: Yale University Press, 1927).

Irving, Washington, *Astoria: Adventure in the Pacific Northwest* (London: KPI, [1839] 1987).

Irving, Washington, *The Adventures of Captain Bonneville* (London: Bohn, 1850).

Irving, Washington, *A Tour on the Prairies*, ed. John Frances McDermott (Norman, OK: University of Oklahoma Press, 1985).

Jackson, W. Turrentine, *The Enterprising Scot: Investors in the American West after 1873* (Edinburgh: Edinburgh University Press, 1968).

Johnson, Robert E., *Sir John Richardson, Arctic Explorer* (London: Taylor & Francis, 1976).

Johnson, Samuel and Boswell, James, *A Journey to the Western Isles of Scotland* and *The Journal of a Tour to the Hebrides* (Mineola, NY: Dover [1775] and [1785] 2008).

Karras, Alan A., *Sojourners in the Sun: Scottish Migrants in Jamaica and the Chesapeake 1740–1800* (Ithaca, NY: Cornell University Press, 1992).

Kelly, Douglas, with Caroline Switzer Kelly, *Carolina Scots: An Historical and Genealogical Study of over 100 Years of Emigration* (Dillon, TX: 1739 Publications, 1998).

Kerrigan, Catherine (ed.), *The Immigrant Experience* (Guelph: University of Guelph Press, 1992).

Landsman, N., *Scotland and its First American Colony, 1683–1765* (Princeton, NJ: Princeton University Press, 1985).

Laurence, Margaret, *The Diviners* (London: Virago, [1974] 1989).

Lavender, David, *Westward Vision. The Story of the Oregon Trail* (London: Eyre & Spottiswood, 1963).

Lavender, David, *The Penguin Book of the American West* (Harmondsworth: Penguin, 1969).

Leakey, John, *The West that Was, from Texas to Montana*, as told to Nellie Snyder Yost (Lincoln, NE: University of Nebraska Press, 1958).

Lewis, Jon E., *The West. The Making of the American West* (Bristol: Sienna, 1998).

Lindsay, Ann, *Seeds of Blood and Beauty. Scottish Plant Explorers* (Edinburgh: Birlinn, 2008).

Lindsay, Ann and House, Syd, *The Tree Collector. The Life and Explorations of David Douglas* (London: Aurum, 2005).

Little, J. I., *Crofters and Habitants, Settler Society, Economy and Culture in a Quebec Township, 1848–1881* (Montreal: McGill-Queen's University Press, 1991).

MacDonald, D. R., *Cape Breton Road* (London: Chatto & Windus, 2001).

MacDonnel, Margaret, *The Emigrant Experience: Songs of the Highland Emigrants in North America* (Toronto: University of Toronto Press, 1982).

MacDougall, Robert, *The Emigrant's Guide to North America*, ed. Elizabeth Thompson (Toronto: Natural Heritage Books, [1841] 1998).

Macfarlane, Robert, *Mountains of the Mind. A History of Fascination* (London: Granta Books, 2003).

Macfarlane, Robert, *The Wild Places* (London: Granta Books, 2007).

MacInnes, Allan, Harper, Marjory-Ann D. and Fryer, Linda G., *Scotland and the Americas, c. 1650–c. 1939* (Edinburgh: Scottish History Society, 2002).

MacKay, Donald, *Scotland Farewell: The People of the Hector* (Toronto: Natural Heritage/Natural History Inc., 1996).

Mackenzie, Eneas, *An Historical, Topographical, and Descriptive View of the United States of America* (Newcastle, 1819).

Mackenzie, George A. (ed.), *Aberdeen to Ottawa. The Diary of Alexander Muir* (Aberdeen: Aberdeen University Press, 1990).

Mackenzie, Osgood, *A Hundred Years in the Highlands* (London: Edward Arnold, 1921).

MacLean, Malcolm and Carrell, Christopher, *As an Fhearann* (Edinburgh, Stornoway and Glasgow: Mainstream, An Lanntair Gallery and Third Eye Centre, 1986).

MacLennan, Hugh, *Two Solitudes* (Toronto: Stoddart, [1945] 1998).

MacLennan, Hugh, *Cross-Country* (Edmonton: Hurtig, [1949] 1972).

MacLennan, Hugh, *Scotchman's Return* (New York: Scribners, [1958] 1960).

MacLeod, Alexander, *Light Lifting* (London: Cape, 2012).

MacLeod, Alistair, *No Great Mischief* (London: Vintage, 2001).

MacLeod, Alistair, *Island* (London: Vintage, [2001] 2002).

Macleod, Donald J., Introduction, Martin Martin, *A Description of the Western Isles of Scotland* (Stirling: Eneas Mackay, 1934).

Macleod, Margaret Arnett (ed.), *The Letters of Letitia Hargrave* (Toronto: The Champlain Society, 1947).

McCartney, Laton, *Across the Great Divide: Robert Stuart and the Discovery of the Oregon Trail* (Stroud: Sutton, 2003).

McGoogan, Ken, *Fatal Passage* (London: Bantam Books, 2002).

McKee, Bill and Klassen, Georgia, *Trail of Iron. The CPR and the Birth of the West 1880–1930* (Vancouver: Douglas & McIntyre, 1983).

McLean, John, *Notes of a Twenty-Five Year Service in the Hudson's Bay Territory* (London: Richard Bentley, 1844).

McLean, Marianne, *The People of Glengarry: Highlanders in Transition 1745–1820* (Montreal: McGill-Queen's University Press, 1991).

McMurtry, Larry, *Lonesome Dove* (London: Pan, [1985] 1986).

McMurtry, Larry, *Dead Man's Walk* (London, Orion, 1995).

McMurtry, Larry, *Streets of Laredo* (London: Orion, 1993).

McPhee, John, *Rising from the Plains* (New York: Farrar, Straus & Giroux, 1986).

Martin, Albro, *James J. Hill and the Opening of the Northwest* (New York: Oxford University Press, 1976).

Meyer, Duane, *The Highland Scots of North Carolina, 1732–1776* (Chapel Hill, NC: University of North Carolina Press, 1961).

Miller, Sally M., *John Muir: Life and Work* (Albuquerque, NM: University of New Mexico Press, 1993).

Moodie, Susanna, *Roughing it in the Bush* (London: Virago, [1852] 1986).

Moodie, Susanna, *Life in the Clearings* (London: Richard Bentley, 1855).

Morton, A. S., *History of the Canadian West to 1870–71* (London: Thomas Nelson, 1939).

Muir, John, *Stickeen. The Story of a Dog* (Boston, MA: Houghton, Mifflin, 1909).

Muir, John, *The Story of My Boyhood and Youth*, ed. Frank Tindall (Edinburgh: Canongate, [1913] 1987).

Muir, John, *My First Summer in the Sierras* (New York: Houghton Mifflin Harcourt, [1917] 1998).

Munro, Alice, *Friend of My Youth* (London: Vintage, 1991).

Munro, Alice, *Open Secrets* (London: Chatto & Windus, 1994).

Munro, Alice, *The View from Castle Rock* (London: Chatto & Windus, 2006).

Munro, Alice, *Selected Stories* (London: Vintage, 2010).

Munro, Neil, *John Splendid* (Edinburgh: B&W, [1898] 1994).

Munro, Neil, *The New Road* (Edinburgh: Blackwood, [1914] 1958).

Murray, Charles Augustus, *The Prairie-Bird* (London: Richard Bentley, 1844).

Murray, Charles Augustus, *Travels in North America* (London: Richard Bentley, [1839] 1854).

Nash, Roderick, *Wilderness and the American Mind* (New Haven, CT: Yale University Press, 1982).

Neatby, Leslie H., *In Quest of the North West Passage* (London: Constable, 1958).

Newman, Peter C., *Company of Adventurers* (Markham: Penguin Canada, 1985).

Newman, Peter C., *Caesars of the Wilderness* (Markham: Penguin Canada, 1987).

Newman, Peter C., *Merchant Princes* (Markham: Penguin Canada, 1992).

Newton, Michael, *We're Indians Sure Enough. The Legacy of the Scottish Highlanders in the United States* (Alexandria: Saorsa Media, 2001).

Nimmo, Ian, *Walking with Murder. On the Kidnapped Trail* (Edinburgh: Birlinn, 2005).

Niven, Frederick John, *Mine Inheritance* (London: Collins, 1940).

Niven, Frederick John, *The Transplanted* (London: Collins, 1944).

Niven, Frederick John, *The Flying Years* (London: Collins, 1974).

Norton, Wayne, *Help Us to a Better Land: Crofter Colonies in the Prairie West* (Regina: University of Regina, 1994).

Oelschlager, Max, *The Idea of Wilderness* (New Haven, CT: Yale University Press, 1991).

'Old Scene Painter', *The Emigrant's Guide, or A Picture of America* (London, 1816).

Oliphant, Laurence, *Minnesota and the Far West* (Edinburgh: Blackwood, 1855).

Ormsby, Margaret A. (ed.), *A Pioneer Gentlewoman in British Columbia. The Recollections of Susan Allison* (Vancouver: University of British Columbia Press, [1976] 1991).

Osgood, Ernest Staples, *The Day of the Cattleman* (Chicago, IL: University of Chicago Press, 1939).

Parker, Anthony, *Scottish Highlanders in Colonial Georgia: The Recruitment, Emigration and Settlement at Darien, 1735–1748* (Athens, GA: University of Georgia Press, 1997).

Pennant, Thomas, *Tour of Scotland 1769* (Perth: Melven Press, [1771] 1970).

Penney, Stef, *The Tenderness of Wolves* (London: Quercus, [2006] 2007).

Preston, Richard Arthur (ed.), *For Friends at Home: A Scottish Emigrant's Letters from Canada, California and the Cariboo 1844–1864* (Montreal: McGill-Queen's University Press, 1974).

Raban, Jonathan, *Bad Land: An American Romance* (London: Picador, 1996).

Rae, John, *Correspondence with the Hudson's Bay Company* (Hudson's Bay Record Society, 1953).

Rae, William Fraser, *Newfoundland to Manitoba* (London, 1881).

Raffan, James, *Emperor of the North: Sir George Simpson and the Remarkable Story of the Hudson's Bay Company* (Toronto: HarperCollins, 2007).

Randall, John (ed.), *Island Emigrants. The History of Emigration from the Hebrides over the Centuries* (Isle of Lewis: Island Book Trust, 2001).

Ray, Celeste, *Highland Heritage: Scottish Americans in the American South* (Chapel Hill, NC: University of North Carolina Press, 2001).

Richards, Eric, *The Highland Clearances* (Edinburgh: Birlinn, 2000).

Richards, Eric and Clough, Monica, *Cromartie. Highland Life 1650–1914* (Aberdeen: Aberdeen University Press, 1989).

Rigg, Suzanne, *Men of Spirit and Adventure. Scots and Orkneymen in the Hudson's Bay Company 1780–1821* (Edinburgh: John Donald, 2011).

Ross, Alexander, *Adventures of the First Settlers on the Oregon or Columbia River* (London: Smith, Elder, 1849).

Ross, Alexander, *Fur Hunters of the Far Northwest* (London: Smith, Elder, 1855).

Ross, Alexander, *The Red River Settlement* (London: Smith, Elder, 1856).

Ross, Alexander, Letters, in *Transactions*, Manitoba Historical Society, available at: www.mhs.mb.ca/docs/transactions/l/rossletters.

Ross, Eric, *Beyond the River and the Bay* (Toronto: University of Toronto Press, 1970).

Ruddock, Ted (ed.), *Travels in the Colonies in 1773–1775, Described in the Letters of William Mylne* (Athens, GA: University of George Press, 1993).

Ruxton, George Frederick, *Life in the Far West*, ed. LeRoy R. Haten (Norman, OK: University of Oklahoma Press, 1964).

Schaefer, Jack, *Shane and Other Stories* (Harmondsworth: Penguin, [1954] 1963).

Schaw, Janet, *Journal of a Lady of Quality*, ed. Evangeline Walker Andrews with Charles McLean Andrews (New Haven, CT: Yale University Press, 1921).

Scott, Abigail, *Journal of a Trip to Oregon*, available at: www.over-land.com/diaries.

Scott, Walter, *The Lady of the Lake* (London: Adam & Charles Black, [1810] 1904).

Scott, Walter, *Waverley* (Oxford: Oxford University Press, [1814] 1986).

Scott, Walter, *Rob Roy* (Edinburgh: Collins, [1817] 1953).

Scott, Walter, *Redgauntlet* (London: Penguin, [1824] 2000).

'Scotus Americanus', *Information Concerning the Province of North Carolina* (Edinburgh: James Knox and Charles Elliot, 1773).

Sheppe, Walter (ed.), *First Man West. Alexander Mackenzie's Journal of His Voyage to the Pacific Coast of Canada in 1793* (Berkeley, CA: University of California Press, 1962).

Service, Robert, *Collected Verse*, vols I and II (London: Ernest Benn, 1943).

Simpson, Thomas, *Narrative of the Discoveries of the North Coast of America* (London: Richard Bentley, 1843).

Spufford, Francis, *I May Be Some Time. Ice and the English Imagination* (London: Faber & Faber, 1996).

Stegner, Wallace, *The Gathering of Zion: The Story of the Mormon Trail* (London: Eyre & Spottiswood,1966).

Stevenson, Robert Louis, *Kidnapped* (Edinburgh: Canongate [1886] 1989).

Stevenson, Robert Louis, *Memories and Portraits* (Glasgow: Richard Drew, [1887] 1990).

Stevenson, Robert Louis, *The Master of Ballantrae* (London: Dent, [1889] 1976).

Stevenson, Robert Louis, *From the Clyde to California*, ed. Andrew Noble (Aberdeen: Aberdeen University Press, 1985).

Stewart, George R., *Ordeal by Hunger: The Story of the Donner Party* (London: Eyre & Spottiswood, 1962).

Stewart, William Drummond, *Altowan, or Incidents of Life and Adventure in the Rocky Mountains by an Amateur Traveller*, ed. J. Watson Webb (New York: Harper, 1846).

Story, Norah, *Oxford Companion to Canadian History and Literature* (Toronto: Oxford University Press, 1973).

Stuart, Granville, *Forty Years on the Frontier, as seen in the Journals and Reminiscences of Granville Stuart, Gold-miner, Trader, Merchant, Rancher and Politician*, ed. Paul C. Phillips (Cleveland, OH: Arthur H. Clark, 1925).

Szasz, Ferenc, *Scots in the North American West 1790–1917* (Norman, OK: University of Oklahoma Press, 2000).

Thomson, Derick, *Gaelic Poetry in the Eighteenth Century* (Aberdeen: Association of Scottish Literary Studies, 1993).

Thoreau, Henry David, 'Walden', in *The Portable Thoreau*, ed. Carl Bode (New York: Viking 1964).

Traill, Catherine Parr, *Lost in the Backwoods* (Whitefish: Kessinger, [1852] n.d.).

Traill, Catherine Parr, *The Female Emigrant's Guide and Hints on Canadian Housekeeping* (Toronto: Maclear, 1854).

Turner, Frederick, *John Muir. From Scotland to the Sierra* (Edinburgh: Canongate, 1997).

Unruh, John D., *The Plains Across: Emigrants, Wagon Trains and the American West* (London: Pimlico, 1992).

Van Every, Dale, *The Final Challenge: The American Frontier 1804–1845* (New York: Mentor, 1964).

Van Vogt, William, *Britain to America: Mid-Nineteenth-Century Immigrants to the United States* (Chicago, IL: University of Illinois Press, 1999).

Waterston, Elizabeth, *Rapt in Plaid. Canadian Literature and Scottish Tradition* (Toronto: University of Toronto Press, 2003).

Whipple, T. K., *Study Out the Land* (Berkeley, CA: University of California Press, 1943).

White, Graham (ed.), *Sacred Summits. John Muir's Greatest Climbs* (Edinburgh: Canongate, 1999).

Wolfe, Linnie Marsh (ed.), *John of the Mountains. The Unpublished Journals of John Muir* (Madison, WI: University of Wisconsin Press, 1979).

Worster, Donald, *A Passion for Nature. The Life of John Muir* (Oxford: Oxford University Press, 2008).

Youngson, A. J. (ed.), *Beyond the Highland Line. Three Journals of Travel in Eighteenth Century Scotland* (London: Collins, 1974).

Index